THE IMPERIAL DRUG TRADE

THE IMPERIAL DRUG TRADE

JOSHUA ROWNTREE

GYAN

Published by

Gyan Publishing House
5, Ansari Road
Daryaganj, New Delhi-110002
Phone: 011-47034999, 9811692060
E-mail: books@gyanbooks.com

Distribution Network
gyanbooks.com
India, USA, Canada, UK, Australia

ISBN: 978-93-7447-489-1 (PB)

First Published, 1903

2nd Impression 2026

Printed at: Gyan Press, Delhi.

THE IMPERIAL DRUG TRADE
Author: JOSHUA ROWNTREE

THE IMPERIAL DRUG TRADE

A RE-STATEMENT OF THE OPIUM QUESTION, IN THE LIGHT OF RECENT EVIDENCE AND NEW DEVELOPMENTS IN THE EAST

BY

JOSHUA ROWNTREE

SECOND EDITION

METHUEN & CO.
36 ESSEX STREET W.C.
LONDON

CONTENTS

PART I

HISTORY

PART II

THE ROYAL COMMISSION

PART III

PRESENT POSITION

INTRODUCTION

A GREAT controversy has long been waged over the opium trade from India to China. Of late, so far as the Press and Parliament are concerned, it has been practically in abeyance. Men once listened to—Earl Shaftesbury, John Bright, Cardinal Manning, Dr. Temple, Sir Joseph W. Pease, and others—have passed away; whilst the proceedings of the Royal Commission on Opium were admirably adapted to stay further unrest on the part of the general public. Sir A. C. Lyall, in the last edition of the *Encyclopædia Britannica*, explains that "the agitation against the drug was laid for a further term of years by the Royal Commission." If so, the term is probably a short one, and nearly over. In truth, the proceedings of the Commission are only impressive so long as they are not examined and understood. When studied, they will be found to lessen the credit usually attaching to such semi-judicial inquiries, and to reflect on the impartiality of British tribunals appointed for temporary purposes.

The Commission was indeed effective for allaying the agitation, largely because it synchronised with a change in the thought of the day, much more important and difficult to grapple with than the inquiry itself. A recrudescence of materialism in the national life threw ethical considerations for a time into the background. Ideals for the betterment of humanity have not prospered. War has cast its deadly shadow over the comity of nations, and selfishness, if only on a sufficiently large scale, has been greatly exalted. The victory for the moment has rested with the forces of organised wealth. These causes have all favoured non-interference in an exceptionally lucrative branch of commerce, carried on with all the prestige of the British Empire. The Chinese obtain the smoke they love, the Indian Treasury obtains the revenue it needs: why should any one meddle?

And yet, passive or active, the controversy remains, and will remain, so long as any trade injurious to the morale of one nation is pushed by another for its own profit,—so long as either the Confucian or the more absolute Christian rendering of the Golden Rule has an influence over the minds of men. The signs of the times suggest that the world is getting through the trough of its recent moral depression,—that truer notes than those of armed force and material gain are already asserting themselves amongst the nations. A readjustment of relations between the Eastern and Western peoples is becoming necessary. The opium question, however skilfully it may be kept in the background, accounts for much of the weakness of England in the esteem of China; whilst it represents a distinct divergence of policy between this country and its new ally, Japan. On these broad grounds alone the problem should be faced fairly and frankly. It is only a hackneyed question to those to whom it is unwelcome, whose fears are stronger than their hopes. Its past certainly cannot be regarded with satisfaction by any school of Englishmen. Lord

Brassey, presiding over the Royal Commission before it had placed itself in the hands of the Government of India, said, "We may take it that we all regard that policy of the past with great regret." The sword has been resorted to again and again without any cleaning of our escutcheon; it is time to try methods that will lift our relationship with China on to a higher plane, promising better results.

The complications time has brought constitute in themselves formidable entrenchments for the protection of the traffic as now carried on. The span of human life is short, as compared with the numbers and length of modern blue-books. This essay is written to assist those who desire to forward mutual helpfulness amongst the nations, and to have a fair knowledge of the opium question, which has played, and may yet play, no unimportant part in our history.

On one point, at least, thoughtful contestants on both sides of the controversy may agree. The final issue is likely to be satisfactory [illegible] the [illegible] as it is the outcome of a knowledge of the [illegible] facts of history and of the experiences of human life, more especially in China. Charges of exaggeration are easy to make, and are not confined to either party. There is a disposition in some quarters to evade the responsibilities of inquiring into the facts, by quietly accepting as true sweeping charges of exaggeration against the opponents of the opium traffic, and against them only. It is human to err in this controversy as in any other; but any one who would bow the opium question out of court on the score of this infirmity on one side only, must be blind to the first principles of justice, or, more probably, have neglected altogether to search into the evidence for himself.

Many pamphlets and treatises have been written upon it, some by writers of great ability and knowledge, but they are difficult to come at now, and history moves persistently forward. The endeavour of the writer has been to sketch briefly the course of the opium trade in the past, with as little contentious matter as possible; to analyse the proceedings of the Royal Commission and Report, so far as they relate to the Indo-Chinese trade and the Chinese opium habit only; and to cite some of the most important evidence that has been given to the world on the larger issues of the question since the publication of the Commission's Report.

It is impossible specifically to acknowledge indebtedness, direct and indirect, to all previous writers and authorities; but the endeavour has been made to give references wherever practicable, in order that the reader may be in a position to consult at first [illegible] original sources of information.

In dealing with the Royal Commission, the writer has made use of some of his criticisms and analyses published at the time in *The Opium Habit in the East*, and elsewhere.

PREFACE
TO THE SECOND EDITION

THE author is indebted to the writers of the numerous reviews of this book, which have appeared from many different standpoints. A second edition offers an opportunity to add a brief résumé of some recent facts of special importance.

The Indian opium revenue for 1904–5, estimated at £2,947,700, reached the sum of £4,069,100. The official "explanatory statement" suggests that "it is unsafe to reckon on a continuance of the exceptional prices realised during the past two years."

Legislation against opium has taken place in the United States, South Africa, and Australasia, as follows:—

An Act of Congress revising the tariff of the Philippine Islands (3rd March 1905) provides (Clause 80) that the Philippine Commission shall have power to prohibit the sale of opium, or to limit its sale, or to adopt such other measures as may be required for the suppression of the evils resulting from the sale and use of the drug. After 1st March 1908, the importation of opium in any form, except by the Government, *and for medicinal purposes* only, shall cease. The revenue from opium was $350,000 at the passing of the Act. This prohibition policy follows from the report of a Commission appointed in 1903 "to visit the various countries of the Orient, and study the methods adopted for the suppressing of the evils growing out of the smoking and eating of opium." The Commission consisted of the chief of the Public Health Bureau, a prominent Filipino physician, and the Protestant Episcopal Bishop of the Islands. The members "started from varying view points," but after five months' travelling and investigation came to unanimous conclusions. The report is condensed, comprehensive, catholic. It says: "The Japanese fear opium as we fear the cobra or the rattlesnake, and they despise its victims. . . . China's curse has been Japan's warning. A non-Christian country is the only country visited where the opium question is dealt with in its purely moral and social aspect."

Of China it is said: "From an economical point of view, it appears that the opium habit is far and away the greatest hindrance existing to the industrial productiveness of Chinese labour." The American treaty obligation to carry no opium into China is endorsed with the remark, that the use of the drug "is an evil for which no financial gain can compensate, and which America will not allow her citizens to encourage even passively."

Turning to South Africa: on the 6th September 1905, Sir George Farrar moved the adjournment of the Legislative Council at Pretoria, to call attention to "the enormous quantity of opium" finding its way into the Transvaal. He urged that "measures should be taken for the immediate stopping of the traffic." Two chemists on the Rand were said to have imported two tons of opium during August for smoking purposes. On 6th October an ordinance was issued, restricting the importation of opium to registered chemists only, according to regulations to be prescribed by permits by the Lieutenant-Governor—under a penalty not exceeding £500, or imprisonment not exceeding six months.

Any person in possession of any such substance . . . except for medicinal purposes, unless under a permit, is liable to similar penalties. Stringent rights of search are given to police constables under certain circumstances, without even the necessity of a written authority.

It is difficult to imagine a more conclusive reply to apologists for the spread of opium in China, than this peremptory rising up of the mine owners of the Rand against the use of opium by their Chinese coolies.

The great Commonwealth of Australia has gone further than the Transvaal. From the 1st January 1906, the import of opium into the Commonwealth has been absolutely prohibited, except for medical purposes, and under stringent conditions.

It has been often pointed out that the opium vice had much to do with the gradual extinction of the native race in Queensland; now alarm has been caused by the foothold the drug has obtained in the slums of Sydney and Melbourne. In May last, the Chinese merchants of New South Wales agreed to abandon the trade, and not only to forego all its profits, but to subscribe funds for the cure of the opium victims. Similar gatherings of Chinese were held at Melbourne and Brisbane. Several of the States are supporting the action of the Commonwealth by drastic provisions against the retail sale. The total loss of revenue is estimated at £100,000.

From China come warnings to Great Britain not to champion the opium traffic much longer. The following paragraph is taken from the *China Times*, January 16, 1906:—

THE PROPOSED OPIUM MONOPOLY

The Viceroys of Chihli, Liang-Kiang, Liang-Kuang, and Liang-Nu, have jointly telegraphed to the Waiwupu (China

Foreign Office), requesting the Board to open negotiations with the British Minister in Peking, with regard to the scheme for the adoption of an Opium Monopoly in the provinces of China, and the gradual reduction of the importation of Indian opium, it being the intention of the Chinese Government to limit the production of home-grown opium, with the hope of getting rid of the opium-smoking evil in China by gradual steps. The Viceroys state that China can never become strong, and stand shoulder to shoulder with the Powers of the world, unless she can get rid of the habit of opium smoking by her subjects, about one quarter of whom have been reduced to skeletons, and look half-dead. Their Excellencies add, that, by adopting the Japanese methods in Formosa, China can be saved in the course of the next thirty years. As Great Britain is the friend of China, she will surely be glad to assist the Chinese Government to stamp out the evil. The Board replied that it would do as suggested.

The Chinese, who are acknowledged experts in combination, have introduced the boycott as a weapon of offence and defence against the West. According to the Press Association, they are pleased with the result of the boycott so far, and the newspapers have advocated its use against Indian opium. In any case it is not questioned that the movement of "China for the Chinese," foretold by Sir Robert Hart, has grown vastly stronger since the close of Japan's victory over Russia. The enrolling of a new army modelled on Japanese lines is proceeding apace, and in that army no opium smoker is accepted (*The Times*, 1st January 1906). It seems probable that timely action alone can save this country from the humiliation of being virtually compelled to discontinue a demoralising trade, at the instance of non-Christian powers.

J. R.

3rd March 1906

THE IMPERIAL DRUG TRADE

PART I: HISTORY

CHAPTER I

EARLY COMMERCE

THE main landmarks in the history of the relations between Great Britain and China are undisputed. Controversies mainly turn on the relative degrees of blame attaching to one party or the other.

Great mistakes have been made by both sides, with immediate results painful to look into, with far-reaching consequences that deserve more thought than they have yet received. As diplomatists cease to be themselves judges and juries, with executioners at call, such mistakes must become well-nigh impossible in the future. Every honest effort to put ourselves in thought in the place of those with whom we are, or have been, at variance, is in itself a step forward to better understandings.

The common idea, that China has always met Western approaches with churlish aloofness and childish arrogance, is not borne out by history; and without the historic key it is vain to attempt to unlock the mysteries of her procedure. Prior to the Christian era, a considerable trade existed between

China and the Roman Empire.[1] The Turks, Arabs, Persians, and Jews followed. Nestorian monks carried silkworms' eggs to Constantinople. The latest, and one of the most impartial of the historians of the East, Captain Brinkley, says: "Up to the middle of the fourteenth century, the attitude of the Chinese towards foreign trade and foreign religions was remarkably liberal, and even hospitable. There was no closing of ports, no persecution of converts to alien faiths, no law against the preaching or propagandism of strange creeds." The long tarriance of Marco Polo and his father in China, the appointment of the former to be Governor of Yangchou, and his employment in various capacities, illustrate this view. When enterprise passed from individual adventurers to companies, troubles began to show themselves. Western faith and civilisation too often forget that they have been peculiarly unfortunate in many of their pioneer representatives. The Portuguese, in return for a kindly welcome by the Chinese (whose "good order, industry, manners, and love of justice," one of their leaders, Mendez Pinto, duly commended), developed into lawless desperadoes and irresponsible conquerors. Sir John Davis, Governor of Hong Kong, wrote in 1845: "Their early conduct was not calculated to impress the Chinese with any favourable idea of Europeans; and when in course of time they came to be competitors with the Dutch and English, the contest of mercantile avarice tended to place them all in a still worse point of view." Dr. Wells Williams confirms this with the remark, "These characteristics of avarice, lawlessness, and power have been the leading traits in the Chinese estimate of foreigners from their first acquaintance with them,

[1] Brinkley, x. 135 *et seq.*

and the latter have done little to effectually disabuse Orientals upon these points."[1] The Spanish conquerors of the Philippines twice resorted to set massacres of the Chinese in those islands.[2] Their coolies returned home only to fan flames of discord against the foreigner. The Dutch at Macao forced the Chinese to labour for them, with great severity. The Russians, on the other hand, entered into a treaty with China, which lasted one hundred and thirty-one years.

The tone of the first official utterance of England to China might well have been had in remembrance by after diplomatists; Queen Elizabeth, addressing the Emperor, announced that "by intercourse and traffic, no loss, but rather most exceeding benefits, will redound to the princes and subjects of both kingdoms, and thus help and enrich one another"; so she sped her mariners, "for the greater increase of mutual love and commerce."[3] Alas, the bearers of this greeting were shipwrecked, and the Emperor never received the letter of the great Queen. When the first English squadron arrived off Macao in 1637, the Portuguese explained to the Chinese that the new-comers were "rogues, thieves, and beggars."[4] The Chinese attacked the strangers, who answered with a bombardment, and the demolition of "what they could." It has been said that in every phase of their intercourse with foreigners, the Chinese show well by the side of the Macao Portuguese. This is not saying much, as the record of the latter could not well be worse. Foreign trade and merchandise were too far beneath the serene atmosphere of the Celestial Government to merit its direct attentions.

[1] *The Middle Kingdom*, vol. ii. p. 427.
[2] Brinkley, x. 178. [3] Martin, p. 2. [4] Brinkley, x. 188.

Early in the eighteenth century it appointed the Hong merchants to act as a medium between the Chinese and the strange traffickers, who came unsought to their shores. The Hong were a syndicate of native merchants, who, in return for a monopoly of foreign trade, stood security for the customs' duties and for the proper carrying on of the over-sea commerce of China.

As the century progressed, and the wars of Europe extended to Eastern seas, the perplexities and annoyances of the Chinese grew fast. It would have taxed the best Western jurists to uphold strict neutrality over warships preying upon the merchantmen of different flags in far-off seas. Might was right, and the Chinese description of the foreigners as "fierce and barbarous," had much to justify it. The British embassies of the Earl of Macartney in 1792, of Lord Amherst in 1816, though undoubtedly intended to bring some order out of chaos, were in vain. China skilfully received the first as from one of its tributary States. The frigate *Alceste*[1] did not retrieve the position by firing on a flotilla and bombarding forts. Mistrust grew, and the estrangement widened. The whole of this narrative of the relations of East and West reads like a history of human error. A change for the worse came over China in its attitude towards foreigners. The rulers of this ancient and self-contained civilisation hardened themselves in their pride, isolation, and subtlety. Their Western visitors, more eager for gold than honour, returned the contempt with interest, and over and over again took the law ruthlessly into their own mailed fists.

All travellers bear witness to the hospitable dis-

[1] In the second expedition.

position of the natives to strangers in early days. The turn of the tide cannot be dissociated from a bitter experience of Western encroachments and brutalities. It is significant that the enmity grew most rapidly in and around Canton, the earliest centre of a European settlement. After it had spread along the coast, travellers inland still experienced kindly receptions as of old. Mr. Medhurst's pages,[1] though hot with insults and injuries received in Hong Kong, show how the moral conditions improved on his leaving the coast, and bear pleasing testimony to the cheerful willingness of the people of the interior. It is well to remember that the history of Japan bears the impress of a similar repulsion following the first impact between the two civilisations. In his great work on Japan, Captain Brinkley, after regretting the contemptuous treatment of the Japanese by foreign nations, concludes thus: "The memory of the evil time survives; the causes of the change suggest a low estimate of Western morality. . . . They now know that the world never took any respectful notice of them until they showed themselves capable of winning battles." In both countries the Chinese proverb was illustrated, "Stir the cane-brake, and rouse the snake."[2]

[1] *China*, pp. 395, 512.

[2] Brinkley, i. 16.

CHAPTER II

THE BEGINNINGS OF THE TRADE

A LEARNED historical statement on opium in China, compiled by Dr. Edkins, of the Chinese Customs' Service in 1889, is reprinted in the Report of the Royal Commission.[1] The drug seems to have been introduced by Arab traders, who dealt in precious stones, spices, drugs, etc. Its original Chinese name "afuyung" is clearly the Arabic "afyun"; "foreign medicine" is still its designation in the Chinese tariff, while it is popularly known as "foreign smoke."

The poppy may have been indigenous, but it is mentioned so rarely in the abundant early literature of the country, that it cannot have filled any conspicuous place in the imagination of the people. It is first described by Ch-en Ts'ang-chi, an author of the first half of the eighth century, who quotes from an earlier writer. The second mention occurs at the end of the century. In a medical work written under imperial auspices in 973, the seeds of the poppy are described as possessing healing properties. A contemporary poem alludes to its narcotic virtues. About 1057, a medical author writes: "The poppy is found everywhere; many persons cultivate it as an ornamental flower"; and he goes on to speak of the seeds as medicine.

[1] *R. C. Report*, vol. i.

In the fifteenth and sixteenth centuries the Chinese were, next to the Arabs, the chief traders in the Indian seas; before the discovery of the passage round the Cape of Good Hope by the Portuguese, the maritime trade to the East was mainly carried on by the Venetians from South-Western Europe to the Persian Gulf and the Red Sea; from Aden to Malacca by Arab merchants, and from Malacca by the Chinese. The Venetians were afterwards supplanted by the Portuguese; the Portuguese by the Dutch, and the Dutch again by the English, each in their turn extending their horizon, and taking a wider sweep for their commerce. Barbosa, who accompanied his relative the famous Magellan, writes in 1516:

"The Chinese are also great navigators . . . they go with all their goods to Malacca . . . for the return voyage they ship drugs of Cambay, much *afiam*, which we call opium, wormwood, saffron, etc." Barbosa mentions that the opium coming from Aden commanded a much higher price than the Malwa drug from Cambay. In 1589, and again in 1616, opium occurs in the tariff of duties on imported goods.

A medical work of 1589 states: "Formerly opium was not much heard of, recently it has been used by some in medical recipes." It is evident the seeds were prepared and used at times for food. Acosta, a Portuguese doctor and naturalist, in a work on the drugs of the East Indies, speaks of the common use of opium to cause sleep, lighten fatigue, and stimulate lust. "Though condemned by reason, it is used so extensively that it is the most general and familiar remedy of degraded debauchees." After stating that this use defeats itself, he continues:

"Such is the opinion not only of all the followers of our medical system, but also of the Arabic, Persian, Turkish, Coringa (Madras coast), Sunda, Malay, Chinese, and Malabar doctors. The worst of it is, that once it has become a habit, they cannot give up their liking for it without great risk of life." The doctor's own experiences were chiefly in India. In the *Travels of Theuenot* (1655), the sentence occurs: "The Chinese are said to have the best preparation of it (opium) in the world."

Bontius, a Dutch physician, who died in Batavia, wrote in 1629, that those nations which use opium seem drowsy, dull in commerce and in arms; but in dysentery, cholera, burning fever, etc., "we should practise medicine in vain without it."[1]

The manufacture of opium in China would seem to date from the latter part of the fifteenth century. Its early use was evidently that of a drug.

A curious glimpse into the transition from Dutch to English commercial supremacy in the East, also from the private adventurer to the company stage of the opium trade, is revealed by Captain Hamilton,[2] who spent forty years in India at the beginning of the eighteenth century. In 1714, the native ruler of Calicut went to war with the Dutch East India Company; after fighting for three years, he was forced to accept very disadvantageous terms, including the payment of a heavy war indemnity and a perpetual tax of 7 per cent. on all pepper exported from his dominions. After observing that "the chief of our English factory, privy councillor to the native ruler, had a great hand in promoting the war," Captain Hamilton continues: "Whether our English East India Company got or lost by that

[1] Edkins. [2] *New Account of the East Indies.*

war, I know not, nor will I pretend to pass judgment on their affairs; but this I know, that the chief lost a good milch cow; for the chiefs of Calicut had vended between 500 and 1000 chests of Bengal opium yearly up in the inland countries, where it is very much used; the water carriage up the river being cheap and secure, the price of opium high, and the price of pepper low, so that the profits were great both ways; for, if I mistake not, the Company paid the highest price for their pepper, and by the unexpected turn of affairs caused by the war, that trade is fallen entirely into the Dutch Company's hands, and it will be a very difficult task to get it out again."

Hamilton describes Patna as "frequented by Europeans, where the English and Dutch have factories. It produces so much opium that it serves all the countries in India with that commodity." The discovery of this "beneficial trade" is ascribed to "one Mr. Lucas, a factor in the Company's service at Malacca, who was advised by a Malay to send some *surat bastaes* dyed blue and some *berams* dyed red, which are both coarse cotton cloth much worn in that country; and opium is as much in request there as tea is with us. In the ten years that he kept that trade wholly to himself, though in other men's names, he got an estate of ten or twelve tons of gold, or about £100,000, and then revealed that secret to the Company, who took that trade altogether into their own hands."

This explains why the Annals of the East India Company contains a despatch from the Company's agent at Borneo, which runs: "Indian produce must be sent on the Company's account only, and not on that of their individual servants in India; the market for opium, for instance, having this year (1703) been totally engrossed, and a sufficient quantity for twelve months brought by a vessel, which had arrived under Sir Edward Littleton's pass from Bengal."

Daniel Defoe, like Hakluyt, was in the habit of conversing largely with the sailors of the port of London. The statements in *Robinson Crusoe* reflect the general knowledge of the time with regard to the trade in the drug. The first edition, published at the "Sign of the Ships," Paternoster Row, in 1719, states:

"I made this voyage to Achim, in the island of Sumatra, and thence to Siam, where we exchanged some of our wares for opium, a commodity which bears a great price among the Chinese, and which at that time was very much wanted there. . . . Returned to Bengale, and I was very well satisfied with my adventure. I observe that our people in England often admire how the officers which the Company send into India, and the merchants, which generally stay there, get such very great estates as they do, and sometimes come home with 60 to 70 thousand pounds at a time."

Speaking of an after voyage, Defoe says: "He told us that our best port would have been to put in at Macao, where we could not have failed of a market for our opium to our satisfaction." And again, "The opium and other goods we had on board would make it appear the ship had been at Bengale."

It is quite clear, then, that opium has long been known in China as a medicine, and that the poppy has been used there, as it is in India, as a vegetable. It is probable that there grew up in some districts a demand for the drug for vicious purposes also. But it is practically certain, from the absence of all mention of any opium habit by the Jesuit missionaries, by travellers, and in the Chinese records, that there was no general consumption of opium before the introduction of opium smoking.

The first account of opium smoking locates it in Formosa. It is given by Huang Yu-pu, a native of Pekin, who had been sent to investigate the island early in the eighteenth century. His observations are quoted in a work on Formosa, published in 1746:

"Opium for smoking is prepared by mixing hemp and the grasscloth plant with opium, and cutting them up small. This mixture is boiled with water, and the preparation mixed with tobacco. A bamboo tube is also provided, the end of which is filled with coir fibres. Many persons collect the opium to smoke mixed with tobacco alone. Those who make it their sole business to prepare opium in this way are known as opium tavern-keepers. Those who smoke once or twice form a habit which cannot be broken off. . . . The aborigines smoke as an aid to vice. The limbs grow thin and appear to be wasting away; the internal organs collapse. The smoker, unless he be killed, will not cease smoking. The local officers have from time to time strictly prohibited the habit. It has often been found that when the time came for administering the bastinado to culprits of this class, they would beg for a brief respite that they might first take another smoke. Opium came from Java."[1]

The rapid spread of the habit of smoking tobacco mixed with opium, resulted in 1729 in an edict

[1] Edkins.

prohibiting the sale, and the opening of opium-smoking houses. Its disastrous physical effects led the Pekin Government to regard it as an alarming social evil. "Sellers of opium were to bear the wooden collar for a month, and to be banished to the frontier. The keepers of shops were to be punished in the same way as propagators of depraved doctrine—strangled after a few months' imprisonment. Their assistants were to be beaten with 100 blows, and banished 1000 miles. Boatmen, neighbours lending help, soldiers, police-runners, all in any way connected with the matter, had punishments assigned them. Magistrates and custom house superintendents were all to bear some penalty. Only the opium smoker was exempted."

This edict was followed by another the next year, for the checking of evil practices amongst the colonists of Formosa. The sale of gambling instruments or of opium for smoking was classed with robbery and instigation to murder, and punished with banishment or death.

Dr. Edkins continues: "Opium selling for smoking purposes has from this time (1729) forward been regarded as a crime by the ruling authorities. From their point of view it is considered as criminal in proportion to the mischief it causes, which is without doubt great beyond computation. The very earliest instance of legislation in the matter . . . was based on local events occurring on the sea-coast a long way from Pekin. The gradual spread of the habit to all the provinces was still in the future, and not before the minds of the legislators. The sale of opium was connected in their minds with gambling, robbery, and false accusation, its special guilt consisted in its being a temptation to evil on the part of the salesman, as the drug was destructive of the comfort, physical health, and life of their victims." The English, as already mentioned, gradually ousted the Portuguese and took the trade into their own hands. The sale is said to have gradually risen to 1000 chests per annum in 1767; the actual figures cannot be ascertained.

Dr. Edkins states that at the conquest of Bengal by Clive, "the minor portion only of the opium imported into China was devoted to smoking. The superintendents of customs would continue to take the duty on opium as a drug. What was contraband they would say was 'ya-pien-yen' (opium for smoking), the drug 'ya-pien' would still pass the customs as medicine. Medicine claimed opium as a most powerful agent, and since the commencement of the trade at Canton and Amoy, whether the merchants were Portuguese, Chinese, Arab, or Dutch, it was as a medicine that it had been sold."

That a conflict between the traders in the drug and the Chinese authorities had arisen in some parts before the time usually assigned to it, is shown by a letter from Mr. Fitzhugh to Mr. Gregory of the East India Company, written in 1782. The importation of opium, he declares, is forbidden "under very severe penalties. The opium on seizure is burnt, the vessel confiscated, and the Chinese possessing it are liable to death. The contraband trade is only carried on through the excess of corruption on the part of the customs' officials."[1]

The opium vice continued to spread rapidly, causing real alarm to the authorities. In order to stem the tide more effectually, a universal edict was issued by the Emperor in 1799, prohibiting the

[1] *Parl. Report*, 1783, vol. vi. App. 77.

importation of the drug, as well as its vicious use among the people.[1] It recites that opium alone was exempted from "the free interchange of commodities" with foreign nations permitted at Whampoa and Macao. It is described as "a substance of whose composition we are unacquainted, the use of which originally prevailed only among vagrants and disreputable persons, but has since extended itself to others, and even to students and officials; their inducement appears to be the power which this substance communicates to those who partake of it, of not closing their eyes for entire nights, and spending them in the gratification of impure and sensual desires, whereby their respective duties and occupations are neglected." The pernicious effects are stated to have been formerly confined to one province. The frequency of suicide through its agency is referred to. "Foreigners obviously derive the most solid profits and advantages" through the traffic, "but that our countrymen should blindly pursue this destructive and ensnaring vice . . . is indeed odious and deplorable in the highest degree."

Probably the edict had some effect at the time; but seventeen years later an observing traveller writes:

"No opium is exposed for sale in the shops, probably because it is a contraband article, but it is used with tobacco in all parts of the empire. The Chinese, indeed, consider the smoking of opium as one of the greatest luxuries; and if they are temperate in drinking, they are often excessive in the use of this drug. They have more than one method of smoking it: sometimes they envelop a piece of solid gum in tobacco and smoke it from

[1] *R. C. Report*, vii. 74.

a pipe with a very small bowl, and sometimes they steep fine tobacco in a strong solution of it, and use it in the same way. The smokers of opium have a very peculiar sottish and sleepy physiognomy, in consequence of the whole visage being turgid with blood." . . . (After smoking) "they fall into a sort of torpor, and continue in it for several minutes, and much longer, when they can command time for its indulgence."[1]

Dr. Abel, who was naturalist to Lord Amherst's embassy, makes no mention of the poppy, either as a crop or as a plant in China, though he is careful to enumerate all crops and plants that he saw.

[1] Clarke Abel, *Journey in China*, p. 214.

CHAPTER III

THE MONOPOLY OF THE EAST INDIA COMPANY

TURNING now to India, it would appear that opium was introduced there, as well as into China, by the Arabs. Monopolies have not been viewed with as much disfavour in the East as in the West. In the days of the Mogul Empire, towards the end of the sixteenth century, opium was farmed as a Government monopoly. With the decay of the empire the monopoly fell through, and the trade languished. In the "privileges and immunities" formerly enjoyed by the Mogul princes, the servants of the English East India Company "now found a compensation for the scanty allowances made to them by their masters in England."[1]

The British opium trade was at first "managed chiefly by the civil servants of the Patna factory, and for their own benefit." When the profits promised to be considerable, the Company took them over for its own gain, leasing the monopoly to one or more native contractors. The system had its disadvantages. It is mentioned incidentally, that notwithstanding a "dreadful famine" in Bengal, "several of the poorer farmers were compelled to plough up the fields they had sown with grain, in

[1] *Parl. Papers*, 1783.

order to plant them with poppies, for the benefit of the engrossers of opium."

The Company in India at this time was Warren Hastings, and he was responsible for the revival of the opium monopoly, with its transference from the account of merchandise to that of revenue. On behalf of this policy he urged that "opium was not a necessary of life, but a pernicious article of luxury, which ought not to be permitted but for the purposes of foreign commerce only, and which the wisdom of the Government should carefully restrain from internal consumption." In view of all that has transpired since, Lord Cornwallis showed a truer insight into the matter when he wrote in 1786: "I suspect even that the opium and other contracts, the terms of which appear so advantageous, are not calculated to promote the real interests of the Company."[1]

In pursuance of Hastings' discriminating ethics, the best opium was reserved for export, the inferior sold for home consumption. The London Directors endorsed the monopoly as to growth and manufacture, but declined to become traders and distributors. Hastings gave the monopoly to a young inexperienced Englishman, by whom it was promptly sold and sub-sold. Hastings also sent cargoes of opium to Malacca and China on account of the Company. The ships were armed and supplied with the Company's soldiers. Some 3450 chests were sent forth under these auspices. The expedition was doomed to disaster. One of the ships was seized by the French; the Chinese market proved to be disappointing, and the total loss was estimated at £20,000. The Company's super-

[1] Cornwallis, *Cor.*, i. 238.

cargoes at Canton were surprised and puzzled at the consignment. They wrote to Calcutta (1782): "The importation of opium being strongly prohibited by the Chinese Government, and a business altogether new to us, it was necessary to take our measures with the utmost caution."[1] They sold the contraband cargoes secretly to two of the Hong merchants, but deprecated, on financial grounds, the course adopted by their superiors, and contended that if any "urgency of need" led to a repetition, long credit must be allowed, as the purchaser "can have no prospect of selling any considerable part of it here." This is clear proof that the opium habit was not as yet generally prevalent throughout China.

The Directors at home condemned the transaction strongly. They had been informed that the importation of opium into China was forbidden under very severe penalties, "under any circumstances it is beneath the Company to be engaged in such a clandestine trade." They positively forbade the sending of opium to China, but favoured the establishment of a trading station in the eastern islands, whence, as they thoughtfully remark, "whatever opium might be in demand by the Chinese, the quantity would readily find its way thither without the Company being exposed to the disgrace of being engaged in an illicit commerce." The commerce, so carefully shielded from any disgraceful exposure, continued for a term of seventy-eight years on the same illicit footing.

Whilst they did not adhere to the policy of Warren Hastings, in which opium appeared as an article for export merely, the Company were

[1] *Parl. Papers*, 1787.

evidently anxious to keep down the opium habit in India. The rules placing the drug along with spirits under the excise, confined the sale in those days (1813) to one or two of the principal towns in each district; collectors were enjoined to discourage "to the utmost extent of their means the sale and consumption of the drug, except for medicinal purposes." In sanctioning these licensing arrangements, the Court of Directors wrote (1817): "It is our wish, not to encourage the consumption of opium, but rather to lessen the use, or, more properly speaking, the abuse of the drug; and for this end, as well as for the purpose of revenue, to make the price to the public, both in our own and in foreign dominions, as high as possible. . . . Were it possible to prevent the use of the drug altogether, except strictly for the purpose of medicine, we would gladly do it in compassion to mankind."[1] Unhappily for these disinterested opinions, the opium revenue grew greatly. The sales rose gradually from 2330 chests in 1788–89 to 4968 in 1809–10; passed this figure in 1821–22; reached 10,570 in 1825–26; and were then forced up to 17,257 in 1835–36.[2] In 1830, the Governor-General wrote: "We are taking measures for extending the cultivation of the poppy, with a view to a large increase in the supply of opium." All vestige of compassion for mankind, at any rate outside India, had been swept away by the silver stream of rupees which poured into the Calcutta Exchequer.

Whilst vigorously prosecuting the manufacture of opium for consumption in China, the fear of disgrace led the Company to pass stringent regulations, for-

[1] *Parl. Report*, 1831. [2] *R. C. Report*, vii. 61.

bidding any of their servants to carry the contraband article to China, under pain of instant dismissal.[1] As a matter of fact, no British ship could trade between India and China without a licence from the Company, and these licences were given with the proviso, that they would be cancelled if the holders failed to obey the orders of the Company's supercargoes at Canton; they were to be cancelled, moreover, if any other opium than that of the Company was put on board. Any British trader or employee found in China without a licence was liable to be seized and imprisoned.[2] An opium merchant, Mr. Jardine, told the Committee of 1840, he did not see how the supercargoes could disclaim participation in the opium traffic, because they used to advance money upon it. Twice in the course of their history the Company refunded a proportion of the purchase money to the purchasers, because the Chinese trade had proved exceptionally disastrous.[3]

Like Bunyan's waterman, *Mr. Facing-both-ways*, the Company resolutely looked one way and rowed the other. A sailing fleet of some of the finest clippers ever built carried the drug to China; their successful voyages were duly chronicled in the Indian papers. In its infancy the trade sought shelter in the Portuguese settlement at Macao, but the reception was not a kindly one, and the opium ships went instead to Whampoa. Here the pressure of corrupt Chinese officials proved too severe, and for a time the storeships were moved to Lintin amongst the network of islands at the mouth of the Canton River. These ships were floating batteries, protected with large guns, small arms,

[1] *China Trade Report*, 1840. [2] *Ibid.*, Q. 1383.
[3] *Ibid.*, pp. 170, 118.

and netting above the bulwarks, capable of defying all the war-junks of the Chinese Empire. The drug, taken out of the chests on board ship, was put into bags for easier transfer, and smuggled on shore in fast boats, known as "crabs," manned in the earlier years of the century by Chinese, but later by desperadoes of other races, armed to the teeth.

The spread of the opium habit along the coast was assisted by trading voyages undertaken for this purpose.[1] A Captain Parkyns is credited with setting the example in the *Merope*. He was followed by Mr. Matheson, then acting as Danish Consul at Canton, who proceeded in 1823 as far as Chin-chow, some 400 miles up the coast, without making any profit that trip; but he developed a considerable trade on sending a ship to the same ports next year. After another successful voyage, the mandarins intervened on behalf of the laws of the land; they burned the houses of those who dealt with the foreign smugglers, and stopped the trade for the time. Better financial results attended similar voyages to Amoy. A Mr. Innes is said to have made 330,000 dollars in one voyage in 1831. A Mr. Majoribanks, emulating him, entirely failed, "because the drug was comparatively unknown." Ultimately, receiving ships were stationed in several places along the coast, just outside the limits of the ports. The officials, in the vast majority of cases, were successfully corrupted, and became willing accomplices in the contraband trade, which went forward with great regularity.

There are records of Chinese memorials in the years 1799, 1812, 1815, and 1820, praying for

[1] Tinling, p. 55.

further measures of repression on the part of the Imperial Government. In 1809, the Governor of Canton published an edict, requiring the Hong merchants, when a ship discharged her cargo at Whampoa, to give a bond that no opium was on board. In 1815, an order was issued to search all vessels at Macao; a similar action in 1820 caused a serious interruption of trade, compelling a separation for some months of licit from illicit merchandise. In 1821, a Chinese edict declared the seizure of one American and three English vessels for opium smuggling at Canton, and the confiscation of half their cargoes. By a subsequent edict the forfeiture was remitted, but they were forbidden either to sell the cargoes, to carry away tea and rhubarb, or to trade any more in the future. The edict on this occasion says: "Yet these foreigners feel no gratitude, nor wish to render a recompense; but smuggle in opium, which poisons the empire. . . . They should rouse themselves to zealous reflection, to bitter repentance, and to reformation, and alter their inhuman unreasonable conduct."

The supercargoes wrote home: "On our secret records your honourable Committee will perceive the measures so frequently threatened by the Chinese Government to check the opium trade."[1] Later (1822) they reported: "These measures have since been persisted in by the Viceroy of Canton with such a degree of pertinacity, as to occasion the most serious interruption of this most important branch of trade." "We were desirous to avoid the slightest implication on the part of the Honourable Company, and at the same time not to oppose unnecessary impediments to the trade." The supercargoes admit

[1] *Parl. Papers*, 1831.

that if put to the test, "the arguments we have taken up, though specious, cannot be maintained."

Up to 1812, the apparent balance of trade was not unfavourable to China. As the opium traffic grew, the drain of native silver in exchange became great, and intensified the hostility of the Chinese to this illicit commerce.[1]

Another cause of the growing alienation is indicated by a House of Commons Committee of 1830, in the apprehension that "towards the English there exists peculiar jealousy and distrust, arising from a knowledge of their territorial acquisitions and military achievements in India, especially those in Nepaul and Ava."[2]

In dealing with the opium trade, the Report proceeds: "The Chinese Government prohibits the use of opium upon a moral principle; but their prohibition, although frequently reiterated in imperial proclamations, is not only disregarded by the people, but also by the Government officers, who appear systematically to connive at the smuggling of opium, and to derive a large profit from the bribes of the smugglers. . . . The trade, which is altogether contraband, has been largely extended of late years. Many of the ships go back in ballast, taking their sale proceeds either in bills or specie, the exportation of which requires a licence from the Chinese authorities. This permission is granted occasionally for dollars, but never for native silver (sycee). Both are, however, constantly exported by private traders to India in spite of the prohibition; and the whole export of silver by different parties has in some years considerably overbalanced the importation of dollars."

[1] *R. C. Report*, vii. 72. [2] *Ibid.*, 100.

Neither moral principles, the forcing of more opium on the Chinese, nor the disorganisation of the monetary system of China, weighed with the House of Commons.[a] The East was a long way off, and matters were left to take their course. This course became a stormy one in 1830. The British refused to surrender to the authorities some Parsees who had beaten a Dutch captain to death; they also refused compliance with the Chinese regulations forbidding European women to come to Canton, and prohibiting the use of Sedan chairs to foreigners. Two East Indian ships left the port without proper clearances, with orders, on passing the forts, to return blank cartridge with blank cartridge, and ball with ball. Various irritating restrictions on the liberty of the merchants followed, and the Canton Committee seriously threatened war. In defiance of orders, they enclosed ground in front of the factory, and ordered up sailors and guns.

The Governor-General of India decided to support the Committee, but the Directors at home intervened to stop hostilities, admitting that China had the right to regulate commercial dealings as she thought fit, and reminding their subordinates at Canton: "It is essential you should clearly understand, that you are not the representatives of the British nation, but of the East India Company."

In 1832–33, the Committee, again defying the authorities, sent a vessel up the coast to open out new markets. The Directors again intervened on behalf of peace and order, but their authority no longer carried much weight with some of the private traders. Mr. Innes did not confine his enterprises

[a] Appendix I. note 1.

to the extension of the opium trade.[1] Wishing to make representations about some private grievance, he entered the apartment of the Chinese superintendent of customs with two friends and a Chinese purveyor. The superintendent was asleep. A member of the household rushed at the intruder and assailed him with a wooden chopper. Mr. Innes demanded the trial of his assailant, and swore that if the man was not arrested before sunset he would set fire to the house of the superintendent. The man was not arrested, and the English merchant accordingly set fire to the mandarin's house with rockets and blue-lights. On the following day the native was punished for assault by the Chinese. Not only was the Englishman never called to account, but his example was actually instanced by Lord Napier to prove that "success has always attended determination."[2] Success is often a curiously deceptive word. The Committee in charge in China began to be anxious about the future of the traffic. "It can never be a recognised trade," they wrote to the Directors, "it is now to all intents and purposes an established one." The smugglers grew bolder and more aggressive, and fights with natives occurred up and down the coast. In 1831, one Chinese was killed, and several wounded, by English and American smugglers. The Committee disclaimed responsibility, and the smugglers remained unmolested. The strain became well-nigh intolerable, and in 1832 the Governor of Canton, who was alleged to be a participant in the smuggling, suggested to the Emperor the alternative of legalising the opium trade. He urged that the consumers smoked to their own injury and were unworthy of regard; that if the

[1] *R. C. Report*, vii. 114. [2] *China Cor.*, 1840, p. 14.

drug were brought in as a medicine, the foreigners would be prevented from raising the price, and this might place "a silent impediment in the way of their avaricious plans and large profits."[1] The memorialist was censured for this proposal. In 1833, an affray between the opium fleet and natives led to another approach to open war. In the account forwarded to the Directors, the Committee "fear that the time has been gradually approaching, and has now arrived, when the system of non-interference has raised up a power, and encouraged a lawless and piratical mode of procedure, which it is absolutely incumbent upon us to put down." In this case, as in many others, the Chinese authorities behaved with studious moderation. The evils continued to grow, and Great Britain did nothing to put them down. The same year further severe laws were enacted against both buyers and smokers of opium.

Never has a great trade sprung up under more extraordinary circumstances. A Government pushed to the utmost the growth of the poppy, and the manufacture and sale of the drug, for the sake of revenue. It licensed the ships that carried the drug, with their captains and crews. It provided that they should be absolutely controlled by its officers in China. It affixed its own stamp to the drug, and took pains that it should be manufactured expressly to suit the taste of the Chinese. Yet because the trade was illegal, it disclaimed and instructed its officers at the receiving port to disclaim all knowledge of the trade. The drug was frequently confiscated, and natives were executed for criminal disobedience to the laws of their country. The smuggling led to piracy; boat crews were armed to the teeth;

[1] *China Cor.*, 1840, p. 153.

a merchant concerned had "known some instances in which the opium boats have been seized, and the crews have had their heads cut off."[1] Still the illusion was kept up. The Government receiving its income from such a source, ostentatiously washed its hands in innocency, and forbade its officials to engage in the later stages of the trade!

The attitude of the receiving nation is little less remarkable. She steadfastly abjured the trade with all its ways and consequences; but her officials, for the most part, as steadily accepted bribes and acted as willing accomplices. On the score of deception there is little to choose between the two, the briber certainly cannot boast himself against the bribed. Before their respective responsibilities can be apportioned, their relative degrees of moral enlightenment and material force behind it must first be determined and allowed for. The amazing extent of the deception practised is clearly revealed in evidence given later by one of the leading opium merchants. Mr. Inglis stated that "it very much horrified the whole foreign community to find that Captain Elliot had for the first time committed his Government to a knowledge of the opium trade, because in the time of the East India Company, the East India Company's factory had most carefully avoided admitting to the Chinese that they knew anything about it, and so had H.M. Government always done, up to that period."[2]

In the official correspondence of that time two forces are constantly seen clashing against one another. On the one hand, a determined striving on the part of the foreigners for the extension of trade, lawful or unlawful, backed guardedly by the maritime

[1] *China Cor.*, 1840, p. 158. [2] *Ibid.*, Q. 745.

power of the West; on the other, a resort to harassing restrictions on trade and on the traders by the frightened officials of the immovable East. The Celestial mind clung closely to commerce, differing in this from the Japanese, but like them perpetually harassed by a dread of the rude aggressions ever following in its wake. One distinction between the two governments should be recognised. The Emperors of China appear to have been immovably hostile to the opium trade.

CHAPTER IV

BRITISH SUPERINTENDENCE

A NEW chapter in the relations of the two countries was opened on April 23, 1834. The Reform Parliament brought the monopoly of the East India Company over the Chinese trade to an end, and gave all English traders liberty to sail the Eastern seas. For more than a generation the Company had carried on a large trade with China, without any Chinese war having been laid to its charge. There is no doubt that it played a double game in the opium trade, and the consequences fell heavily upon its successors. Nevertheless it had maintained some hold, though a lessening one, over its traders. The British Government committed the grave mistake of sending out superintendents of trade, without giving them any real powers, either over the merchants, or the motley crews for whom they were nominally responsible.

These superintendents were appointed to protect British traders "in the peaceful prosecution of all lawful enterprises, and to avoid all that might unnecessarily irritate the feelings or revolt the opinions of the Chinese people or Government." In sending out Lord Napier as Chief Superintendent, Lord Palmerston instructed him to seek to extend trade; to discourage adventurous traders, but never to lose sight of the fact that he had "no authority to interfere with or prevent them."[1]

The superintendents were ordered to take up their residence at Canton,—no such permission had been given by China, nor was it even asked; no communication was sent in advance informing the punctilious Chinese of the new arrangements. The substitution of Government officials for Company traders was very distasteful to the authorities at Pekin, still more so the refusal to communicate through the Hong merchants as aforetime. "The petty affairs of commerce are to be directed by the merchants themselves," wrote the Governor of Canton; "any changes in the trade of the said barbarians" should come from the merchants.[2] The intervention of the British Government was held to be unwarranted and suspicious. Instead of allaying this suspicion, the steps now taken decidedly enhanced it. "Even England," the Governor remonstrated, "has its laws, how much more the Celestial Empire." Each side contrived to exasperate the other; the Governor kept emphasising the breach of decorum in the attempt to thrust officials on them without any previous sanction. Lord Napier—who had already informed his Government that all Chinese could read—posted placards appealing to the Cantonese "against the ignorance and obstinacy of their Viceroy."[3] The Viceroy retaliated by calling Lord Napier a "lawless foreign slave," and Lord Napier writing home designated the Viceroy "a presumptuous savage." Lord Napier's residence was surrounded by the Chinese; two frigates came up the river to his assistance, and hostilities took place,

[1] *China Cor.*, 1840, p. 3. [2] P. 18.
[3] P.

attended with loss of life—and followed by an interruption of trade.

A few weeks later, Lord Napier retired to Macao, where he died of fever, aggravated by his difficulties and disappointments. Mr. Davis filled the gap until the appointment of Sir George Robinson as Chief Superintendent. The trade, licit and illicit, was resumed, and the dangers arising out of the latter grew apace.

In an able memorandum drawn up by the Duke of Wellington (1835), the Government acknowledged the failure of its Chinese policy: "It is quite obvious that the attempt made to force upon the Chinese authorities at Canton an unaccustomed mode of communication with an authority of whose powers and of whose nature they had no knowledge, which commenced its proceedings by an assumption of power hitherto unadmitted, had completely failed, . . . as it is obvious that such an attempt must invariably fail, and lead again to national disgrace."[1] On Lord Napier's death, the Chinese called upon the British merchants to select a commercial man as director of all affairs of trade, urging: "This is an affair of buying and selling; it is not what officers can attend to."[2] The director was to control the barbarian ships, and prevent the smuggling going on at Lintin, where nearly forty vessels were then anchored, "which neither come up to trade, nor yet get under weigh."[3] The Emperor was informed that the "barbarian ships which clandestinely sell opium on the outer seas are daily increasing; just when the laws were being established to bring them to order, there came this mad, mistaken, barbarian eye.[4] If at this time indulgence should be shown

[1] *China Cor.*, 1840, p. 51. [2] P. 55. [3] P. 48. [4] Lord Napier.

them, they will then advance step by step, begetting other foolish expectations."[1] Renewed endeavours were made to deter natives from trading with foreigners, except through the responsible Hong merchants, who in the main kept aloof from the opium traffic. The "native bandits" who dealt with the opium ships were to be suppressed; the strange merchants that "by nature have no other object but gain," were to be persistently watched. In forwarding these numerous edicts, Mr. Davis adds: "It remains now to be seen whether the native Government, having its attention at length awakened by the increased amount of smuggling transactions . . . will endeavour to give greater efficacy to its edicts."[2]

In 1835, the Chinese issued revised regulations for foreign trade, and complained bitterly of the growth of smuggling. Their grievance cannot be disputed; its long continuance only emboldened the smugglers. Mr. Innes, encouraged by his previous successes in carrying on private war, publicly threatened reprisals on Chinese commerce for an alleged injury to some of his merchandise. When the matter was referred to the Home Government, Lord Palmerston pointed out that Mr. Innes would have rendered himself liable to penalties for piracy, and that "the Government would not have interfered on his behalf."[3] In a despatch reviewing the extent of smuggling and consequent scuffles along the coast, Sir George Robinson indicated the weak points in the position which Lord Palmerston took up in regard to the opium traffic: "Whenever H.M. Government direct us to prevent British vessels engaging in the traffic, we can enforce any order

[1] *China Cor.*, 1840, p. 65. [2] P. 76. [3] P. 112.

to that effect, but a more certain method would be to prohibit the growth of the poppy, and manufacture of opium in British India."[1]

Sir George Robinson took up his residence in a cutter at Lintin, in the midst of the smuggling fleet. As if to add to the difficulties, the Indian Government took extraordinary pains to promote the growth of the poppy, which resulted in a large extension of the opium trade.

In the same year a scheme for legalisation was again brought forward, and the English representative sent the news home with feverish joy. An official memorial to the Emperor[2] recited the growth of the habit and its many evils. At Lintin, seven or eight large receiving ships were constantly anchored. "Fast crabs" or "scrambling dragons" plied up and down the river, "well armed and manned with some scores of desperadoes, who ply their oars as if they were wings to fly with. All the custom houses and military posts are heavily bribed. If they happen to encounter any of the armed boats, slaughter and carnage ensue. "Smoking," the memorial states, "is destructive of time, injurious to property, and yet dear to one as life." "The individuals themselves clearly see the evil effects of it, yet cannot refrain." But the smokers are unworthy of consideration as compared with the "waste taking place in the resources, the very substance of China." A guarded legalisation is recommended, but even in this memorial the absolute necessity of prohibiting opium to all officers, soldiers, and scholars is insisted on, as essential to the safety of the State. Two officials, to whom the memorial was submitted, reported in the same strain. They

[1] *China Cor.*, 1840, p. 120. [2] P. 156.

advised that the prohibition of the poppy should be relaxed, since "there was no better way of shutting out the importation of opium by foreigners." The Chinese drug was said to be milder and less injurious; the habit was still to be strictly prohibited to officers, scholars, and soldiers. Counter memorials from other dignitaries protested against any pulling down of dikes. "It would be impossible to permit the drug to the common people and prohibit it to the army and literati; its use by the soldiers would be the ruin of the empire."[1] A deficiency in property might be supplied, but "it is beyond the power of any artificial means to save a people enervated by luxury. In the people lies the very foundation of the empire." Foreigners proved themselves presumptuous and violent by riding in sedan chairs, consorting with Chinese prostitutes, levelling graves to make a road at Macao, and by their lawless trading in the high seas, etc.; but if only the native accomplices were "awed and purified," the strangers would surely succumb.[2] The principal provincial authorities were practically unanimous against legalisation, and the Emperor decided to persevere with the policy of exclusion.

A notice to leave China was served on eight of the principal opium traders, whilst their Chinese accomplices were severely dealt with. Captain Elliot, who was now in charge, transmitted all these memorials to Lord Palmerston. He considered the last edict "an intolerably injurious aggression," and announced his intention of interposing if the gentlemen in question were expelled. Ultimately they were allowed to remain.

Of the many men who have served England with

[1] *China Cor.*, 1840, p. 170. [2] P. 177.

self-sacrificing devotion abroad, few should have more allowance made for them than Captain Elliot. He was sent out with absurdly limited powers. He sought to have them enlarged in vain. He asked for the assistance of a special commissioner, and it was denied him. He was expected to keep on good terms with the Chinese, with British merchants, and with armed British smugglers, and to persuade them all to keep on good terms with each other. The breakdown that inevitably followed cannot fairly be laid to his charge.[1]

Even before he had entered on the duties of chief superintendent, a warning despatch from Captain Elliot forecasts the actual course of events in which he was doomed to play so prominent a part. "Sooner or later the feeling of independence, which the peculiar mode of conducting this branch of trade has created upon the part of our countrymen in China, will lead to grave difficulties. A long course of impunity will beget hardihood, and at last some gross insult will be perpetrated that the Chinese authorities will be constrained to resent; they will be terrified and irritated, and probably commit some act of cruel violence, that will make any course but armed interference impossible to our Government."[2]

Six months later a despatch ends with the ominous suggestion: "It seems likely that the visits of men-of-war at this crisis . . . would have the effect either of relaxing the restrictive spirit of the Provincial Government, or of hastening onwards the legalisation measure."[3]

Before taking up his quarters at Canton, Elliot frankly stated his opinion of the opium traffic, and the embarrassment it produced on trade generally.

[1] Appendix I. note 2. [2] *China Cor.*, 1840, p. 137. [3] P. 155.

Writing to Lord Palmerston on 21st February 1837, after expressing his regret for "the fact that such an article should have grown to be by far the most important part of our import trade," and "the wide-spreading public mischief which the manner of its pursuit has necessarily entailed," he concludes: "Perhaps your Lordship may be led to think that a gradual check to our own growth and imports would be salutary in effect. . . .

"It cannot be good that the conduct of a great trade should be dependent upon the steady continuance of a vast prohibited traffic in an article of vicious luxury, high in price, and liable to frequent and prodigious fluctuations."[1]

Two years later, when his forecast was all but fulfilled, Elliot made the following retrospect of the illicit traffic, which had at length roused China to take the law into her hands: "The manner of the rash course of traffic within the river probably contributed most of all to impress on the Chinese Government the urgent necessity of repressing the growing audacity of the foreign smugglers, and preventing their associating themselves with the desperate and lawless of their own large cities. . . . While such a traffic existed in the heart of our regular commerce, I had all along felt that the Chinese Government had a just ground for harsh measures towards the lawful trade, upon the plea that there was no distinction between the right and the wrong."[2]

The sundering of the old personal relations with the East India Company, and the advent unannounced of representatives of England, insistent on diplomatic equality with the Court at Pekin,

[1] *China Cor.*, 1840, p. 190. [2] P. 343.

widened the breach between the two powers. The Chinese saw on their shores and in their harbours strong and defiant strangers, whose one visible motive was the greed of gain. The English statesmen turned their gaze away from the lawlessness of their countrymen, and, with little more knowledge of the Chinese mind than the latter had of the English, they pressed for a full recognition of Western equality. Lord Palmerston instructed Captain Elliot to go past the Hong merchants to the Chinese officials in person. Sealed packets, delivered by the merchants, were finally arranged as a compromise.

Captain Elliot honestly tried to steer a *via media*, and for a time succeeded. As soon as he arrived at Canton, early in 1837, the authorities urged him to send away the opium-receiving ships from their anchorage outside the port. The Governor issued an edict (4th August) stating: "A memorial has been laid before the Emperor, representing that more than ten English vessels are constantly anchored outside the port, . . . that the illicit trade—the importation of opium and the exportation of sycee silver—depends entirely on these vessels, and that they form also places of refuge for proscribed smugglers.[1] The Emperor accordingly directs that the resident foreigners be immediately required to send them away, also that steps be taken to punish all natives engaged in the smuggling of opium." Captain Elliot declared that his orders applied only to the legitimate trade of Canton, also that his Government had no "formal knowledge" of any other traffic. On 17th August a second and more insistent edict was issued; as no reply was forthcoming, a third edict appeared on 18th September, in which the

[1] *China Cor.*, 1840, p. 234.

superintendent was censured for his incapacity to deal with the situation. Chinese patience at length became ironical: "The vessels having been so long anchored off the coast, that the great Emperor has been informed respecting them, and the superintendent having resided for some years at Macao, how can he be ignorant of the circumstances and places of their anchorage?"[1] "The King of the said nation being apprehensive lest merchants and seamen coming hither should infringe prohibitions, or transgress the laws, and so bring shame upon their country, he specially sent Superintendent Elliot to Canton to keep them under control and restraint. . . . We fear he is unfit to bear the designation of Superintendent."[2] A further document expressed a fear that "gain-seeking desires had cauterised their souls."

The Hong merchants made a personal appeal to Captain Elliot to acknowledge the receipt of these edicts, and explain his position in regard to the opium traffic. He replied, admitting he was personally aware of an extensive illegal traffic; he had heard of the existing conditions with "concern and apprehension, and desired humbly to express an earnest hope that sure and safe means of remedying a hazardous state of things may speedily be devised"; he had not, however, received, direct from the authorities, any official protest to transmit to his Sovereign.[3] The authorities saw the force of this argument, and sent him an official memorandum "to bring to the knowledge of his King."

All the time that Captain Elliot was trying to "save the face" of his nation to the Chinese (to use one of their own expressions), he was sedulously

[1] *China Cor.*, 1840, p. 237. [2] P. 239. [3] P. 240.

endeavouring to arouse the power he represented to a just and more alert appreciation of the true position in the East.

He kept the Government informed of the vigorous measures against native smugglers, which had been so far successful in the immediate object as to divert the trade almost entirely into European channels. The first effect was an increase in the coast traffic, and consequent collisions with mandarin police boats, "in which there is every reason to believe that blood has been spilt ever and anon."[1] Secondly, a "complete and hazardous change" had overtaken the Canton trade. "The opium trade is now carried on (and a great part of it inwards to Whampoa) in European passage-boats belonging to British owners, and furnished with a scanty armament, which may rather be said to provoke or to justify search accompanied by violence, than to furnish the means of actual defence. . . . An outbreak of piracy might bring about another Ladrone (pirate) war, directed against Europeans as well as Chinese. . . . That the main body of the inward trade (about three-fifths of the amount) should be carried on in so hazardous a manner to the safety of the whole, is a very disquieting subject of reflection."

"The actual state of things cannot be left to the turn of events, without such deeply rooted injury to the national character in the estimation of this huge portion of mankind, as it is painful, indeed, to reflect upon. . . . The natural consequences of the present system is the corruption of all, both high and low, and the infecting of the coasts with evil men, both foreign and native."

"Upon the whole," he concludes, "it seems to me

[1] *China Cor.*, 1840, p. 242.

that the time has fully arrived when Her Majesty's Government should justly explain its own position with respect to the prevention or regulation of this trade; give its own counsels, or take its own alternative course." While Elliot was anxiously waiting for the Home Government to adopt some policy with regard to the illicit China trade, the Canton authorities, trembling under the imperial displeasure, tried to make the superintendent also "tremble intensely!" Three months had elapsed, and the receiving ships still defied the four previous edicts. A fifth was now issued, ordering their departure within a month, and a written report of the fact for communication to Pekin. In case of non-compliance, the edict hinted darkly at stoppage of trade, and the degradation of the Hong merchants. "Further, seeing that the said superintendent, in the discharge of his official duties, sits hand-bound, idly looking on at the unrestrained and illegal practices of depraved foreigners, even kicking against our commands, and resisting the imperial pleasure, we shall find it difficult to believe that he is not guilty of the offence of sheltering and giving licence to these illegalities. We will assuredly proceed to expel and drive him back to his own country."[1]

In December, the Cantonese proceeded to request the naval commander-in-chief to expel the receiving ships; they had previously taken steps to cut off supplies from the mainland. "We have for some time past," they report to the Emperor,[2] "made seizure of opium dealers and smugglers of every description without mercy, in order to prevent the exportation of sycee silver and the importation of

[1] *China Cor.*, 1840, p. 251. [2] P. 257.

opium, and thus to put a stop to this contraband traffic. . . . We have now been earnestly engaged in these measures for one year. We dare not yet say that our efforts have had the full effect to be desired. But with regard to the existing state of things in the provincial city, it may be observed that the price of sycee silver is at present very low; and that opium, one ball of which formerly cost the traitorous natives about thirty dollars, brings now only from sixteen to eighteen dollars."

Readers of the voluminous despatches from China to London during the years 1833–39 (the outbreak of the war) cannot but sympathise with the representatives of England in China. They were dealt with as inferiors, and kept at a distance by the arrogant but frightened Chinese. They resided amongst merchants who, on their own confession, "never paid any attention to any law." For six months every year they were responsible for fleets of ships engaged in smuggling, and manned with motley crews doing whatsoever it pleased them to do in the innumerable inlets and estuaries of an unguarded coast. Their authority depended on their own tact and judgment. Their power of control over their countrymen was to a large extent illusory. They were supposed to have succeeded to the powers of the East India Company's Committee. No Englishman might trade in China without the permit of that Committee; but when the monopoly vanished, the permits vanished also, and nothing took their place.

Lastly, they were sent to the East in the interests of a trade half of which was absolutely illegal. That half they were supposed to know nothing about, but everybody knew that it was deemed to be essential to the Indian Revenue. The situation was an impossible one, but the Home Government, with the exception of the Duke of Wellington,[1] refused even to consider it.

[1] See p. 31.

CHAPTER V

THE BREWING OF WAR

IN February and March 1838, the number of British boats in the illicit traffic between Lintin and Canton increased largely.[1] Deliveries of opium, almost under the walls of the Governor's palace, were frequently attended with conflicts of firearms between these boats and the Chinese preventive vessels. European boats were now first visited and searched for the drug.

In April a Chinaman was executed outside Macao "for traitorous intercourse with foreigners, and for smuggling opium and sycee silver," to warn and intimidate the foreigners.

A visit from Admiral Maitland, with two men-of-war, led to the usual friction over entering the port.[2] The Chinese apologised for firing on a boat, and the visit closed with complimentary messages on both sides. With regard to smuggling, now reaching dangerous dimensions, the admiral took no action. He referred complaints against the irregularities of British subjects to Captain Elliot as the civil authority. Elliot, it will be remembered, had already explained that he was only responsible for the legitimate traders.

On 3rd December, two coolies landing boxes of

[1] *China Cor.*, 1840, p. 299. [2] P. 308–319.

opium at Mr. Innes' factory were arrested. Mr. Innes was ordered to leave, and told that his factory would be pulled down.[1] The foreign traders, "with becoming spirit," according to Captain Elliot, determined to resist such a sentence, which was not carried out. On 12th December, the authorities proceeded to execute a Chinese, convicted of selling opium, in the square in front of the factories. This was also resisted as an "unprecedented and intolerable outrage." The crowd of natives was not at first inimical to the merchants, but "some rash foreigners provoked the people by assailing them with sticks"[2] which led to serious rioting. On hearing of this, Lord Palmerston inquired by what right the execution had been prevented.

The Hong merchants now complained bitterly, and declared they could not carry on legitimate trade until this dangerous and objectionable traffic had been suppressed. Captain Elliot thereupon convened a public meeting of the whole foreign community. He pointed out the "distressing degradation of the whole foreign character, the painful fact that such courses exposed us more and more to the just indignation of this Government and people";[3] he then gave notice that he should require all British boats engaged in the illicit traffic to leave the river within three days, and should offer his aid to the Government in suppressing the evil. The next day he issued a formal notice to this effect, stating that "H.M. Government will in no way interpose if the Chinese Government shall think fit to seize and confiscate." His pacific policy was scouted by some of his countrymen, and smuggling boats still lay at Whampoa flying the British flag. Elliot then

[1] *China Cor.*, 1840, p. 323. [2] P. 324. [3] P. 332.

addressed the Governor of Canton, informing him of his notice and its failure, and requesting him to issue confirmatory orders. "The continuance of this traffic," Elliot concluded, will involve the whole foreign community in some disastrous difficulty; . . . his gracious Sovereign would not interpose for the protection of their property, on behalf of those British subjects who continue to practise these dangerous disorders." After some diplomacy between the Governor and Captain Elliot, the latter was able to report the departure of all the British boats from Whampoa; trade, which had been temporarily stopped, was reopened. In an official notice issued to British subjects the same day, the chief superintendent once more declared his opinion "that in its general effects the illicit trade—which he heartily hopes has ceased for ever—was intensely mischievous to every branch of the trade, that it was rapidly staining the British character with deep disgrace, and, finally, that it exposed the vast public and private interests involved . . . in our commercial intercourse to imminent jeopardy." Looking steadily on its effects on British interests and character, he had "further resolved to shrink from no responsibility in drawing it to a conclusion."

In reporting the steps he had taken to Lord Palmerston, Captain Elliot wrote: "Till the other day, my Lord, I believe there was no part of the world where the foreigner felt his life and property more secure than here in Canton, but the grave events of the 12th ult. have left behind a different impression. . . . And all these desperate hazards have been incurred for the scrambling and, comparatively considered, insignificant gains of a few reckless individuals, unquestionably founding their conduct upon the belief that they were exempt from the operation of all law, British or Chinese."[1] He further wrote: "There is certainly a spirit in active force amongst British subjects in this country, which makes it necessary that the officer on the spot . . . should be forthwith vested with defined and adequate powers for the reasonable control of men whose rash conduct cannot be left to the operation of Chinese laws, and whose impunity is alike injurious to British character and dangerous to British interests."[2] "As the danger and shame of its pursuit (opium smuggling) increased, it was obvious that it would fall by rapid degrees into the hands of more and more desperate men, and stain the foreign character with constantly aggravating disgrace in the sight of the whole of the better portion of this people. . . . If the well-founded hope of improving things honourable and established is not to be sacrificed to the chances which may cast up, by goading this Government into some sudden and violent assertion of its authority, there is certainly no time to be lost in providing for the defined and reasonable control of H.M. subjects in China."[3]

A concise despatch[4] from Lord Palmerston of 15th June 1838, at last referred to the cause of difficulty between the two countries: "With respect to the smuggling trade in opium which forms the subject of your despatches of 18th November and 19th November and 7th December 1837, I have to state that Her Majesty's Government cannot interfere for the purpose of enabling British subjects to violate the laws of the country in which they trade. Any loss, therefore, which such persons may suffer in

[1] *China Cor.*, 1840, p. 327. [2] P. 339. [3] P. 327. [4] P. 258.

consequence of the more effectual execution of the Chinese laws on this subject, must be borne by the parties who have brought that loss on themselves by their own acts."

"With respect to the plan proposed by you in your despatch of 19th November for sending a special commissioner to Chusan, to endeavour to effect some arrangement with the Chinese Government about the opium trade, H.M. Government do not see their way with sufficient clearness to justify them in adopting it at the present moment."

This despatch was not received by Captain Elliot until January 1839, more than two years after his urgent complaints had been sent home. Unfortunately, he never published this despatch, and the sweeping repudiation of the whole traffic by the Home Government remained unknown to those primarily concerned. They doubted Elliot's authority as well as power to carry out any policy of repudiation, and events proved their suspicions to be correct.

For the indifference of the Home Government to the appeal of its representative for special aid in a grave crisis, no excuse has ever been offered. The natural results followed.[1]

The Chinese continued their efforts for the suppression of the opium trade, and the smugglers grew more defiant. In Mr. Dane's narrative it is admitted that "the Emperor and his advisers were by this time in desperate earnest." A proclamation[2] from the Governor of Canton announced the appointment of a high officer as special commissioner, charged with the one duty of suppressing the illegal traffic: "His purpose is to cut off utterly the source of this noxious abuse, to strip bare and root up this enormous evil;

[1] Appendix I. note 3. [2] *China Cor.*, 1840, p. 347.

though this axe should break in his hand, or the boat should sink from beneath him, yet will he not stay his efforts till the work of purification be accomplished."

In this case Chinese eloquence was little at fault. It is said that a special commissioner had been appointed only three times during the dynasty. Commissioner Lin was no common man. Mr. Dane speaks of his "arrogance and hatred of foreigners." Captain Brinkley, with more impartiality, describes him as "a straightforward, resolute, and practical man." In an account of the destruction of the drug surrendered, Mr. King, an American merchant, has recorded his favourable impression of Lin: "From the whole drift of the conversation and inquiries during the interview, it seemed very evident that the sole object of the commissioner was to do away with the traffic in opium, and to protect that which is legitimate and honourable." Mr. King and his wife were treated with marked kindness by Lin, by reason probably of King having always abstained from the opium trade. Mr. Inglis also testified that Lin was sincere in his efforts to put an end to the trade.

There were doubtless individual cases of insincerity, but no one who studies the correspondence of this period at all thoroughly, can doubt the deep-rooted reality of the repugnance to opium smoking and opium smuggling among the better portion of the Chinese Government and people.

"There seems," wrote Captain Elliot to Lord Palmerston, "no longer any room to doubt that the Court has firmly determined to suppress, or more probably, most extensively to check, the opium trade. The immense, and it must be said, most unfortunate increase of the supply during the last four years, the rapid growth of the East Coast trade, and the continued drain of silver have greatly alarmed the Government." [1]

The execution of another native for smuggling opium took place in front of the factories in the presence of Chinese troops. Captain Elliot issued a public notice protesting against the execution, and warning the Chinese Government of unpleasant consequences.

It was at this juncture that the imperial commissioner arrived on the scene. After the custom of his country, he issued his proclamations broadcast. Addressing the foreign merchants, he asked: "Why do you bring to our land the opium, which in your land is not made use of, by it defrauding men of their property, and causing injury to their lives? I find that with this thing you have seduced and deluded the people of China for tens of years past; and countless are the unjust hoards you have thus acquired. Such conduct rouses indignation in every human heart, and it is utterly inexcusable in the eye of Celestial reason." [2]

Lin's State documents might have won praise from Carlyle. They are lengthy, but never dull. A few sentences only from his proclamation to the public must suffice here:

"Of all the evils that afflict mankind, the greatest are those that he perversely brings upon himself. . . . Reptiles, wild beasts, dogs, and swine do not corrupt the morals of the age so as to cause one anxious thought to the Sovereign. There are, however, men who do."

Lin then describes the slavery of the smokers, who require "what is called renovation"—the leak

[1] *China Cor.*, 1840, p. 343. [2] P. 350.

that grows in the rich man's cup, the cold and want that visit the wives and children of the poor, the sloth and impotency of soldiers and officers—the general befooling of a people who submit to be duped by the poison of the foreigners. A sage had said, "When the bulk of the people are joyfully hastening to their ruin, and when it is not in the power of the gods or devils to change their course, man can do it." And if it be asked how, Lin gives the reply—"By killing, in order to stay killing."

Alas! the killing came soon enough, and yet the plague was not stayed. In an address drawn up by Commissioner Lin, to be forwarded to Queen Victoria, the paragraphs occur:—

"In the ways of Heaven no partiality exists, and no sanction is allowed to the injuring of others for the advantage of one's self. . . . Your honourable nation, though beyond the wide ocean, acknowledges the same ways of Heaven, the same human nature, and has the like perception of the distinction between life and death, benefit and injury. . . . But there is a tribe of depraved and barbarous people, who, having manufactured opium for smoking, bring it hither for sale, and seduce and lead astray the simple folk, to the destruction of their persons and the draining of their resources. Formerly the smokers thereof were few, but of late the practice has spread, . . . and daily do its baneful effects more deeply pervade this rich, fruitful, and flourishing population. . . . Hence those who deal in opium, or who inhale its fumes within this land, are all now to be subjected to severest punishment, and a perpetual interdict is to be placed on the practice so extensively prevailing.

"We have reflected that this poisonous article is the clandestine manufacture of artful schemers, and depraved people of various tribes under the dominion of your honourable nation. Doubtless you, the Honourable Sovereign of that nation, have not commanded the manufacture and sale of it. . . . We have heard that in your honourable nation, the people are not permitted to inhale the drug. . . . It is clearly from a knowledge of its injurious effects on man that you have directed severe prohibitions against it. But what is the prohibition of its use in comparison with the prohibition of its sale and manufacture, as a means of thoroughly purifying the source. Though not making use of it one's self, to venture on the manufacture and sale of it, and with it to seduce the simple folk of this land, is to seek one's own livelihood by the exposure of others to death. Such acts are bitterly abhorrent to the nature of man, are utterly opposed to the ways of Heaven. . . . We would now then concert with your Honourable Sovereignty, means to bring to a perpetual end this opium, so hurtful to mankind, we in this land forbidding the use of it, and you, in the nations under your dominion, forbidding its manufacture. . . . Will not the result of this be the enjoyment by each of a felicitous condition of peace?"[1]

The uprising of the Chinese Government from useless edicts to active measures for ending the ills they had so long uneasily accepted, placed Captain Elliot in a peculiarly painful position. He had clearly foreseen the coming breach. He had not shrunk from laying the blame on his lawless countrymen. He had urged his Government to send out a commission to avert the rupture. He had proved his own powers to be insufficient. He had publicly absolved himself from the consequences

[1] *Chinese Repository*, 1839, vol. vii.

of the continued and increasing illegalities; but when the storm broke he was not strong enough to ride it, and he could not stand alone.

The merchants, so many of whom had wilfully provoked the war, were after all his own countrymen, and he did not hesitate to range himself beside them. The British, indeed, had so long been a law unto themselves, that they looked upon the Chinese as the aggressors. The execution in front of the factory seems to have alarmed Captain Elliot to such an extent, that he imagined the lives and property of the merchant community to be in danger. Captain Elliot now explained[1] that before the arrival of Lin, he had considered the expediency of formally requiring all British opium ships to leave the coast of China, but decided against it. He had concluded some months ago, that "the determination of the Court to put down the trade was firmly adopted." When called to Canton by Lin's vigorous measures, it was his purpose, either "to cause the opium merchants to make solemn promises to abstain from the traffic in the future," or to assent on behalf of H.M. Government, if they were forthwith expelled. He contemplated these grave responsibilities with intense uneasiness, but, mindful of the character of the trade, "should not have shrunk from this if he could have obtained from the Chinese reasonable securities for the future, and moderate explanations concerning the past." The trade was one "which every friend of humanity must deplore," but, he inconsequently concludes, Lin's proceedings classed his case "amongst the most shameless violences which one nation has ever yet dared to perpetrate against another," and so the die was cast.

[1] *China Cor.*, 1840, p. 385.

Two days later, Elliot wrote to the commissioner: "It has been a great satisfaction to Elliot to know that the merchants of his own and other foreign nations at Canton have sincerely pledged themselves to your Excellency to discontinue a trade which the Emperor has strictly forbidden. Assuredly they will faithfully fulfil their obligations. . . . Their characters are gone for ever if they violate their solemn pledges to this Government."[1] Elliot might well have hesitated before endorsing such pledges. Lin demanded that every particle of opium should be given up to be destroyed, that the foreigners should sign a bond to the effect that their vessels should never again dare to bring opium; should any be brought the cargo should be forfeited, and the parties should suffer the extreme penalty of the law. Three days were allowed for compliance with these demands. Captain Elliot warned British subjects that he had no confidence in the intentions of the Government, and that they should prepare to resist any act of aggression. The merchants made no reply within the time specified. Before its expiry, coercive measures were taken. On 19th March communication with Whampoa was prohibited. On the 21st all boats were prevented from leaving Canton. An offer to surrender 1030 chests of opium, on the understanding that the remainder should be sent back to India, and that the trade should cease in future, was rejected the same evening. The Chairman of the Merchants' Committee was sent for, but refused to give himself up to the Chinese. On 24th March a blockade of the entire foreign community was instituted. Captain Elliot applied for passports, expressing his conviction that peace was

[1] *China Cor.*, 1840, p. 394.

placed in imminent jeopardy "by these unexplained and alarming proceedings."[1] Lin insisted on the surrender of the opium. On 27th March, Elliot, "constrained by paramount motives affecting the safety of the lives and liberties of all foreigners here present in Canton, and by other very weighty causes," enjoined the surrender to the Government of China of all the opium; "proof of British property, and value of all British opium, to be determined upon principles, and in a manner hereafter to be defined by the British Government."[2] This circular was complied with. For some months past opium had been unsaleable, owing to the energetic measures of suppression; the merchants were not averse to find a purchaser in the British agent. The whole of the opium surrendered, 20,281 chests, valued at between two and three millions, was destroyed with extraordinary precautions between 3rd May and 23rd May, under the personal superintendence of Commissioner Lin. After 30th March the blockade was withdrawn as regards food, but maintained in other respects, until the surrender of the drug was complete.

Lin insisted, in accordance with his first announcement, on the signing of bonds against future trading in opium, on penalty of death. Many of the merchants, including Americans, had already pledged themselves. The British superintendent firmly refused to have anything to do with such a bond.

On 13th April, Elliot wrote[3] to the Portuguese at Macao, placing himself and all British subjects under their protection, and offering armed assistance against China. The Portuguese had already signed bonds pledging themselves to bring no more opium into

[1] *China Cor.*, 1840, p. 367. [2] P. 374. [3] P. 406.

their settlement. On 16th April, Elliot applied to the Governor-General of India for as many armed vessels as could be spared.

Mr. Innes continued to smuggle opium defiantly.[1] Captain Elliot complied with an order to expel him; but when Lin further demanded the banishment of sixteen merchants, conspicuous as opium importers, Captain Elliot identified himself with them by accompanying them, when they left Canton. The tension between the English superintendent and the Chinese high commissioner grew more strained. The former sought to remove all British commerce to the Portuguese settlements. He published a manifesto to the Chinese, stating that it would be derogatory to forget "all the insults and wrongs which have been perpetrated." The latter sought to retain it at Canton, purged of all complicity in the offending drug.

A serious riot among the Hong Kong sailors, in which a Chinese was killed, precipitated the outbreak of war. Elliot conducted a trial on board ship, notifying the mandarins they might "be present," but no Chinese went. He failed to find the guilty person. Five men convicted of riot only were sent home, but released on arrival in England, the law officers holding that Elliot had exceeded his judicial powers.

Supplies were now cut off from the British at Macao, who thereupon retreated to Hong Kong. A British passage-boat was attacked, and seven Lascars killed. The imperial commissioner issued another edict complaining that the foreigners "have withstood the prohibitory enactments . . . have continued to linger at Macao . . . the empty store-

[1] Appendix I. note 4.

ships have remained anchored in the outer seas, and newly arrived merchant vessels neglecting to surrender what opium they have brought, have collected together at Hong Kong . . . whereby occasion was given in a drunken brawl to cause the death of Lin Weihe, one of the people of the empire . . . Superintendent Elliot has withstood commands, and sheltered the murderer."

By this time Captain Elliot had made up his mind for war. He refused to receive official communications from the commissioner, and wrote again to the Portuguese Governor of Macao, proposing to return thither with 800 or 1000 men at his disposal. The Governor had no wish for such guests, and refused to depart from "the maintenance of neutrality." [1]

On the 4th September, Captain Elliot fired upon some junks which prevented a regular supply of provisions. Repenting of his rashness, the same night he decided to discontinue hostilities. He admitted, in an apologetic despatch, that he had been betrayed by "feelings of irritation into a measure, that he was sensible, under less trying circumstances, would be difficult indeed of vindication." Shortly after, however, supposing that a missing English boat had been cut off, he declared a blockade of the port and river of Canton. The boat duly returned, and the blockade was withdrawn, not without complaints against such high-handed proceedings from some American, as well as Portuguese, merchants. Captain Elliot was a good man, but not great in a crisis.

Throughout these complicated and embittered relations, the one underlying element of disturbance

[1] *China Cor.*, 1840, p. 446.

continually reasserts itself. Negotiations were re-opened through the Portuguese,[1] and China put forth three conditions as essential to any understanding:—

1. All opium in the ships at Hong Kong to be surrendered.

2. The murderer of Lin Weihe to be given up, or the seamen concerned sent to trial before Chinese law—one only to answer for the crime.

3. The opium-receiving ships to depart beyond the Great Ladrone; all persons banished from China to depart immediately.

The negotiations were finally broken off by the high commissioner, owing to further outrages and lawlessness on the part of the foreigners. He announced that war vessels would be sent to Hong Kong "to surround and apprehend all the offenders, those connected with the murders, and those connected with opium, as well as the traitorous Chinese concealed on board the foreign vessels."

In a further parley between Captain Elliot, with two men-of-war, and a Chinese admiral, with twenty-nine junks, the junks were ordered to withdraw to a more distant anchorage. In default, the British ships opened fire, and destroyed four of the Chinese vessels. Great Britain and China were now at war.

"I have proceeded," Elliot wrote to Lord Palmerston, "to the uttermost verge of my authority, if I have not exceeded it, in my attempt to discover and bring to justice the murderer of the innocent native . . . and I am unaffected by the commissioner's charge of countenancing the illicit traffic in opium.

"If my private feelings were of the least important consequence upon questions of a public and important nature, assuredly I might justly say, that

[1] *Additional Cor.*, p. 6.

no man entertains a deeper detestation of the disgrace and sin of this forced traffic on the coast of China than the humble individual who signs this despatch. I see little to choose between it and piracy; and in my place, as a public officer, I have steadily discountenanced it by all the lawful means in my power, and at the total sacrifice of my private comfort in the society in which I have lived for some years past.

"But whilst I have endeavoured to fulfil my duty to H.M. Government in the public course of repression I have pursued, it does not consort with my station to sanction measures of general and undistinguishing violence against H.M. officers and subjects; and to a mode of working out objects, right or wrong, which set all obligations of right and justice at defiance."

In stating the issues of peace and war, Elliot places in the one scale "the disgrace and sin of a forced traffic with a friendly nation"; in the other, a mode of putting an end to it by the nation concerned, "which set all obligations of moderation and justice at defiance." The one evil had been at work for a generation, the other a few weeks. The one was the work of unbidden strangers in a foreign land; the other of a conservative people in their own defence. The scales of history assuredly dip in their favour. The punishment fell without measure on them alone.

CHAPTER VI

THE OPIUM WAR

THE British Government supported Captain Elliot with forces to carry on war, but repudiated the financial responsibility he had assumed for the surrendered opium. The Emperor ascribed the coming of the expedition to the extermination of the opium traffic and stoppage of trade. He grandiloquently ordered his officers to exterminate the barbarians, and not allow them to sneak into the harbours. Rewards were offered for the capture of British war vessels, and prices set on the heads of officers and crews. A few months later, when the natives were hard pressed and negotiations were proposed, a quaint proclamation ends thus: "You ought all quietly to plough your fields and read your books, taking care of yourselves and your families. If indeed these barbarians do not distress you, you must not again search for and seize them."

It has been truly said that Ouchterlony's history of the war enables any who desire it to sup full of horrors; this is equally true of other contemporary accounts.

The *Spectator* writes (5th November 1842): "It is pure butchery, without risk at any time beyond casual incidents; and now it would seem without even the idea of risk."

The one-sided character of the proceedings is

illustrated in the following account of the sack of Chusan:—

"On 4th July 1840, General Birrel, with three ships of war and three transports, arrived in the anchorage of Chusan harbour. An attempt was made that evening to obtain the surrender of the island without bloodshed; but as no arrangement could be come to, and the Chinese next morning indicated a resolution to resist, the *ultima ratio regum*, a fire of round and grape shot, was resorted to, which soon drove the Chinese from their forts and war-junks with great slaughter. Troops were landed, and an assault on the capital of the island was resolved on for the next day, and preparations made for battering down the walls. Meanwhile shot and shell, for "the purpose of trying the range," were thrown in, which occasioned great slaughter among the unoffending inhabitants. During the night, however, the Chinese troops and nearly the whole of the inhabitants evacuated the town, and the British entered it the next morning without resistance. The whole loss on the part of the British in this affair was one man wounded. . . . Notwithstanding strict orders had been issued to respect private property, the sailors were allowed to leave their boats and to plunder the town. In a short time they had reduced it to a perfect wreck, wantonly destroying what they could not carry off. Great quantities of liquor, called Samshu, were found in the town, and the soldiers got so completely intoxicated that they had to be carried into the ships by whole companies, and almost regiments, in a state of insensibility."[1]

[1] *Edinburgh Magazine*, January 1841.

The *India Gazette* adds:—

"A more complete pillage could not be conceived than took place. Every house was broken open, every drawer and box ransacked, the streets strewn with fragments of furniture, pictures, tables, chairs, grain of all sorts,—the whole set off by the dead or the living bodies of those who had been unable to leave the city from the wounds received from our merciless guns. . . . The plunder ceased only when there was nothing to take or destroy."

Captain Loch writes of a stand made by some Tartar soldiers at Chin-kiang-foo: "The firing brought the General up, who resolved to sweep the town from house to house. As we marched along the walls, I saw, what as a novice in this description of warfare shocked me much, old men, women, and children cutting each others' throats, and drowning themselves by the dozen; and no one either attempting, or apparently showing any inclination, to save the poor wretches; nor, in fact, regarding them with more notice than they would a dead horse carried through the streets of London."[1]

Sir Henry Pottinger is reported to have said at a dinner of Liverpool merchants: "I wish I were permitted to say all I could respecting the moral character and high sense of honour of these people (the Chinese). They really put me to the blush when they reasoned with me on the injustice of the case, and the wanton atrocities committed by our men. They entreated me, on my return, to get our Government to restrain our sailors from committing such unnecessary acts of violence; for it appears that fieldpieces loaded with grape had been planted at the end of long narrow streets thronged with

[1] *Closing Events of the Campaign in China.*

men, women, and children; that they were mowed down like grass, and that gutters flowed with their innocent blood. It is no wonder that the Chinese have such a horror of the English, and that they call us barbarians."

Prolonged and able debates took place in both Houses of Parliament.[1] It was pointed out that the appeals from the British representatives in China for additional powers over British subjects, and for securing better relations between the two Governments, had received little attention in all the five years which had elapsed.

Sir William Follet could find no trace, except in the single minute by the Duke of Wellington, that the affairs of China had occupied the thoughts of the Ministry for a single hour.

Sir George Staunton, armed with special knowledge, traced back the unfortunate occurrences to the decision of the Committee in 1832, that it was not expedient to relinquish the opium revenue.

Mr. Charles Buller, on behalf of the Government, dated our error from the period when the China trade was thrown open to the public "on a footing in which it was utterly impossible for it to continue with honour and security."

Lord Palmerston stated that he "would be the last to defend a trade which involved the violation of the municipal laws of the Chinese, and which furnished an enormously large population with the means of demoralisation"; but he questioned the sincerity of the Chinese, and upheld the British representative.

The division gave a majority of nine to the Government.

[1] Hansard, vol. liii.

In the Upper House, Earl Grey contrasted Captain Elliot's strong denunciation of smuggling with his disavowals of all formal knowledge and responsibility. Lord Melbourne, in defence of the Ministry, regretted much, condoned more, and promised nothing.

Of contemporary opinion outside Parliament, three extracts may be quoted.

Dr. Arnold wrote to a friend: "Ordinary wars of conquest are to me far less wicked than to go to war in order to maintain smuggling, and that smuggling consisting in the introduction of a demoralising drug which the Government of China wishes to keep out, and which we, for the lucre of gain, want to introduce by force. In this quarrel we are going to burn and slay in the pride of our supposed superiority."

In a letter to Mr. Gladstone thanking him for his speech against the war, Baron Bunsen wrote: "You can scarcely be aware what good you have done, in enabling the friends of England abroad to maintain their ground against her numerous enemies, all throwing that (opium) question in our face, as proving the humbug and hypocrisy of all pretended Christian profession and works of the English nation."

A leading article in the *Times* ran (3rd December 1842): "We think it of the highest moment that the Government of Great Britain should wash its hands once for all, not only of all diplomatic, but of all moral and practical responsibility for this (the opium) traffic; that we should cease to be mixed up with it, to foster it, or to make it a source of Indian revenue. . . . We owe some moral compensation to China for pillaging her towns and slaughtering her citizens, in a quarrel which never could have arisen if we had not been guilty of this national crime."

The cessation of hostilities brought with it a cessation of scruples, and a more secure continuance of the illegal trade which had led up to the war.

A résumé of a Chinese account of the war has been given to the world by Consul Parker. To the translator it is an illustration of the extraordinary faithfulness with which the Chinese endeavour to perfect their history. To the reader it will more probably be a striking illustration of their extraordinary fairness.

The account begins with a memorial to the throne in 1838, which pointed to the growing consumption of foreign opium as the root of China's troubles; silver was becoming scarce, the revenue was in confusion, peculation was rife, trade disorganised. Opium came from England, and though these foreigners were ready to weaken China and absorb her wealth by encouraging its use, they forbade smoking amongst themselves. They were now ruining the bodies and fortunes of China with their abominable poison.

The Emperor remitted the matter to all high provincial authorities. Without a single exception they recommended the most stringent measures. Lin was sent as special imperial commissioner, and discovered an extensive system of bribes. The English alone had a separate trading company, with a consular officer sent by their King to "manage the whole concern." Lin demanded from the foreigners a surrender of all the opium; it was agreed to give three catties of tea for each one of opium.[1] The

[1] Appendix I. note 5.

Emperor ordered the total destruction of the drug. Americans and others gave the required bonds; Elliot refused either to receive the tea, or give the bonds. Then a Chinese was killed. Elliot, though he had no intention of deliberately disobeying, only tried five black barbarians, not the real criminal. Lin, in accordance with the law, cut off the supply of fuel and provisions. Elliot, being exasperated, sent for two men-of-war, and, under pretext of demanding food, "engaged our naval force in battle." A law condemning opium smokers to strangulation, and opium dealers to decapitation, had now been in force the best part of a year; "as the watch kept all over the empire was very strict, over half the smokers were already cured."

Elliot had sent home for troops, and the Queen directed Parliament to deliberate upon the matter. The official body was for war, the mercantile interest was for peace. Discussion went on for several days, without result; at last lots were drawn in the Lo Chang Temple (division before the Lord Chancellor?); three tickets were found in favour of war. Lin had caused this war by his excessive zeal. The foreign chief, Bremer, arrived at Tientsin with five ships. First he demanded the value of the "produce" opium, as he afterwards plainly called it. The reply suggested that "adhering to the principle of rigidly excluding opium, these concessions should be conditional upon opium not coming."

The foreign chief, Bremer, said, "Lin is one of China's best viceroys, an able and plucky man, though he does not understand foreign ways. You can stop the opium trade, but you cannot stop all our trade." By this time the Tinghai fleet had come, and flags struck up in the boats advertised opium for sale all along the river. On the other hand, the English did not kill the Cantonese, and always released all local braves taken prisoner, and prohibited all looting.

In summing up, Wei-Yuan intimates that it was the closing of trade, not the forced surrender of opium, that brought on the war. Lin's demands were too exacting. He should have executed the rear-admiral for corruption, secured the goodwill of other foreigners, purchased ships, guns, etc. "What enemy would then have dared to attack us? How could opium then have ventured into China? Our guns on the heights could not do much against a contrary wind. . . . All our leaders now lost courage, submitting to everything, and not alluding at all to the rule about opium being excluded. The English were overjoyed. Of late the opium business is greater than ever. . . . The barbarian pirate war lasted two years; no one, strange to say, ever recommended a strictly defensive attitude. We should have resolutely adhered to the opium interdiction."

To this Chinese magistrate the war was a defective struggle, rashly begun against an evil fate; *the root of it all was the drug.*

With an intimate knowledge of both West and East, the latest English historian of these times writes: "It was not because China entertained any project of terminating their commerce, and driving them from her coasts, that she instructed Commissioner Lin to adopt the measures which finally involved her in war. It was because they had introduced into their commerce an unlawful element, which threatened to debilitate her people morally and physically, and to exhaust her treasure. But for opium smuggling by British subjects, the war would never have taken place, so far as human intelligence can discern. History can only have one verdict in the matter."[1]

[1] Brinkley, xi. 14. See also Appendix I. note 6.

CHAPTER VII

TREATY OF NANKIN

THE first negotiation for peace, known as the "Treaty of the Bogue," failed; the Emperor refusing to pay a dollar for the opium, or to yield an inch of territory. Amoy, Tinghai, Chunhai, and Ningpo were then taken by the British. Captain Elliot was replaced by Sir Henry Pottinger. The latter issued a manifesto of British grievances, the acts of Commissioner Lin heading the list. It alleged that the opium had been given up by the British merchants, in order to escape death.

On the 29th August 1842, a treaty of peace was signed. Opium was carefully ignored, except in the 4th Article, which provided, that the Emperor of China agrees to pay the sum of six millions of dollars as the value of the opium which was delivered up, "as a ransom for the lives of H.B.M.'s superintendent and subjects, who had been imprisoned and threatened with death by the Chinese high officers." The treaty ceded Hong Kong to Great Britain, abolished the exclusive trading of the Hong merchants, granted fifteen million dollars for debts due to English merchants and expenses of the war, and threw open five ports to English trade.

The cession of Hong Kong, "for the purpose of careening and refitting ships," began the unseemly struggle of the West for the partition of China.

The hard fate meted out to Chinese officials who fail to be successful was visited upon Commissioner Lin, as the following admonition proves:—

"Lin Tseh Sen, you received my imperial orders to examine and manage the affairs relating to opium; from the exterior to cut off all trade in opium, from interior to seize perverse natives, and thus cut off supplies to the foreigners. You have proved yourself unable to cut off this trade, it appears you are no better than a wooden image."

Following the treaty closely, came a supplementary treaty. Amongst its provisions is the following:—

Art. 12. "A fair and regular tariff of duties and other dues having now been established, it is to be hoped that the system of smuggling which has heretofore been carried on between English and Chinese merchants (in many cases with open connivance of Chinese custom-house officers) will entirely cease; and the most peremptory proclamation to all English merchants has been already issued on this subject by the British plenipotentiary, who will also instruct the different consuls to strictly watch over and carefully scrutinise the conduct of all persons (British subjects) trading under his superintendence. In any positive instance of smuggling transactions coming to the consul's knowledge, he will instantly apprise the Chinese authorities of the fact, and they will proceed to seize and confiscate all goods, whatever their value or nature, that may have been so smuggled."

The description of the proclamation seems a little overdrawn. Sir Henry Pottinger had merely pointed out publicly,[1] that "opium being an article the traffic in which is well known to be declared illegal and

[1] *China Repository*, 1843, vol. xii.

contraband, any person who may take such a step (trading in opium at the treaty ports) will do so at his own risk, and will, if a British subject, meet with no support or protection from H.M.'s consuls or other officers."

Sir Henry Pottinger afterwards told the British merchants, "that they had not in any single iota or circumstance striven to aid him in his arrangements, but had thrown serious difficulties and obstacles, if not positive risk, in the way of his arrangements." But even here, the said merchants might plead the general disposition of the British Government in their favour. Though an Order in Council, 24th February 1843, forbade British ships to violate the treaty by trading outside the treaty ports,[1] when Captain Hope, of H.M.S. *Thalia*, stopped two or three opium ships from proceeding above Shanghai, he was recalled from his station and ordered to India, where he could not "interfere in such a manner with the undertakings of British subjects."[2]

Lord Palmerston instructed Rear-Admiral Elliot and Captain Elliot "to endeavour to make some arrangement with the Chinese Government for the admission of opium into China, as an article of lawful commerce."[3] They were not to make this a demand, nor threaten compulsion, but to point out that "it is scarcely possible that a permanent good understanding can be maintained," with the opium trade on its then footing. "It is wholly out of the power of the British Government to prevent opium from being carried to China; if none were grown in any part of the British territories, plenty would be produced in other countries,"—"illegal trade is always at-

[1] *China Repository*, 1843, xii. 446. [2] Wells Williams, ii. 582.
[3] *Parl. Papers*, 1857.

tended with acts of violence." Writing to Sir Henry Pottinger, Lord Palmerston says, he was to avail himself of "every favourable opportunity strongly to impress upon the Chinese plenipotentiary . . . how much it would be for the interest of that Government to legalise the trade."

The victorious nation had in various ways acknowledged the unsatisfactory character of the opium trade, *per se*. Its only concern now was to assist it by legalisation. The ethics of the Emperor of China rose higher. In a manifesto, he said, "I cannot prevent the introduction of the flowing poison; gain-seeking and corrupt men will for profit and sensuality defeat my wishes, but nothing will induce me to derive a revenue from the vice and misery of my people."[1] This continued to be the position of the Chinese Government until after the close of the second war.

The best extenuation that can be offered for the British is the connivance and corruption of most of the Chinese officials, and the tacit spread of poppy cultivation in China. It must be remembered that the provinces of China have many of the powers of independent kingdoms; that the government of the empire rests on the moral sanction of the governed to an extent little understood by outsiders; and, moreover, that in our own country at that time smuggling was carried on in wholesale fashion, the enactment of death penalties notwithstanding.

The excuse, that the real grievance with China was the exportation of her silver, will not bear investigation. It was not until 1827 that the balance of trade turned against the Chinese, and caused the outflow of silver. In the years 1821–24,

[1] *Parl. Report* (China), 1847, p. 292.

strenuous efforts were made by the Government for the suppression of the opium trade. The great outflow of silver after 1827 undoubtedly inconvenienced and alarmed the Chinese. It aggravated, but did not supplant, the fear of the drug, and its consequences to the nation.

In the negotiations, Sir Henry Pottinger introduced the forbidden, and yet vitally important, subject,—"the great cause that produced the disturbances which led to the war, *i.e.* the trade in opium" as a topic for private conversation; the incident is thus described by Captain Loch:

"They (the Chinese commissioners) then evinced much interest, and eagerly requested to know why we would not act fairly towards them by prohibiting the growth of the poppy in our dominions, and thus effectually stop a traffic so pernicious to the human race. This, he (Sir Henry Pottinger) said, in consistency with our constitutional laws, could not be done; and, he added, that even if England chose to exercise so arbitrary a power over her tillers of the soil, it would not check the evil, so far as the Chinese were concerned, while the cancer remained uneradicated among themselves, but that it would merely throw the market into other hands. It, in fact, he said, rests entirely with yourselves. If your people are virtuous, they will desist from the evil practice; and if your officers are incorruptible and obey your rulers, no opium can enter your country. The discouragement of the growth of the poppy in our territories rests principally with you, for nearly the entire produce cultivated in India travels east to China. If, however, the habit has become a confirmed vice, and you feel that your power is at present inadequate to stay its indulgence, you may rest assured your people will procure the drug in spite of every enactment."[1]

Whether the Chinese were duly impressed by this unfolding of Western ethics as applied to conduct is not stated. It is to be hoped their knowledge of "our constitutional laws" had not proceeded far enough to debar them from following the extraordinary propositions laid down by Sir Henry Pottinger. He had, however, been expressly told by the Home Government to impress the Chinese plenipotentiary, by all the arguments which would naturally suggest themselves to his mind, and this was the result. The Chinese Commission was unwilling to make any representation to the Emperor. They promised that the officers of China should be enjoined to confine their jurisdiction, in respect of opium, "to the soldiery and people of the country, not allowing them to make use of it."[2]

Even superficial students of these events must recognise that the Emperor of China was whole-hearted in his desire to suppress the opium trade.

Hong Kong now became the basis of supply for the drug to Canton, and the illegal trade grew apace.

Two years later, Sir Henry's successor, Sir John Davis, renewed the efforts for legalisation. "Such a happy measure," he explained, would remove all chances of unpleasant occurrences, whilst providing "an ample revenue for the Emperor";[3] but the voice of the charmer found no entrance. The Chinese would not ratify that which they durst no longer resist. Commissioner Keying's reply was, that such a measure "would certainly put a value on riches,

[1] Loch, *Campaign in China.*

[2] *Parl. Papers* (Opium Trade), 1857, p. 12. [3] *Ibid.*, p. 15.

and slight on men's lives, and I am apprehensive that the great Emperor would not get over this."

Sir John Davis wrote: "The trade is virtually tolerated, a state of things very different from that which existed previous to the war. The position in which Great Britain stands is materially changed. . . . They have distinctly declined a conventional arrangement for the remedy of the evil, and expressed a desire that we should not bring the existing abuse to their notice." [1]

The victory rested with England, and forms part of the measure of her responsibility.

A well-informed writer wrote in 1857: "It is not to be denied that upon the whole the Government of China and the authorities at the various ports have faithfully adhered to the stipulations of the treaty," with the one exception of free access to the city of Canton.[2] As a matter of fact, the Chinese text of the treaty did not contemplate foreigners dwelling within the walled city of Canton, or having access to it. The people there became increasingly hostile to foreigners, and the authorities had some reason on their side in desiring to keep them apart.[3]

In 1845, Lord Stanley, speaking of China, said, "I believe, so far as our later experiences have gone, that there is no nation which more highly values public faith in others; and up to the present moment, I am bound to say, there never was a government or a nation which more strictly and conscientiously adhered to the literal fulfilment of the engagements into which it had entered."

It would be impossible to say anything like this

[1] *Parl. Papers* (Opium Trade), 1857, p. 20.

[2] *Fraser's Magazine*.

[3] Brinkley, xi. 179.

of Great Britain's pledge against smuggling in the 12th Clause of the supplementary treaty.

In the correspondence of Sir John Davis, similar complaints to those of Captain Elliot against his own countrymen appear. Writing, November 1846, he says: "I am not the first who has been compelled to remark, that it is more difficult to deal with our own countrymen at Canton than with the Chinese Government." The British admiral, Cochrane, writes from the *Agincourt*, Hong Kong, a week later: "If the merchants would believe that their best, and by far most efficient protection is to be found in their own circumspect conduct, in treating the people with urbanity and goodwill, and avoiding, rather than seeking, sources of conflict, they will soon practically discover in these measures more persuasive advocates with the Chinese than in all the force I could bring against them."

Two months later, Sir John Davis writes: "I may add, that the subjects of every other civilised government get on more quietly with the Chinese, and clamour less for protection, than our own." And again, on 15th February 1847, he writes to Lord Palmerston: "Not that I have any expectation of occurrence of acts of disobedience and disorder, if our own people will only behave with common abstinence." The war had led those who desired the application of force further on a down grade.

There was only one possible result to the continuance of the illicit trade under the real but unacknowledged protection of England; but the Chinese faced loss and trouble for many years, rather than take the plunge. Whilst Chinese convicted of dealing in the drug, or using it, were "continually paraded in gangs, with iron shackles upon their necks and feet, in Canton, the Government of India and its English merchants fared sumptuously as the result of the war. The *Sir Edward Ryan*, armed with fifteen guns and seventy men, made a net profit of £50,000 in one opium cruise. The sale was at once legalised by the British in Hong Kong, and within three months of the peace the *Hong Kong Gazette* predicted that another rupture was inevitable, unless China followed suit.

CHAPTER VIII

SMUGGLING RENEWED

ONE of the last documents issued by the East India Company on its Chinese trade ran:

"To attempt to maintain a purely commercial intercourse such as that with China by force of arms, would in a pecuniary point of view be anything rather than a matter of profit, even if justice and humanity would allow us for a moment seriously to contemplate such a step."

It would have been well for both countries if the British Government, in taking the trade over for its subjects without restriction, had been equally far-sighted. The evils of smuggling became yet more rampant along the Chinese coast after the Treaty of Nankin. The war had won great concessions from China, had given England a trading centre, and opened important ports. The smuggling trade had greatly increased, and the hostility to foreigners also. But China and lawful commerce remained unbenefitted. So ruinous had productive trade become, that a Select Committee of the House of Commons was appointed in 1847, to inquire into our commercial relations with China.

Sir Henry Pottinger had hastened to Manchester in 1842, to explain how he had "opened up a new world to their trade, so vast, that all the mills in Lancashire could not make stocking stuff sufficient for one of its provinces." China's sage, Lao Tzu, had given "a truer prediction," although it was 2500 years previously, in the saying: "Where troops have been quartered, brambles and thorns spring up. In the track of great armies there must follow lean years."

The Committee found that trade with China had been for some time in "a very unsatisfactory position," with a declension of exports in "nearly every branch of manufacture."[1] The one exception is dealt with in the following passage:—"The opium trade, however, already flourishes at Foochowfoo, with its usual demoralising influences on the population, and embarrassing effects upon the monetary condition of the place. The latter would be diminished by the legalisation of the traffic; the former, we are afraid, are incontestable and inseparable from its existence."

The war, which was to open the door to lawful and beneficent British industries, had totally failed to do so. Even so late as 1857, when another war was thought necessary on behalf of British interests, *The Times* (27th February) had to point out that "the exportation of British manufactures into that country has not increased since 1842; the inevitable result being that for want of a good trade, a bad trade has thriven: opium, for clothing, and smuggling for open traffic." The more reasonable explanation would appear to be, that because of a bad trade, good trade had not thriven. Hong Kong was described[2] as "an Alsatia of refuge for all the outlaws and conspirators of the mainland; the resort of pirates—who devastate the coast and their port—for refitting and rearming, where men, arms and

[1] *Parl. Report* (China), 1847, p. iii.
[2] *Edinburgh Review*, April 1857.

ammunition, the best adapted for their lawless purposes, could always be obtained at the lowest cost; . . . and our laws, or their administrators, are unfortunately wholly and hopelessly powerless to deal with this monster evil." As against these opinions, or in their support, may be set the opinion of the British Resident at Hong Kong, quoted regretfully by Earl Grey; that the recent colonial ordinance had been of great advantage, because it had increased the coasting trade "in cotton, opium, and other products."[1] This colonial ordinance had other results also. In granting a British register to Chinese who were tenants of the British Crown in Hong Kong, it became the cause of the circumstances which led to the second Chinese war. The ordinance was alleged by some authorities to be illegal, as contravening an Act of the Imperial Parliament, by which it was impossible for any colonial authority to confer the rights of a British vessel upon any ship not owned by a British subject.

It would seem to be more than a coincidence that at Shanghai, where foreigners were least known, the relations of British and Chinese were the most amicable, and that Canton, where the intercourse had been the longest and closest, was ever the storm centre between the two peoples. Several disturbances, some provoked, some unprovoked outrages against "foreign devils," occurred in successive years after the treaty. Lord Palmerston's foreign policy made much of self-assertion. Animated apparently by this spirit, Sir John Davis, then Governor of Hong Kong, after a Fatshan mob had stoned six Englishmen, waited not to make any demands, but ordered out his forces, bombarded some forts, blew

[1] Hansard, 9 Mar. 1857.

up their powder magazines, and spiked 827 cannon. Upon this fiery foray, the Governor of Canton, Keying, appropriately observed, "If natural tranquillity is to subsist between Chinese and foreigners, the common feelings of manhood, as well as the first principles of Heaven, must be considered and conformed with."[1] Within six months of the raid, six Englishmen were massacred within three miles of Canton. Yet this was the district where the policy of armed force had been pushed the farthest. It led to a general imitation of the armed opium smugglers on every hand. The Portuguese excelled in fitting out lorchas, which were used for all kinds of evil practices, and the very name of foreign lorchas stank in the nostrils of the Chinese. From England's resolve to keep the opium revenue intact, her representatives were continually placed in the unhappy position of expressing views worthy of a great Christian nation, and then of straightway acting in defiance of them. No one had spoken more strongly against the monstrous system of licensing Chinese lorchas to carry the British flag than Sir John Bowring. As he expressed it, "a vessel no sooner obtains a register than she escapes Colonial jurisdiction, carries on her trade within the waters of China, engages probably in every sort of fraudulent dealing, and may never again appear to render any account of her proceedings, or be made responsible for her illegal acts." Under a doubtful law, leading to undesirable enterprises by indefensible means, Sir John Bowring—whose hobby was said to have been peace in England—plunged this country into its second war with China. The lorcha *Arrow*, built, owned, and manned by Chinese, had been captured

[1] Brinkley, vi. 189.

by pirates and used by them, recaptured, and sent for resale under the colonial ordinance; and had been registered in the colony, obtaining for a specified time the rights of a British ship. On the fateful morning of the 8th October 1856, these rights had expired. This legal lapse was not known to the Chinese officials. Independently of this, they held she was not a British vessel. It is stated (though this is contested) that she was still flying the British flag. She had a British captain, a young fellow, retained for the sake of his nationality. China was torn by rebellion. Taipings (sworn to desist from opium) and Imperialists—both assisted by foreigners—fought one another with the utmost ferocity. The British were greatly irritated by being kept at arm's length at Canton, and Sir John Bowring had persuaded himself that the assertion of British power in a visible form in that city would accomplish great results. As the *Arrow* lay off Canton, a man recognised in one of her crew a pirate by whom he had been recently attacked and plundered. Accordingly he lodged an information. The Chinese authorities boarded the *Arrow*, arrested the whole crew, and, it is said, hauled down the British flag. Mr. Consul Parkes demanded the surrender of the men. They were surrendered, but were not accepted, because of the low grade of the official in charge. Sir John Bowring demanded, in addition, an apology, and a promise against such acts in future. Yeh, the responsible official, promised not to repeat such acts, but refused to apologise. He believed the lorcha to be screening piracy under the British flag. He suggested that such difficulties would not recur if English registers were no longer sold to Chinese subjects. Consul

Parkes, a very able official, who had been brought up in "the gunboat policy," advocated active measures; "for it appeared to me" (he writes) "that the insolence of the commissioner had been carried too far."[1]

Sir John Bowring rose to the occasion. As he afterwards wrote: "Of course the magnitude of our demands grows with the growth of our success. All diplomacy is the exemplification of the Sibyl's story—all wise diplomacy." After receiving the assurance that there should not be any repetition of the mistake, he wrote to Consul Parkes: "Can we not use this opportunity to carry the City Question? If so, I will come up with the whole fleet. I think we have now a stepping-stone from which with good management we may move on to important consequences." There was one difficulty, however, in the way—"I do not think the admiral will make war, and we must consider, not what we might, but what we can do." Three days later Sir John was able to write: "The admiral has left me in excellent disposition, and we must write a bright page in our history." Yeh's letters show that he understood from the first all that was intended.

The British entered Canton by a breach they made for themselves, the Chinese burnt the foreign factories, reinforcements were sent for from England, and so the second war was entered upon. The pity of it was long drawn out, for the Indian Mutiny intervened, with its absorbing claims; so the Chinese tree "was girdled and left for the present." In the meantime a French missionary had been tortured and massacred, so when the British axe was at last applied, the French came also to assist. The *Arrow*

[1] Brinkley, xi.; Lane Poole, *Sir Harry Parkes*.

affair, in truth, affords a sorry justification for war, in the light of history. It was but "a match to a mine."[1] On the 25th April 1854, Sir John Bowring had himself described the two "most important subjects of grievance" as "non-admission into Canton city," and "absence of personal intercourse between the officials of the two countries." Time was not against England in either of these matters Writing two months after the first entry into Canton, Consul Parkes states: "As yet there is no war with China, but simply at Canton, and that because the commissioner chose to declare it." But Consul Parkes himself describes how the admiral, on the 23rd and 24th, entered and dismantled various forts . . . on the 27th and 28th, he "fired slowly on the residence of the commissioner." It was not until the 28th that the commissioner penned his war proclamation, calling on his countrymen "to exterminate the English barbarians." Should a man be specially reflected upon for declaring war after his house had been slowly shelled for a couple of days by foreigners?

"On 11th October, Sir John Bowring wrote to Consul Parkes: 'It appears on examination that the *Arrow* had no right to hoist the British flag. The licence to do so expired on 27th September, from which period she has not been entitled to protection.'" And the next day: "I will reconsider the regranting the register of *Arrow* if applied for, but there can be no doubt that after the expiry of the licence, protection could not be legally granted." Yet, on the 14th, Sir John wrote to Commissioner Yeh: "There is no doubt that the lorcha, *Arrow*, lawfully bore the British flag under a register granted by me."

[1] Brinkley, xii. 8.

CHAPTER IX

THE SECOND WAR

THE opium war of 1839–42 is said by one able writer to have been "really waged to put a stop to grievances which had been accumulating for 150 years!"[1] According to some opinions, a second war became needful on similar grounds, fifteen years after the first. Here again justice requires that the grievances of both sides should be weighed before any decision is arrived at. The West was in a great hurry to make money out of the East, and gunboats were found to clear the way quickly. When the reports as to the *Arrow* proceedings reached England, the Law Lords were divided on the case. Lord Lyndhurst and Lord St. Leonards said, "in no respect whatever was she a British ship." The Lord Chancellor and Lord Wensleydale upheld the legitimacy of the colonial register. In the Commons, Mr. Cobden moved a resolution condemning the war. The debate, lasting four nights, was of a high order. The resolution was carried by fourteen votes. Lord Palmerston appealed to the country, and the war wave carried all before it. Even in times of peace the better characteristics of the Chinese people are little known, and less appreciated. It is to be feared that the *Calcutta Review* was not far wrong in declaring that it was not easy for the

[1] Colquhoun, *China in Transformation*.

public to look upon a war with China as a serious business at all. "The general feeling, strange to say, was one of jocosity." Lord Palmerston said, in his electoral address, "An insolent barbarian wielding authority at Canton, violated the British flag, broke the engagement of treaties, offered rewards for the heads of British subjects in that part of China, and planned their destruction by murders, assassination, and poison." The statement must not be accepted as a judicial pronouncement. English ministers have the exigences of general elections to excuse them, which Chinese ministers have not. A comparison between this appeal and a memorial from inhabitants of Canton to the English nation is instructive. The document runs:

"Your nation has traded at Canton for more than a century, during which it may be said that between you and ourselves, the Cantonese, there have been relations of friendship and not of hostility. The late affair of the lorcha was a trifle; it was no case for deep-seated animosity as a great offence that could not be forgotten; yet you have suddenly taken up arms, and for several days you have been firing shell, until you have burned dwellings and destroyed people in untold numbers. It cannot be either told how many old people, infants, and females have left their homes in affliction. If your countrymen have not seen this, they have surely heard, have they not, that such is the case? What offence has been committed by the people of Canton that such a calamity should befall them? Again, it has come to our knowledge that you are insisting on official receptions within the city. This is doubtless with a view to amicable relations, but when your only proceeding is to open a fire upon us which destroys the people, supposing that you were to obtain admission into the city, still the sons, brothers, and kindred of the people whom you have burned out and killed will be ready to lay down their lives to be avenged on your countrymen. Nor will the authorities be able to prevent them. There is another point. Although shell have been flying against the city for several days, burning buildings and destroying life, no fire has been returned by the troops. This is really friendly and conceding; it is enough to content you. And as you resorted to hostilities for a small matter, so now, for the sake of the people's lives, you may suspend them; and, considering what has been achieved at the present stage of proceedings there, allow them to terminate. Why add another difficulty to the existing one, and so cause an interruption of the friendly understanding between our countries?"[1]

Canton fell, and Viceroy Yeh, taken captive by Consul Alcock, was transported to Calcutta, where he died. The Peiho forts were captured, and Tientsin occupied.

The Earl of Elgin, an honourable and humane man, was sent out to finish the war, and to negotiate a treaty with China. He was instructed by the Earl of Clarendon to ascertain whether the Government of China would revoke its prohibition of the opium trade. The Treaty of Tientsin, signed on the 26th June 1858, contained no reference, however, to opium. The cause of the omission is honourable to Lord Elgin. He had "a strong, if not invincible repugnance, involved as Great Britain was in hostilities at Canton, and having been compelled in the north to resort to the influence of threatened

[1] Hansard, cxliv. 1190.

coercion, to introduce the subject of opium to the Chinese authorities."[1] An eye-witness testified, "for the first eight, nine, or ten months, he (Lord Elgin) never referred to opium as a possible item of negotiation at all. He referred to it as a thing deplorable, from what he saw—from what he saw in the streets; from the emaciation and wretchedness of the opium smokers he came across."[2]

The diplomatist, with supreme power, clear instructions, and strong backing, yet could not bring himself to tell the Chinese that the time had come when they must legalise this lucrative, but demoralising traffic. It is one of the few gleams of light on English diplomacy throughout this long history. Unfortunately Lord Elgin's aversion to the drug trade led to nothing more than a little delay. England had never even considered the possibility of an honestly restrictive policy, and she did not do so now. Lord Elgin found an interesting interlude in a visit to Japan, to arrange the first treaty between Great Britain and those islands. It expressly prohibited the importation of opium into Japan.

On Lord Elgin's return to China, Mr. Reed, plenipotentiary of the U.S., who had gone to the East opposed to the opium trade, was so strongly impressed with the hollowness and danger of the existing state of things, that he addressed a long letter to Lord Elgin on the question. Mr. Reed urged that there were only two courses open: either to urge the authorities to suppress the trade, to assure them that no assistance, direct or indirect, should be given to any one seeking to evade the process, and to put a stop to the growth and export

[1] *China Cor.*, 1859, p. 396. [2] *R. C. Report*, i. p. 90.

of opium from India; or to urge the Chinese to admit the drug under a tariff. Mr. Reed said he was confident his Government would do ready justice to the high motives which would lead to the former course if that were adopted, and would rejoice at the result. "No one doubts it is very pernicious and demoralising. I am confident your Excellency will agree with me that its evils, as the basis of an illegal, connived at, and corrupting traffic, cannot be overstated. It is degrading, alike to the producer, the importer, the official, whether foreign or Chinese, and the purchaser."[1]

Lord Elgin knew prohibition to be hopeless. He had, indeed, only the second alternative open to him, and now adopted it. His delegates, Messrs. Oliphant and Wade, proposed the legalisation of the opium trade to the Chinese delegates; and Treasurer Wang admitted the necessity for a change. The official Report states: "China still retains her objection to the use of the drug on moral grounds, but the present generation of smokers, at all events, must and will have opium. To deter the uninitiated from becoming smokers, China would propose a very high duty; but as opposition was naturally to be expected from us in that case, it should be made as moderate as possible."[2] The Chinese were informed that "according to the data before Lord Elgin, a duty of from 15 to 20 taels a chest would be a fair rate." The Chinese named first 60, then 40, then 30 taels per chest. "After much discussion, chiefly upon the probable increase of smuggling in the event of the imposition of too high a duty, it was agreed to put down 30 taels per chest as the duty to be levied"—*i.e.* about 8 per cent. on average value.

[1] *China Cor.*, 1859, p. 394.

[2] *Ibid.*, p. 401.

Lord Elgin wrote to Lord Malmesbury: "It is hoped by this arrangement, on the one hand, a term will be put to the scandals and irregularities to which a contraband trade at the ports necessarily gives birth; and, on the other, that occasion will not be furnished for the still greater scandals and irregularities which would inevitably arise, if foreigners were entitled under the sanction of treaties to force this article into all districts of the interior of China."[1]

The drug which the Chinese Government had objected to so tenaciously for so long a time, and at such a costly price, now had its admission legalised, at a less duty than England then levied on Chinese silks or teas.

Lord Elgin's mission, shared, as has been said, by France, was closely watched also by the United States and Russia, who, though not joining in the war, joined very readily in the Western gains out of it. Both of the two latter nations, in entering into treaties with China, specifically excluded opium from the articles of trade.

Much importance was attached by England and France to a formal ratification of the Treaty of Tientsin just concluded at Pekin. The Chinese agreed to a visit with a moderate escort only. The envoys determined to proceed in force. The Chinese forts on the Peiho baffled the hostile fleets; and, as a consequence, the third Chinese war was entered upon—to be ended by a treaty signed at Pekin.

During some negotiations, Consul Parkes and an escort were captured by the Chinese under treacherous circumstances, and cruelly treated as captives, twenty-two out of twenty-seven perishing. Two days

[1] *China Cor.*, 1859, p. 425.

afterwards Lord Elgin ordered the destruction of the Summer Palace, which numbered thirty main edifices, containing priceless treasures, in an enclosure of twelve square miles. The palace is said to have been previously looted by the French. There seems to be an abnormal brutality about all warfare in China. The Allies, on landing at Pehtang, were well received by the inhabitants. Consul Parkes tells how the commanders proclaimed promises of protection on entering the town. Notwithstanding these, the place was "thoroughly pillaged," and a number of people, principally women, committed suicide, to escape, as they feared, a worse fate. A justification of the war at the time, describes it as "chasing away the darkness of heathenism, and substituting for its iron rule the benignant sway and gentle influence of Christianity."[1]

The price China had to pay for peace was a heavy one. The Allies insisted on money indemnities, as well as territorial acquisitions. The jealousy of the Powers had grown. England obtained an additional piece of land at Hong Kong, and secured the legalisation of opium and of Christianity. France not to be behind-hand, secured a grant of all the Catholic churches, and an enforced restoration of all land once owned by Christians, and alienated by various methods even in remote periods.

Lord Elgin's letters[2] prove that he was acutely sensitive to the baser side of the British controversy with China, as the following extracts show:—

Dec. 22, 1857.—"When we steamed up to Canton and saw the rich alluvial banks covered with luxuriant evidences of unrivalled industry and natural

[1] *Fraser's Magazine*, Feby., 1857.

[2] *Letters and Journals of Lord Elgin.*

fertility . . . I thought bitterly of those who, for the most selfish objects, are trampling underfoot this ancient civilisation."

Dec. 9.—"Nothing could be more contemptible than the origin of our existing quarrel. . . . I have hardly alluded in my ultimatum to that wretched question of the *Arrow*, which is a scandal to us, and is so considered by all, except the few who are personally compromised."

"The Chinese do not want to fight, but they will not accept the position relatively to strangers under which alone strangers will consent to live with them. The English do want to fight."

Dec. 24.—"One of the gunboats got ashore yesterday, within a stone's throw of Canton. The officers had the coolness to call on a crowd of Chinese who were on the quays to pull her off, which they at once did! Fancy having to fight such a people!"

Dec. 25.—Christmas Day. Canton "doomed to destruction, through the folly of its own rulers, and the vanity and levity of ours."

June 12, 1858.—"I have seen more to disgust me with my fellow-countrymen than I saw during the whole course of my previous life, since I have found them in the East, among populations too timid to resist and too ignorant to complain."

Aug. 30.—(After Jeddo) "quitting the only place I have left with any feeling of regret since I reached this abominable East; abominable, not so much in itself, as because it is strewed all over with the records of our violence and fraud."

Nov. 6.—"In our relations with China we have acted scandalously, and I would not have been a party to the measures of violence which have taken place if I had not believed that I could work out of them some good. . . . What was really meritorious was, that it (the treaty) should have been obtained at so small a cost of human suffering. This is what discredits it in the eyes of almost all here."

In addressing the Shanghai merchants, Lord Elgin said: "Uninvited, and by methods not always of the gentlest, we have broken down the barriers behind which these ancient nations sought to conceal from the world without the mysteries, perhaps in the case of China the rags and rottenness, of their waning civilisations. Neither our consciences nor the judgment of mankind will acquit us, if, when asked to what use we have turned our opportunities, we can only say we have filled our pockets from among the ruins which we have found or made."

To the Protestant missionaries at Shanghai, Lord Elgin condemned reckless men up and down the coasts, "who bring discredit on the Christian name; inspire hatred of the foreigner where no such hatred exists; and, as some recent instances prove, teach occasionally to the natives a lesson of vengeance which, when once learned, may not always be applied with discrimination." And at a dinner at the Mansion House on his return, he gave his opinion that "the occasional misconduct of our own countrymen and other foreigners in China is perhaps the very greatest difficulty with which the Queen's representatives there have to deal."

CHAPTER X

LEGALISATION

GREAT BRITAIN had at last accomplished its desire, so long worked for, so little avowed. The Government of India was no longer to be the chief accomplice, the unsleeping partner, of Chinese smugglers. The great drug trade was regularised by law. China had yielded to a steady continuous pressure, which it had not the strength to resist.

It has been claimed by some of those who took part in the negotiations, that opium played a very subordinate part, and that the Chinese rather welcomed than objected to the final act of legalisation. Mr. Lay's account has been quoted in Parliament as follows:—"The preparation of the tariff devolved on me. When I came to opium, I inquired what course they proposed to take in respect to it. The answer was, 'We have resolved to put it into the tariff as foreign medicine.' I urged a moderate duty in view of the cost of collection, which was agreed to. This represents, in strict accuracy, the amount of extortion resorted to."[1]

Mr. Oliphant, one of the Commission, adds that he informed the Chinese commissioner of his instructions from Lord Elgin, "not to insist on the insertion of the drug in the tariff, should the Chinese Government wish to omit it. This he declined to

[1] *Parl. Debates*, 1889, p. 1188.

do. I then proposed the duty should be increased beyond the figures suggested in the tariff, but to this he objected, on the grounds that it would increase the inducements to smuggling. I trust that the delusion still existing that the opium was extorted from China may be finally dispelled."

The other English commissioner, Sir Thomas Wade, stated,[1] that "as to the duty, it would be an abuse of words to say that there was any negotiation at all."

These three statements, no doubt, accurately describe the final drafting of the tariff. The only comment a student of these events has to offer is, that they are too limited in their scope to carry the much wider conclusion suggested. The details may be correct, the perspective surely errs; before it can be put right, it is necessary to take a wider survey. This was done very effectively by Sir Thomas Wade himself, whilst still a responsible official, and before any wrangling over opium had engaged him "on the other side." In a despatch in 1868, he wrote:

"Nothing that has been gained was received from the free-will of the Chinese; more, the concessions made to us have been from first to last extorted against the conscience of the nation—in defiance, that is to say, of the moral convictions of its educated men—not merely of the office-holders, whom we call mandarins, and who are numerically but a small proportion of the educated class, but of the millions who are saturated with a knowledge of the history and philosophy of their country. To these, as a rule, the very extension of our trade must appear politically, or, what is in China the same thing, morally, wrong; and the story of foreign

[1] *R. C. Report*, i. 70.

intercourse during the last thirty years can have had no effect but to confirm them in their opinion."[1]

It is difficult to understand how any reader of history can come to any other conclusion than Mr. Harold Gorst's: "As to the fact that we did, inch by inch, force commercial relations upon a country which desired to remain closed to the outside world, there can be no reasonable doubt."[2]

The fullest and best-informed evidence on the attitude of the Chinese Government to the opium question after the wars had ceased and legalisation was an accomplished fact, is to be found in a confidential despatch of Sir Rutherford Alcock's, which reports a private conversation between himself and three ministers of the Foreign Board at Pekin.[3] After discussing the relations then (1869) existing between China and foreign States, the conversation turned on the hostile animus shown by the literati and official classes to foreigners, apart from religious questions. "Wen Seang asked, 'How could it be otherwise? They had often seen foreigners making war on the country, and then again, how irreparable and continuous was the injury they had inflicted on the whole empire by the foreign importation of opium.' He added, 'If England would consent to interdict this, cease either to grow it in India, or to allow their ships to bring it to China, there might be some hope of more friendly feelings. No doubt there was a very strong feeling entertained by all the literati and gentry as to the frightful evils attending the smoking of opium, its thoroughly demoralising effects, and the utter ruin brought upon all who once gave way to the vice. . . . If England ceased to

[1] *Tientsin Cor.*, 1868, p. 432. [2] *China*, p. 212.
[3] *E. I. Finance Report*, 1871, p. 267.

protect the trade, it could then be effectually prohibited by the Emperor, . . . and it would eventually cease to trouble them; while a great cause of hostility and distrust in the minds of the people would be removed.' "

This interview convinced Sir Rutherford Alcock that the Chinese Government were determined to make an earnest effort to induce the British Government to prohibit it altogether, and to take it out, in fact, of the list of goods in which trade was permitted. This conversation was followed by an official memorandum from the Chinese Foreign Office, foreboding the alternative policy on the part of China, if England persisted in the trade. The document runs: "The writers have on several occasions, when conversing with His Excellency, referred to the opium trade as being prejudicial to the general interests of commerce. . . . Day and night the writers are considering the question; the more they reflect upon it, the greater does their anxiety become, and they cannot avoid addressing H.E. very earnestly upon the subject. That opium is like a deadly poison, that it is most injurious to mankind, and a most serious provocative of ill-feeling, is, the writers think, perfectly well known to H.E. . . . The officials and people . . . all say, that England trades in opium because she desires to work China's ruin, for, say they, if the friendly feelings of England are genuine, since it is open to her to produce and trade in everything else, would she still insist on spreading the poison of this hurtful thing through the empire? There are those who say, 'stop the trade by enforcing a vigorous prohibition against the use of the drug.' . . . A strict enforcement of the prohibition would necessitate the taking of many lives. Now, although the criminals' punishment would be of their own seeking, bystanders would not fail to say that it was the foreign merchant seduced them to their ruin by bringing the drug, and it would be hard to prevent general and deep-seated indignation; such a course would tend to arouse popular anger against the foreigner. There are others, again, who suggest the removal of the prohibition against the growth of the poppy. . . . We should thus not only deprive the foreign merchant of the main source of his profits, but should increase our revenue to boot. . . . Such a course would be practicable, and indeed the writers cannot say that, as a last resource, it will not come to this; but they are most unwilling that such prohibition should be removed, holding, as they do, that a right system of government should appreciate the beneficence of Heaven, and seek to remove any grievance which afflicts its people; while to allow them to go on to destruction, although an increase of revenue may result, will provoke the judgment of Heaven and the condemnation of men. . . . Again, the Chinese merchant supplies your country with his goodly tea and silk, conferring thereby a benefit upon her; but the English merchant empoisons China with pestilent opium. Such conduct is unrighteous. Who can justify it? What wonder if officials and people say that England is wilfully working out China's ruin? The wealth and generosity of England are spoken of by all, . . . how is it, then, she can hesitate to remove an acknowledged evil? The writers hope that H.E. will memorialise his Government to give orders in India and elsewhere to substitute the cultivation of cereals or cotton. Were both nations rigorously to prohibit the growth of the poppy, both the traffic in and the consumption of opium might alike be put an end to. To do away with so great an evil would be a great virtue on England's part. She would strengthen friendly relations and make herself illustrious."[1]

Sir Rutherford Alcock afterwards found that Li Hung Chang had instituted the rival policy in his province; and he was satisfied in 1871 that the Chinese Government were "seriously contemplating, if they cannot come to any terms with the British Government, the cultivation, without stint, in China, and producing opium at a much cheaper rate. Having done that, they think they will afterwards be able to stamp out the opium produce among themselves."[2]

In his evidence given before the Committee on East Indian Finance of 1871, Sir Rutherford Alcock further stated his firm conviction that "whatever degree of honesty may be attributed to the officials and to the central Government, there is that at work in their minds, that they would not hesitate one moment to-morrow, if they could, to enter into any arrangement with the British Government, and say, 'Let our revenue go; we care nothing about it. What we want is to stop the consumption of opium, which we conceive is impoverishing the country and demoralising and brutalising our people.'"[3] He believed the Chinese Government were perfectly sincere in their desire to put an end to the consumption. "I must say that my own impression is that they were infinitely better off without the opium."[4]

Sir Rutherford Alcock thought, "The very fact

[1] *E. I. Finance Report*, 1871, pp. 268, 269. [2] *Ibid.*, p. 273.
[3] P. 273. [4] P. 276.

that they had been compelled by the superior force of foreign governments to admit opium against all the moral feeling and judgment of the nation, and against their own, as an article of commerce, and to derive a revenue from it, must very much damage the Government in the estimation of the people; first as a sign of deplorable weakness, and next as an indication of want of courage to do what was necessary for the welfare of the nation."[1]

When asked whether we forced the Chinese by treaty to take opium, Sir Rutherford Alcock answered, "That is so in effect."[2] To the Chairman's question, "We have forced the Government to enter into a treaty to allow their subjects to take it?" his reply was, "Yes, precisely."[3] "If they now said, 'We will not renew the treaty except on the condition of excluding opium altogether,' they must be prepared to fight for it." Sir Rutherford Alcock admitted that the treaty was undoubtedly imposed on them by our superior force. "There are many things in that treaty which they never would have assented to of their own accord."[4] He advocated an agreement between the two Governments to diminish the supply of opium annually at a fixed rate.[5]

Lord Elgin took the same view of the treaty when he wrote in a despatch reviewing his work in China: "The concessions obtained in the treaty from the Chinese Government are not in themselves extravagant, but in the eyes of the Chinese

[1] *E. I. Finance Report*, 1871, p. 275. [2] *Ibid.*, p. 279.
[3] P. 283. [4] P. 284.
[5] After his return home, Sir Rutherford Alcock engaged himself, like Sir T. Wade, in defending the British Government against anti-opium reflections, but his official evidence is left undisputed.

Government they amount to a revolution. . . . They have been extorted therefore from its fears."[1] This was penned three months before the tariff was fixed, but holds good of the diplomatic relations of the two countries as a whole.

[1] *China Cor.*, 1859, p. 345.

CHAPTER XI

THE CHEFOO CONVENTION

IN 1869, Sir Rutherford Alcock completed a painstaking Commercial Convention, revising several of the provisions of the Treaty of Tientsin. The Chinese sought to raise the duty on opium from 30 to 50 taels per chest. The opium merchants, deeming their craft in danger, took the alarm; the Indian Government followed suit; and in spite of Sir Rutherford Alcock's efforts, including a visit to India, Lord Granville yielded to the pressure of the trade, the Liberal Government refused its ratification, and the Convention fell through. It is well to record the opinion of Sir T. Wade on this incident. In an official report of 1877, after explaining Lord Elgin's intentions in his treaty, that "if the Chinese would but include opium in the tariff, they were to be free to do what they pleased with it" in the matter of inland transit dues, he writes: "The rejection" (of Sir R. Alcock's Convention) "greatly added to our difficulties. It was the first instrument affecting British trade that had not been extorted from the Chinese by force of arms. It was the first in which there was at least a show of reciprocal interchange of concessions. It was the result of two years of negotiations. It was not wonderful, therefore, that its rejection without a trial . . . should show itself in renewed obstructiveness."

In 1876, Sir Thomas Wade negotiated the Chefoo Convention.[1] Under the Elgin Treaty the Chinese had imposed inland transit dues on opium of amounts varying from 16 to 80 taels per chest. Sir Thomas Wade provided that the inland transit dues and the import duty should be collected together at the port,—the total amount to be 110 taels. This involved a practical surrender by the provinces of their right to put a prohibitive duty on the drug in the interior; but it represented a great increase of duty on entering the country, and much more certainty of collection. As a matter of fact, the right of the authorities to tax opium as they pleased up the country, was vitiated by the frequency of smuggling, and the inability of the officials to cope with it. Sir T. Wade mentions that the Chinese believed they lost £300,000 per year by the unfettered smuggling from Macao and Hong Kong alone. If the authorities in London were always feeble over opium, those at Calcutta were always strong. A long apologetic despatch of Sir Thomas Wade to the Viceroy concludes by timidly proposing an increase of 20 to 40 taels only.[2] The Indian Government received the suggestion with dismay. Sir Thomas Wade admitted that the Chinese had originally proposed a likin of 150 taels. This was gradually reduced to 130, 120, 110, 80, and finally 70. The agreement was signed on 13th September 1876. The German and other embassies made some demur in order to gain further concessions for their trade, but the more serious obstruction came from India. The agreement represented a give-and-take policy between the two countries. China was to open four more

[1] *China Cor.*, 1882, p. 72. [2] *Ibid.*, p. 67.

ports for residence to foreigners, and six places of call. On the other hand, she was to obtain a higher and more certain tax on opium. She opened the ports, and fulfilled her part at once; but year after year passed by, and no acceptance of the Convention was forthcoming from England.

Even after opposition on the part of India was formally withdrawn in 1881, the reluctance to allow China to tax the drug on the basis agreed upon continued. When negotiations were finally renewed, the Chinese, now strengthened by Sir Robert Hart as their adviser, made a stand for 80 taels per chest. Earl Granville fought for 70 taels, and also for the foreigner's right of going with his drug into the interior. At last, on 9th February 1885, Great Britain acceded to the Chinese terms, which, it was alleged, "may entail a considerable loss of revenue on India," on the understanding that beyond the stipulated levy, "foreign opium shall pay nothing that native opium does not pay."[1] Perhaps the most cynical exposition of England's real attitude was given by Lord Salisbury in the House of Lords (9th May 1879): "With respect to opium," he said, "the Convention proposes what would undoubtedly be a very drastic remedy—that the collection of likin should be placed in the same hands as those which collect the custom. In that case smuggling would be absolutely barred, and the tax upon opium might be raised to any amount provincial governors pleased. That would be a result which practically would neutralise the policy which hitherto had been pursued by this country in respect to that drug." Has any missionary or philanthropist ever put the case against England more severely?

[1] *China Cor.*, 1885, p. 9.

When the nine years of haggling were over, England plumed herself on having conceded everything to China, and claimed that all suspicion as to a forced drug traffic was now for ever swept away. Lord Kimberley announced that "the agreement now under negotiation is of the Chinese Government's own proposing, and includes all that they desire." This emboldened the Royal Commission to say, "The existing regulations therefore must be taken to be in accordance with the wishes of the Chinese Government."[1] But a reference to the text of the despatch shows that the construction which any ordinary reader would put upon this, is a misapprehension of the facts of the case. The satisfaction of the Chinese Government had reference only to the details of the additional article of agreement as compared with the regulations previously in force, and does not apply to the general question of the import of opium.

The Society for the Suppression of the Opium Traffic accepted Lord Kimberley's view at the time, but pointed out that the evil results of the past were still operative in China. The idea of any final clearance of responsibility lacks all sense of historic proportion. China had emerged from an eighteen years' scramble with a larger share of the booty than she had at one time expected, and said polite and pleasant things in consequence. But during the process she had asked for half as much again, and had pointed out, with her profound trading instinct, that her utmost requests would only give her a jackal's share of the profits on the drug, as compared with the lion's share retained by the Indian Government. Sir Thomas Wade mentions that even during

[1] *R. C. Report*, vi. 52.

the negotiations China sent an intelligent officer to Calcutta to sound the Indian Government on the practicability of gradually extinguishing its interest in the traffic.[1] There are frequent admissions in the official correspondence, that the shadow of the opium war still hung over the diplomatists of the country. As it was, they would never have been allowed to raise the duty, but for the equivalent given in the opening of new ports to commerce, including the drug; so that any boast as to giving China complete freedom only shows how easy it is to forget, where pecuniary interests are concerned, what freedom means to other countries.

The great difficulty Englishmen have in thinking of China in terms of freedom as a self-governing nation, was strikingly illustrated before the Royal Commission by both Sir Thomas Wade and Mr. Lay.

Sir Thomas Wade said, "If the Chinese Government were minded to raise the duty, or to make fresh arrangements regarding the revenue, there is not a shadow of doubt that we should not, as in former days when there were no relations at all, meet them with a direct negative; we should not refuse any proposition they might make without consideration."[2]

The naïve statement that we should not now refuse to China the right to decide her own drug tariff "without consideration," shows the extraordinary part that our superior force has played in past days. Mr. Lay, who denounced the pretence that we had forced opium on the Chinese as "fustian," said, "They have encouraged our opium, and we, by allowing the Chinese to overtax it, have

[1] *China Cor.*, 1882, p. 80.

[2] *R. C. Report*, i. 92.

stimulated the growth of the native article enormously in every province. I think that the most short-sighted policy that ever was pursued on our part." To Mr. Lay it was still folly to "allow" the Chinese to deal with their own excise.

By the Treaty of Shanghai, following the deplorable outbreak and war of 1901–02, a unification of import and transit dues has been made universal. Opium is exempted from the new surtax at the ports, and remains at the old figure. One advance along the line of restriction for the sake of the health and character of the community, may be gladly chronicled. Morphia, the cheapest and handiest form of the drug, has been finding a ready acceptance in China. In 1901, 138,567 oz. were imported. The Shanghai Convention now absolutely prohibits the general importation of the drug, and limits its admission strictly to medicinal purposes. Morphia had already been put under a similar ban at Hong Kong, where the opium farmers had protested against it. The people liked it, but it was at once pronounced to be a dangerous heresy from the proper opium habit, and was stamped out accordingly. The precedent is not without significance.

The general position of the British opium trade remains as left by the Chefoo Convention. A curious misunderstanding with regard to it, shown by the late Royal Commission, was set right by Dr. Maxwell.[1]

The present freedom of China was assumed by the Commission in the first instance, and was disputed by Dr. Maxwell. He said, "I want to say very definitely, my Lord, that I hold China is not

[1] *R. C. Report*, i. Q. 250.

free, and that I think such statements as those of Sir James Ferguson and . . . Mr. Curzon that China if it pleased could be in the same position as Japan—that China, to-morrow, could issue an edict prohibiting opium, are quite inconsistent with what, I think, most people understand by treaty obligations. At the present time China is bound to us in England." The Chairman observed those gentlemen "were the official representatives of the Foreign Office speaking in their official position, and on their official responsibility in the House of Commons." "Well," Dr. Maxwell replied, "I speak from the point of view of China," and, having the terms of the Chefoo Commission in his pocket, he proceeded to show that if China terminated the Chefoo agreement, the Treaty of Tientsin would revive, and China would not be free to deal with opium as she might wish. Sir James Lyall truly said, "That is quite contrary to what has been said in Parliament." The point was eventually referred to the Foreign Office, and a letter from the Foreign Office states: "This arrangement (that at present in force) was to remain binding for four years, after which either party might give twelve months' notice to terminate it. And in the event of its termination, the arrangements under the regulations attached to the Treaty of Tientsin (1858) should be revived."[1] Dr. Maxwell was therefore right. It is only needful to add here that Sir David Barbour's evidence at Calcutta showed that the Indian Government is by no means prepared to assent to the doctrine of giving China a free hand in the administration of her own affairs. He said, "If we abandon our treaty rights in China and allow the Chinese to

[1] *R. C. Report*, vol. i. App. iv.

impose any import duty they please on Indian opium, the whole, or practically the whole of the Indian revenue from the export of opium to China will be lost to India."

There are occasional indications that China is not satisfied with the present opium duties, and is not free to act as she may herself wish in the matter. On the 16th of August 1902, *The Times* correspondent at Hong Kong telegraphed:

"For several months, despite Lord Cranbourne's declarations that the Foreign Office had received no consular notification in corroboration of this statement, the opium trade has been completely stopped at Canton and Swatau, where the officials are endeavouring to levy an extra tax of 200 dollars per chest. A similar attempt to levy a tax at Nankin, after the Japanese war, failed, the officials attempting to collect it from the proprietors of the smoking shops, who, however, resisted. The Canton and Swatau authorities desire, contrary to Clause 5, to open packages and levy an additional tax at the point of import, which is not the place of consumption, thus avoiding friction with the divan owners, and leakage in the hands of subordinate collectors. Coming while the new treaty is under negotiation, this attempt is significant."

It is said that the tax was not levied equally on home-grown and imported opium, and thus came within the terms of the clause, which reserves the right of the Chinese authorities to levy a further tax "when the package shall have been opened at the place of consumption, provided that it be not other than or in excess of such tax or contribution as is or may hereafter be levied on native opium." [1]

[1] *Friend of China*, July 1903.

Lord Cranbourne, in replying on behalf of the Foreign Office, stated that this particular tax was so levied as not to bear with equal incidence on the native and foreign trade, and that it contravened Clause 3 of the Additional Article; because it was to be levied at the port and while the packages were still unopened for consumption. The Shanghai correspondent of *China's Millions* recently stated that the Imperial Government had increased the tax on locally grown opium, as also on tobacco and wine.

The consular reports confirm the desire of the Chinese to raise the taxation on opium. In the General Report for 1902, it is mentioned that a tax on the prepared drug was instituted, but with many irregularities. "Consequent protests on behalf of H.M. representatives led, in not a few instances, to its abandonment. . . . All things considered, one might have looked for a larger demand for Indian opium when the enhanced cost of native grown opium, owing to scarcity and taxation, is taken into account."

From Wuchow it is reported that "the new, heavy tax on native opium, though it may have the effect of increasing the import of the Indian drug, is a serious blow to the piece-good trade, and therefore to be deplored." At Hankow the "figures for native opium fell nearly half, owing partly to poor crops, partly to the imposition of a tax on prepared opium collected on the crude drug." So the case now stands in China.

CHAPTER XII

OPINION IN PARLIAMENT

A HOUSE of Commons Committee in 1832 reported: "In the present state of the revenue of India, it does not appear advisable to abandon so important a source of revenue, a duty upon opium being a tax which falls principally upon the foreign consumer, and which appears upon the whole less liable to objection than any other which could be substituted."[1] The then "present state of the Indian revenue" has remained equally potent ever since, and the foreign consumer has never come inside the pale of consideration, except very recently, when morphia threatened to undermine the more costly opium habits.

In 1843, Lord Ashley, afterwards Earl of Shaftesbury, moved the following resolution in the Lower House, viz.:—

"That the continuance of the trade in opium, and the monopoly of its growth in the territory of British India, are destructive of all relations of amity between England and China, injurious to the manufacturing interests of the country by the very serious diminution of legitimate commerce, and utterly inconsistent with the honours and duties of a Christian kingdom, and that steps be taken as soon as possible, with due regard to rights of

[1] *East India Co. Report*, 1831–32, iii. 10.

governments and individuals, to abolish the evil."[1] Lord Ashley had for two years been a Commissioner of the India Board of Control. He was, therefore, not unacquainted with Eastern affairs. His introduction to the opium question is thus described in his Journal:

"*Feb.* 13, 1843.—On Saturday last, Samuel Gurney and Mr. Fry called on me to lay the state of the opium trade with China before me, and request that I would submit it to Parliament. I agreed in all they said, for I had long thought and felt the same. . . . They told me, and gave most excellent proofs of their correctness, that the Government were not averse to the abolition of the opium monopoly, though fully aware of its extreme difficulty; that the Board of Trade were actually favourable, and that Peel positively condemned the contraband trade."

In the House, Lord Ashley said, "I am fully convinced that for this country to encourage this nefarious traffic is bad, perhaps worse than encouraging the slave trade . . . the opium trade destroys the man both body and soul; and carries a hideous ruin over millions, which can never be repaired." His speech, the first great indictment of the trade in Parliament, was described by *The Times* as "far more statesmanlike" than those by which it was opposed. Sir Robert Peel stated that the negotiations then proceeding would be impeded by such a resolution, and therefore Lord Ashley withdrew his motion. He entered in his diary: "Very remarkable, not one person even attempted to touch the morality of the question; that seemed to be tacitly, but universally surrendered."

[1] Hansard, vol. lxviii.

In 1857, Earl Shaftesbury renewed his attack in the House of Lords, by moving that two questions be submitted for the opinion of Her Majesty's judges: 1st, Whether it was lawful for the East India Company to derive a revenue from the opium monopoly; 2nd, whether it was lawful for them to sell the opium for the direct purpose of being smuggled into a friendly country. After debate, the motion was withdrawn, on the understanding that the Government would take the opinion of the law officers of the Crown, including the Company's standing counsel. The answer they gave (20th August) to the first was, "Yes." The reply to the second: "We think, now that opium is made contraband by the law of China, and that its importation into China is made by Chinese law a capital crime, the continuance of the Company's practice of manufacturing and selling this opium in a form specially adapted to the Chinese contraband trade, though not an actual and direct infringement of the treaty, is yet at variance with its spirit and intention, and with the conduct due to the Chinese Government by that of Great Britain as a friendly Power, bound by a treaty which implies that all smuggling with China will be discountenanced by Great Britain." This opinion is not pleasant reading. It pronounced Great Britain's conduct in regard to opium to be neither straightforward nor friendly. Nothing, however, was done to make it either or both. But China was continually pressed to legalise the drug.

In 1870, Sir Wilfrid Lawson moved: "That this House condemns the system by which a large portion of the Indian revenue is raised by opium."

47 members supported him, 151 voted with the Government against the motion.

In 1875, Mr., now Sir J., Mark Stewart moved: "That the imperial policy regulating the opium traffic between India and China should be carefully considered by Her Majesty's Government, with a view to the gradual withdrawal of the Government of India from the cultivation and manufacture of opium." For the resolution, 57 voted; against, 94.[1]

In reply to an anti-opium deputation in 1876, Lord Salisbury said, "The Government does not view with any favour an extension of the system, and there is no project of the kind in existence. Without taking the view as to its moral condemnation which is held by many persons present, I feel that there are inconveniences of principle connected with it which would have prevented any government in the present day from introducing it. I entirely disclaim any intention to push the Bengal system farther."

In 1886, Sir J. W. Pease brought forward another anti-opium resolution, when the previous question was carried by 126 to 66. In 1889 a similar motion, submitted by Mr. Samuel Smith, was rejected by 165 to 88. In 1891, Sir J. W. Pease moved: "That this House is of opinion that the system by which the Indian opium revenue is raised is morally indefensible, and would urge upon the Indian Government that it should cease to grant licences for the cultivation of the poppy, and the sale of opium in British India, except to supply the legitimate demand for medical purposes; and that they should at the same time take measures

[1] Hansard, vol. ccxxv., 25th June.

to arrest the transit of Malwa opium through British territory."[1] 160 members voted with Sir J. W. Pease, and 130 against. This victory of the assailants of the drug was followed up in 1893 by Mr. Alfred Webb, who moved the following resolution, viz.:—

"That, having regard to the opinion expressed by the vote of this House on the 10th April 1891, that the system by which the Indian opium revenue is raised is morally indefensible, and which urged the Indian Government to give practical effect to that opinion by ceasing to grant licences, and by taking measures to arrest the transit of Malwa opium through British territory, and recognising that the people of India ought not to be called upon to bear the cost involved in this change of policy, and that oppressive taxation and the stoppage of expenditure necessary for the welfare and progress of the Indian people must be avoided, this House is of opinion that a Royal Commission should be appointed to inquire both in India and in this country, and to report as to (1) What retrenchments and reforms can be effected in the military and civil expenditure of India; (2) by what means Indian resources can be best developed; and (3) what, if any, temporary assistance from the British Exchequer would be required in order to meet any deficit of revenue which would be occasioned by the suppression of the opium traffic."[2]

Mr. Gladstone, on behalf of the Government, moved a counter resolution in these terms:—

"That, having regard to the strong objections urged on moral grounds to the system by which

[1] Hansard, ccclii., 10th April 1891.

[2] *Parl. Debates*, 30th June 1893.

the Indian opium revenue is raised, this House presses on the Government of India to continue their policy of greatly diminishing the cultivation of the poppy, and the production and sale of opium, and desires that an humble Address be presented to Her Majesty, praying Her Majesty to appoint a Royal Commission to report as to—

"1. Whether the growth of the poppy and manufacture and sale of opium in British India should be prohibited, except for medical purposes, and whether such prohibition could be extended to the Native States:

"2. The nature of the existing arrangements with the Native States in respect of the transit of opium through British territory, and on what terms, if any, these arrangements could be with justice terminated:

"3. The effect on the finances of India of the prohibition of the sale and export of opium, taking into consideration (*a*) the amount of compensation payable; (*b*) the cost of the necessary preventive measures; (*c*) the loss of revenue:

"4. Whether any change short of total prohibition should be made in the system at present followed for regulating and restricting the opium traffic, and for raising a revenue therefrom:

"5. The consumption of opium by the different races, and in the different districts of India, and the effect of such consumption on the moral and physical condition of the people:

"6. The disposition of the people of India in regard to (*a*) the use of opium for non-medical purposes; (*b*) their willingness to bear in whole or in part the cost of prohibitive measures."

Mr. Gladstone's resolution was adopted by 184

votes to 105,[1] the anti-opiumists voting against the Government.

The Prime Minister's proposals extended the inquiry from an investigation of ways and means to the whole range of the opium question in India. The China trade and its effect on the Chinese, which were the source of the controversy, are not mentioned in the resolutions. The personal investigations of the Royal Commission were, so far as the effects of the opium habit are concerned, diverted from the larger issue at stake to a minor one. The opium habit in India differs widely from that which obtains in China. In the former country the drug is taken as a pill, in the latter it is smoked. In India the use of opium for other than medical purposes is admitted to be exceptional. The opium exported to China exceeded that retained for home consumption in the proportion, according to the Commission, of twelve to one.

The official resolutions pressed upon the Government to continue their policy of greatly diminishing the cultivation of the poppy, etc. This was in accord with the statements made on behalf of the previous Government.

Mr. W. H. Smith, the Leader of the House of Commons, in speaking on Sir Joseph Pease's motion, said (10th April 1891), "The course which the Government of India had taken during the last five

[1] It should be remembered that the House of Commons was at this time in the throes of the Home Rule Bill. Mr. Gladstone was eager to avoid any occasion of division. When the House met that day, the anti-opiumists had grounds for thinking that the Government resolution No. 1 would commence with the word "when" instead of "whether." As the afternoon wore on they were informed that a colleague of Mr. Gladstone's absolutely refused to assent to this. The negotiations therefore fell through, with the result already indicated.

years was to diminish the area of cultivation in India by 20 per cent. That must be taken as an indication of the policy of the Government in its administration of India." And again, "the policy of the Government had been greatly to diminish the cultivation and consumption of the drug in India. That had been their distinct policy during the past five years, and it would be preserved in the future." On the same occasion, Sir James Fergusson added, "I freely admit that the Government of India have never denied that it would be very desirable that this source of revenue should be altered. They have taken measures to reduce it; they have diminished the number of licences, and they have diminished the area on which the poppy was grown. One hundred thousand acres less are now under poppy in Bengal than ten years ago."

Two successive Governments, therefore, representing the two great parties in the State, both specifically affirmed that the opium policy of the empire was one of restriction and diminished output. When the Commission reached India, they discovered that nothing was known of such a policy. Some care was taken to avoid arousing opinion in England by extending the cultivation, but restriction was only enforced when the markets made it advisable for the sake of revenue. As a matter of fact, the statistics show that during the ten years from 1891–92 to 1901–02, the area under poppy in India has increased by 112,000 acres. The number of chests manufactured in the Bengal factories has increased by 10,576. (The late Secretary of State for India has since justified this extension by the findings of the Majority Report of the late Royal Commission.)

The Commission was appointed as follows:—

Chairman, The Right Hon. Lord Brassey, K.C.B; Sir James B. Lyall, G.C.I.E., K.C.S.I.; Mr. Arthur N. Fanshaw, Director-General of the Post Office of India. Sir Lachhmeswar Singh Bahadur, Maharajah of Darbhanga; Mr. Haridas Veharidas, late Dewan (Prime Minister) of Junagarh. Mr. Arthur Pease; Mr. Henry J. Wilson, M.P.; Sir William Roberts, M.D.; Mr. Robert G. C. Mowbray, M.P.; Secretary, Mr. J. Prescott Hewett, C.I.E. On the return of the Commission to this country, Mr. Hewett was recalled to India, and Mr. Baines, who was in England, took his place as Secretary.

In 1895, some three weeks after the Commission had reported the result of their labours, Sir J. W. Pease moved a resolution, reciting the presentation of the Commission's Report, and reaffirming the resolution that the opium revenue is indefensible. The discussion naturally centred round the Report; Sir J. W. Pease said "no one could look at the Report without seeing who drew it up, and for what purpose. The Government of India thanked the Commission for their trouble in strengthening the hands of the Government."[1] Mr. John E. Ellis asked for a copy of the letter of the Viceroy presented to the Commission, and the returns as to the use of opium in the native army collected, but never presented, and said "such procedure would not have been allowed by a single Private Bill Committee upstairs."

Sir Henry Fowler, Secretary of State for India, said he had not had time to read the Report, and protested against hasty attacks on the Commission, composed as it was of distinguished men of great

[1] *Parl. Debates*, May 1895.

knowledge and experience. Mr. Mowbray generally defended the Commission. 59 members voted for the resolution, and 176 members against.

No debate on the subject has since taken place in Parliament.

Opinion in Parliament is in the main the reflex of opinion in the country. The movement there against the opium trade has proceeded on similar lines to that of former days against the slave trade, to that of recent times against intemperance. The enlarged electorate of to-day is more slow to move on questions beyond its own surroundings than the restricted middle class constituencies of fifty years ago. Probably it is not less just when a great issue is clearly brought before it. The conscience of multitudes of thoughtful people has found expression in strong resolutions against the trade, passed in the Wesleyan Conference, the General Assembly of the Free Church of Scotland, the Convocation of the province of York, the Congregational Union, the Baptist Union, the Primitive Methodist Conference, by the Unitarians, the Society of Friends, and other bodies. By some of these, resolutions have been passed repeatedly up to the present time.

PART II: THE ROYAL COMMISSION

CHAPTER I

THE NON-JUDICIAL COMMISSION

THE Commission spent three months in India, sent schedules of questions to the Straits Settlement, Hong Kong, and China, and returned to England in the early spring of 1894, without the two native Indian commissioners.[1] On the 22nd April 1895, a lengthy notice of their Report appeared in *The Times* three days before it was presented to Parliament. Part I. was only obtainable by the public on 4th May. The press notices, quite naturally, were founded upon the account furnished to *The Times*. The Commission added seven large blue-books and a memorandum to English literature on opium. Of the 2556 pages, barely one-fifth relate to China. The index is unfortunately imperfect, and misleading in places. The books contain a vast amount of information of very unequal value, and as trackless as an Indian jungle. They furnish the fullest statement of the case of the Indian Government which has yet been obtainable. The evidence as to the use of the drug in India (marshalled from the official standpoint) is of real value. Only one aspect of the Commission as a

[1] *R. C. Report*, vii. 321.

whole, and one department of its labours, can be dealt with in this volume, viz. (1) the character of the inquiry, and (2) its bearing on the Indo-Chinese trade.

This chapter is devoted to the character of the proceedings of the Commission.

With regard to the judicial sanction ordinarily attaching to a Royal Commission, it may be said that such a body has never yet been elevated in this country into a Court of Conscience to deal *ex cathedrâ* with questions of international morality. Their function has rather been to collect and sift information and thought for others to work upon. Their most frequent fate was described by Lord Salisbury with accustomed frankness when he said, "I have witnessed the appointment of a great number of Commissions, but my impression is that a very small percentage have received any notice from legislators or from Parliament. . . . I think I know several Commissions now pending that have not the slightest probability of any action being taken upon them."[1] Royal Commissions are nevertheless expected to set a high standard of impartiality and independence in the collecting of evidence, even if they do little else. It has been shown that two ministries in successive Parliaments had been misled, and had misled others, as to the opium policy actually being pursued. Such a discovery at the outset of their work should have made a Royal Commission doubly careful to push home its inquiries thoroughly, to summarise the facts collected guardedly, and, above all, to hold the scales between officials and the non-official public with perfect evenness. The Opium Commission failed in all these respects.[2]

The inquiry covered the growth, manufacture

[1] Hansard, lxxii. 1472. [2] Appendix I. note 7.

and sale of a drug alleged to be injurious in its unrestricted use. The grower, manufacturer, and vendor in this instance was the Indian Government. It was, in fact, the defendant in the suit. It behoved the commissioners, therefore, whilst treating that Government with every consideration and respect, to observe a strictly impartial independence throughout its proceedings; and especially to make clear beyond all question to the residents and natives of India, that every well-intentioned witness might communicate freely with the Commission, and be assured of the complete protection which a British court of justice ever extends to the humblest person appearing before it. Instead of this, the Commission was staffed from first to last by able gentlemen of the Indian Civil Service; it handed over its arrangements to Indian officers, and was personally conducted by them. Witnesses in the employ of the States were debarred from communicating with it, except through certain specified channels. Its Report was drawn up in the India Office in England, and histories of the opium question were compiled for the occasion from the same source, and published *in extenso* with the Report. To any student of English blue-books, the introduction of Eastern methods of conducting an inquiry are not without interest. One characteristic passage in the Majority Report, bearing on China, runs thus: "We agree in not recommending any action tending to the destruction of the trade, but if at any time the Chinese Government declares its wish to prohibit the import, . . . we shall hold ourselves at liberty to reconsider it."[1] No English Secretary could ever dream of depicting his Commission as

[1] *R. C. Report*, vi. 96.

continuing permanently in power, undisturbed even by time itself.

It is fair to state that the Commission needed no pressure to place itself in the very capable charge of the Indian Civil Service. On the 11th August 1893, the Secretary of State for India sent a telegram to the Viceroy, on behalf of the Commission, desiring the latter to "arrange the course of inquiry, places to be visited, and witnesses."[1] This surrender of independent initiation at the outset evidently surprised the Viceroy. He replied, "We had not intended to arrange the course of inquiry and the places to be visited, as we supposed the Commission would do so; but we will now prepare a programme." After this a very effectual programme of hospitality, travel, and evidence was prepared; and the Commission was taken thoroughly in hand, apparently completely to the satisfaction of its members, with the exception of Mr. H. J. Wilson, M.P. In order that the right keynote might be struck at the outset, a letter was laid before the Commission, when it met in Calcutta, from the Viceroy himself.[2] It contained a statement in favour of the existing system, and against interference with that system, as likely to lead to serious trouble. It was a printed letter, but, strange to say, no trace of it is to be found in the printed proceedings, except in a protest by Mr. Wilson, M.P. It is of the essence of a British Royal Commission that it shall obtain its evidence at first hand, and with perfect freedom. In India these conditions were reversed. Even the Governments of the Presidency of Madras and of the North-West Provinces were ordered to communicate with the Commission by way of Calcutta,

[1] *R. C. Report*, vi. 362. [2] *Ibid.*, vi. 161.

submitting abstracts of the proposed evidence to an official there in the first instance.[1]

Some refreshing illustrations of the working of the official mind are to be found in App. iv. vol. ii., which sets forth the questions issued by Lieutenant-Colonel Abbott to the Rajputana States and the accompanying correspondence. Colonel Abbott first prepared a note of his own opinions, then drew two series of questions for witnesses upon them, for the use of the political officers "to draw their attention, and through them the attention of the Durbars, to the serious importance of the subject." The note runs: "I propose that all witnesses be examined at headquarters by the Durbars, with the aid of Political Officers, and that the written replies of the Durbars to the questions asked of them be based on the information which these witnesses supply. These same witnesses should, of course, be sent to appear before the Commission, and should reach Ajmere a week in advance of it, in order that I may become acquainted with all, and see if each one understands on what points he is required to give evidence."[2]

Colonel Abbott thus instituted two preliminary examinations before the real one, and, in addition, the abstracts were forwarded to the Government. The success attending these rehearsals was evidently great. It is to be regretted that space precludes full justice to some of the results; three quotations from three witnesses must suffice. "If the supply of opium were suddenly stopped, nearly all consumers over fifty years of age (moderate included) would be dead within a month."[3] "If the supply of opium

[1] *R. C. Report*, v. 368, 370.
[2] *Ibid.*, iv. 386.
[3] *Ibid.*, Q. 21,128.

were suddenly stopped, nearly all consumers over fifty years of age (moderate included) would be dead within a month or so."[1] "If the supply of opium were suddenly stopped, nearly all consumers over fifty (moderate included) would die within a month."[2] It is not to be wondered at that the Maharajah of Karauli should write, "I have the pleasure to inform you that my friend Colonel Abbott will furnish you with informations, other than those that have been put down in the papers, regarding this State, as he has kindly consented to represent the Rajputana States";[3] or that the evidence of L. L. P. Munsarim, Salt Department, Dalia State, should conclude, "This is the general opinion, but whatever Government thinks is right."[4] Such methods of dealing with evidence would discredit a departmental inquiry.

The importance of presenting a good claim for prospective damages on the part of the Native States, whenever the opium trade should be cut off, was taken up with much alacrity.

It is not likely that any stress will ever be laid on the figures sent in, except for purposes of amusement. It may be worth while giving some illustrations in support of this position. The Shapura claim includes the following:—

Compensation to money-lending classes—	Rs.
On account of loss of yearly business .	9,250
Loss by bad debts	25,000
Loss of credit	5,000
	39,250[5]

[1] *R. C. Report*, Q. 21,150. [2] *Ibid.*, Q. 21,156. [3] *Ibid.*, iv. 388.
[4] P. 424. [5] P. 396.

The Kishengarh claims add— Rs.

For consumer—extra expenses of living, on account of great rise in price of opium . . . . . . 75,600[1]

Compensation was also claimed for the escorts who would no longer have to escort opium, and for the boxes which would no longer be required to hold it.

The under-mentioned official notes by Lieutenant-Colonel Robertson on some of the statements of claim which he submitted to the Commission make further analysis of the claims unnecessary here.

Sailana.

"The land revenue derived from opium has been reduced from Rs.160,475 to Rs.60,000, as the total revenue of the State is only Rs.150,000. The loss to cultivators was given by the State officials as Rs.128,380; this amount I reduced to Rs.40,000."

Jhabua.

"Loss to the State estimated at Rs.43,329. As the total revenue under all headings is only Rs.17,809 I reduced the estimate to Rs.14,494."

Multhan.

"Losses to cultivators and traders were not given by the State. They were assumed by me."

It is difficult, in reading the communications made to the Native States, to blame them for the compensation estimates they submitted. The fault is the fault of their prompters. A study of the five volumes shows, in the words of Sir James Lyall, that in the greater part of British India, and in a very

[1] *R. C. Report*, iv. 397.

large part of the Native States, through the instrumentality of the Government, the growth of the poppy has already been extinguished,[1] but all the inquiries made under this head failed to discover, even by hearsay, one single case of a cultivator or landowner who had received any compensation whatever on account of the prohibition. Some consideration has no doubt been shown to the governments of States which for customs reasons have been persuaded to relinquish the growth. In *Moral and Material Progress of India*, 1888–89, p. 9, appears this statement: "The Native States have engaged so to manage their opium cultivation and production, as to safeguard the British revenue, and in exchange for this service they receive either money compensation, or other concession."[2] Only one illustration of this occurs in the case of a Native State in Bombay. It was provided by treaty that it should give up poppy cultivation: should receive Rs.31,500 from the British Government; and should on its part maintain a preventive establishment at an annual cost of Rs.12,500.[3]

For the Bengal cultivators and traders no claim was put in or formulated. The authorities prefer to retain the absolute right of prohibition whenever and wherever they may wish to exercise it.

So all-pervading was the paternal care of the Indian Government, that the one member of the Commission, Mr. H. J. Wilson, who apparently took some pains to procure and to encourage independent evidence, had publicly to complain because of it.[4] Mr. Wilson had called at Gya, on a Baptist missionary. Shortly afterwards an inspector of police called

[1] *R. C. Report*, Q. 2699. [2] *Ibid.*, Q. 102. [3] *Ibid.*, ii. 369.
[4] *Ibid.*, iii. 10.

on the same missionary, and asked who his visitor was, where he had been, whom he had seen, and particularly if he had spoken to any opium cultivators. It turned out that Mr. Dane, who was accompanying the Commission on behalf of the Government, and who afterwards came to England to assist in the Report, had told the resident magistrate that "anti-opium people had been about, hunting up evidence."[1] The magistrate at once set the inspector to inquire, with the result mentioned. Mr. Wilson publicly objected to being "shadowed" in the discharge of his duties. The Chairman said nothing should be done comparable to shadowing in Ireland, but added nothing to vindicate the freedom of witnesses from Government interference.

Statistical tables set forth in official documents are supposed to be above suspicion. On p. 12, however, a table is given to show that a "sudden apparent increase" in the consumption of opium in Gujarat eighteen years ago was in reality due to the substitution of licit opium for contraband.[2] "The results are to be traced in the following table." The table shows the totals as follows:—

Average of 3 years 1874–77	1877–78	1878–79	1879–80	1892–93
lb. 4490	4068	13,417	36,352	40,413.

The distinct inference is that when once the licit opium had gained the day, the consumption became regular and normal. The real facts are that between 1880 and 1892 the consumption shot up to 65,929 lbs. and then fell again.[3] The figures omitted vitiate the whole table so far as the meaning attached to it in the Report is concerned.

Amongst further instances of the curious partiality

[1] *R. C. Report*, iii. 24. [2] *Ibid.*, vi. part i. [3] *Ibid.*, iv. 280.

of the Report, the following may be mentioned here. In Part 70, millowners are introduced to prove "the general prevalence of moderation."[1] They are said to have given evidence to the general effect that they had never to dismiss a hand for excess in opium-taking. Three references are given, but these references only prove that the use of opium is very exceptional. Other witnesses add, "As a rule, working people have no habit of using opium. Examination of people employed in a mill will prove this."[2] "Amongst the principal operatives in the mills the use of opium is almost unknown." "How many hands do you employ?" "Between 3500 and 4000. I do not find a single one taking opium." And yet the Commission drags in mill-owners to prove "a general prevalence of moderation"!

Paragraph 62 runs: "A few witnesses, chiefly missionaries, stated before us that they believed this practice (administering the drug to infants) to be productive of great infant mortality."[3] This declaration is supported by seven references. One does not relate to mortality at all. Any one studying the evidence may see that there are at least twenty-two distinct references by different witnesses to abnormal infant mortality from this cause. Of these only seven are missionaries. There are at least forty witnesses who speak decidedly of the evils to infants resulting from the habit; only twelve are missionaries. The child-life of India is entitled to more careful consideration than the Commission bestowed upon it.

Paragraph 73,[4] after relating that the information, as to opium being largely used for suicides, was based as a rule on "vague report," continues: "One or two

[1] *R. C. Report*, vi. 19.
[2] *Ibid.*, Q. 13,192
[3] *Ibid.*, vi. 16.
[4] *Ibid.*, vi. 20.

witnesses, however, quoted statistics in support of their opinion." As is shown in the Appendix—*six* witnesses (half of whom were official) quoted statistics in this connection.[1] It is significant that just before the Report appeared in print, a paper on "The Necessity for an Act restricting the Free Sale of Poisons in Bengal," by Surgeon Captain Evans and Assistant-Surgeon C. Lal Rose, Chemical Examiners to the Government of Bengal, read at the Indian Medical Congress (February 1895), showed that suicide by poison was "about nineteen times more prevalent in Calcutta than in England"; that "poison now accounts for 70 per cent. of the suicides, as against 20 per cent. in 1850"; and that opium "has been known to be responsible for the majority of cases of suicide." The Commissioners' report on this head is discredited, first, by the evidence on which it professes to be based; and, secondly, by official evidence which they failed to procure.

Turning for a moment to a different kind of transgression, the Report states: "We do not feel that we are called upon as a Commission to pass a judgment on the disputed facts of history, nor are we qualified to do so."[2] It then at once proceeds to pass judgment in a very halting fashion. Any one who traces carefully the proceedings of the Commission, will agree that it was not qualified to pass such judgment, by virtue of the hearings which it gave under this head; though, naturally, outsiders cannot appraise the initial qualifications possessed by the Commissioners.

The printed proceedings suggest that the Commission varied its estimate, both of its own attainments and requirements with different witnesses, and on

[1] App. I. note 8.
[2] *R. C. Report*, vi. 51.

succeeding days. What actually occurred in this connection is briefly as follows:—

Professor Legge, the second witness heard, was speaking from personal knowledge as to the effects of the opium war in China, when the Chairman interrupted him, and said, "We may take it that we all regard that policy of the past with great regret, and that we accept the statement made on behalf of the late Government by Sir James Fergusson, that such a course of policy as that would never be permitted again; that, I think, is agreed.[1] Dr. Legge therefore of necessity did not pursue the subject. Dr. Maxwell, who followed, was requested by the Chairman to make any statement as to the diplomatic relationships of the two countries "briefly, and in answer to one question," giving as a reason for such limitation, "These are matters all outside the purview of the Commission purely inquiring into the opium question."[2]

Under considerable difficulties, Dr. Maxwell succeeded in persuading the Commission not to take even an official statement in the House of Commons for granted. He was, however, restricted in his historical evidence to the clearing up of this one point.

When Mr. H. N. Lay, C.B., gave evidence six days later, he was encouraged to make a general statement on the history of the question, and gave it to the extent of some eight closely-printed columns.[3] Sir Thomas Wade, G.C.M.B., was invited on the day following to cover the whole ground (as his past knowledge of China fully entitled him to do), and he complied with the invitation in upwards of twenty columns of evidence, mainly in defence of

[1] *R. C. Report*, Q. 206. [2] *Ibid.*, Q. 246. [3] Q. 1189.

the past policy and action of England.[1] The Chairman, in receiving it, observed, "We were very anxious to have the position of the past cleared up."[2] When Mr. M'Laren, a former president of the Edinburgh Chamber of Commerce, with a lifelong knowledge of Chinese trade, referred to the opium war and its effect upon commerce, the Chairman interrupted in the middle of a sentence with the remark, "I do not think we want to go any further into the history of the Chinese wars. We have heard very full statements on both sides, and we do not want to pursue that subject further. It has practically nothing to do with the question which has been referred to the consideration of this Commission." Readers will search in vain for the "full statements on *both* sides" which the Chairman doubtless had in his mind. The final volumes, however, overflow with further presentations from the official standpoint, by two of the gentlemen in the Indian Civil Service assisting the Commission. Mr. Baines contributes a history of the anti-opium movement in England; and Mr. Dane a history of opium in China, reaching to 186 pages.[3] Mr. Dane states that his history was "written by request." Mr. J. E. Ellis, M.P., in referring in the House of Commons to these departures from the usual course of Royal Commissions, said Lord Brassey had informed him that no request had been made (by the Commission), either to Mr. Baines or to Mr. Dane, to write these papers, but that when they appeared it was thought desirable to put them in.[4]

The facts, then, are these:—Three independent witnesses, each with special knowledge of China, were

[1] *R. C. Report*, Q. 1288.
[2] *Ibid.*, Q. 1302.
[3] *Ibid.* vii. 28–163.
[4] *Parl. Debates*, 24th May 1895.

debarred from dealing with the history of the opium trade, either because the Commission had already been fully informed, or because the subject had really nothing to do with the question before it. Then official evidence on the subject at great length was welcomed, as being exactly what the Commission desired; and finally, the Report is mightily enlarged by special histories written for the occasion from the Indian standpoint, but not at the Commission's request.

It is clearly right that the case for the Government of India should be presented with completeness and efficiency. It is as clearly wrong that its officers should have been charged with the procedure of the Commission, should have laid down its itinerary, supervised the great bulk of its evidence, drafted its Report, furnished its histories, and, in so doing, robbed its findings of any judicial value.

This chapter ought not to close without some reference to the treatment accorded to different classes of evidence.

Englishmen are bound to dissent from the method of appraising the value of a witness adopted by two of the Commissioners representing the Government of India on the inquiry. When Mr. S. C. K. Ratman, B.A., had given his evidence, Mr. Fanshaw said, "What is your pay as assistant-schoolmaster in the High School?" The answer was, "I have no objection to answer the question; but may I ask whether you put that question to all European witnesses who have been examined?" "I wish for a reply." "My pay is Rs.75."[1] Mr. Fanshaw and Sir James Lyall asked similar questions on other occasions.

[1] *R. C. Report*, Q. 26,522.

In a more general way readers of these volumes are continually made sensible of a certain condescension to missionaries, or of reflections upon them as witnesses. In view of the great knowledge of the social life of the people accorded to them by several of the consuls in China, and in view of the debt that the sciences of language and ethnology owe to them (generously acknowledged by Darwin, Max Müller, and others), it is difficult to find any justification for this exceptional treatment. There are undoubtedly missionaries and missionaries, as there are magistrates and magistrates, governors and governors. An official offering a guarded defence of the opium habit, and relying chiefly on negatives, finds it easier to do so in calm and measured language, than a missionary who denounces the habit after watching the downfall of some fellow-creatures under it. But allowing for the different class of testimony offered, for the greater aloofness of the official, for the more personal environment of the missionary, it would be very difficult, if not impossible, to prove that the former class has any advantage whatever over the latter on the score of accurate observation, or in the avoidance of manifest prepossessions. Missionaries are mainly concerned with the uplifting of individuals; officials with the upholding of institutions. Both standpoints, and all the opinions more or less incidental to them, should be fairly and fully considered in the interests of the community as a whole. Where monetary interests are involved, the weight of evidence from those directly interested should be discounted, as it would be in a court of justice. Another class of witnesses held in suspicion by the compilers of the Report are total abstainers. The public are cautioned: "Of the native witnesses (India) adverse to opium nearly all were total abstainers."[1] "We are bound to take notice of the circumstance that most of the missionary witnesses were total abstainers, and some were ardent workers in the cause."[2] After such announcements it seems to be thought that little more need be said,—that these were hardly witnesses who need count! On the surface of things it is not apparent why the opinions of men who do not take stimulants are of less value on the opium habit than the opinions of men who do. The curious assumption of superiority on behalf of those who take alcohol rests apparently on what may be termed the foundation axiom of the whole Report, namely, that there "is a universal tendency amongst mankind to take some form of stimulant with which to comfort or distract themselves."[3] It was evidently a comfort to the framers of the Report to think so.

Elsewhere the Report points out that "of the vast population of India, both Hindoos and Mahomedans generally regard the use of alcohol as disreputable, and more or less contrary to their religion";[4] that "both opium and alcohol are prohibited by the Buddhist religion; and that the custom of the country is generally opposed to the use of any stimulant by women.[5] If heads were counted, the commissioners and their axiom might turn out to be in a minority. In any case it is hardly seemly to slight the best thought of those to whom they were sent; or wise to challenge intelligent Hindoos and Chinese to regulate their conduct by the drinking customs of the West. They might even happen to discover that another Royal Commission has been inquiring into the

[1] *R. C. Report*, vi. 94. [2] *Ibid.*, vi. 93.
[3] P. 16. [4] P. 87. [5] P. 18.

drinking habit in England, and has reported "it is undeniable that a gigantic evil remains to be remedied, and hardly any sacrifice would be too great which would result in a marked diminution of this national degradation."[1]

The representatives of "the trade" in England were in this instance more judicial in their pronouncements than the representatives of "the trade" in India.

It would not be fair to throw the blame on the secretaries for these many departures from judicial treatment. They were loyal to the Government who lent them to the Commission, and recalled them as it saw fit. The members of the Commission, on the other hand, may claim that it was quite impossible for them to check the voluminous reports in the time allotted for the purpose. The Commission was, in truth, as unique in its form of closure, as in its peregrinations in the East under the tutelage of those whose business it was sent to investigate. The Chairman stated to his colleagues, in January 1895, that, in the report he was about to submit, he did "not suppose that there will be found much room for amendment," and that, taking this view, he did "not anticipate that our further deliberations need occupy many days";[2] . . . "having received two communications from the Secretary of State (for India) within the last few days, I feel that my duty calls for some decided course of action. . . . I shall, in any case, relieve the Commission from further collective work on the 26th." Mr. Wilson replied on the 21st, stating that "four new chapters, apparently intended to form part of the Report, have

[1] *Report on Liquor Licensing Laws*, p. 2.
[2] *R. C. Report*, vi. 160.

been circulated within the last few days; a further chapter has come to hand this morning; and at least three or four portions, or chapters, have yet to be supplied." He therefore entered his protest against the adoption of any chapters or documents "which its members have not had adequate means and opportunity to consider and approve." With this, the curtain fell on the procedure of this non-judicial Commission. If there ever were any minutes of its proceedings, they have not been published.

CHAPTER II

OPIUM SMOKING

THE inquiry into opium smoking in India bears closely on the opium vice in China, and must therefore be briefly referred to here. The drug is used very differently in the two countries. Indians are an abstaining people; probably not 2 per cent. of the population resort to opium as an indulgence. Those who take it swallow it in the form of pills. Opium smoking has hardly been known until its recent introduction into some of the large towns. One would have supposed that science was in a position by this time to show with some exactness the merits, or demerits, of smoking opium, as compared with swallowing it; but any one turning to the folios of the Commission for light, will come away disappointed. Sir William Roberts represented, no doubt, admirably, the old school of medicine, which greatly exalted stimulants. To the lay mind, his scientific philosophy consisted in this, that every man is entitled to his own "euphoric agent," and that no one is the worse for indulging in it, whatever it be, provided he keeps within his tolerance. Unfortunately, Sir William nowhere suggests how the load-line of safety is to be found. Every one must find this out for himself, and take all the risks of shipwreck in the process.

Twenty-four medical witnesses appearing before

the Commission expressed opinions upon this particular question. Of those, four consider that smoking is not more injurious than eating, and twenty consider that it is. Sir George Birdwood was clear that smoking opium was "as innocuous as smoking hay, straw, or stubble," "opium eating, of course, one can easily understand, may be harmful."[1] Dr. Martyn Clark said, "The smoking of a drug is bound to be a very much more deadly thing than the eating of it." Mr. Garde, L.M., adds, "The effects of smoking are more instantaneous and more energetic."[2] At a meeting of the Calcutta Medical Society, it appeared to be assumed throughout that smoking was more injurious than eating.[3] The non-medical official witnesses also agree, with hardly an exception, in condemning the smoking habit. Mr. Lyall complained, "The Anti-Opium Society has not distinguished between the smoking and eating of opium as I think it should have done."[4] Mr. Stoker said, "A very clear distinction should always be observed between opium smoking and opium eating";[5] and the Hon. A. Caddell observed, "The distinction is, I think, fully justified by the effects of the two habits on the people of these provinces."[6] When we come to the expression of Indian native opinion, for one voice raised in defence of opium smoking there are a hundred against it. Mr. Gupta, the Excise Commissioner, stated that smoking "is regarded as a degrading habit."[7] Mr. Brownrigg, settlement officer in Oudh, says it "is popularly esteemed vicious."[8] Mr. W. H. Cheetham said that six people, out of a population of 3000, who indulged

[1] *R. C. Report*, Q. 1561. [2] *Ibid.*, Q. 16,935.
[3] *Ibid.*, App. xxi. vol. ii. [4] *Ibid.*, Q. 3195. [5] Q. 3527.
[6] Q. 19,120. [7] Q. 4975. [8] Q. 14,352.

in smoking were "regarded as outcasts by the rest of the community."[1] Mr. Ogilvie, an ardent official defender of the practice of eating, says of smoking, "This use of opium is generally reprobated."[2] In a despatch on the consumption of opium in 1892, the Commissioner for Excise, Central Provinces, says, "Every effort should no doubt also be made to put a stop to the smoking of opium in all its forms, practices which are universally condemned as degrading and pernicious by all native opinion with which I have come in contact."[3] This is true of native opinion as expressed before the Commission.

Nothing can be more confirmatory of the strength of opinion against opium smoking than the fact that it is illegal in many of the Native States. Mr. Crosthwaite, agent to the Governor-General in Central India, said the rulers of the Native States "forbid opium smoking. I asked several of them, and they said that if a man smokes opium he becomes yellow, and dries up, and is perfectly useless. They did not condemn it on moral grounds; they merely said it destroys the man, and on that ground they felt bound to prohibit the smoking of opium."[4] Lieutenant-Colonel Robertson said, "In the two principal States, Gwalior and Indore, for instance, it (opium smoking) is a penal offence."[5] "I have no doubt that anybody found smoking in the public places would be prosecuted and punished criminally." Mr. Kershaw, opium superintendent of the Baroda State, was asked, "You say that the use of madak and chandu is made penal in the Baroda State by the Gaekwadi Act I.?" and replied, "Yes, opium smoking is not allowed."[6]

[1] *R. C. Report*, Q. 5804. [2] *Ibid.*, Q. 15,698. [3] Q. 88.
[4] Q. 21,829. [5] Q. 21,870. [6] Q. 22,533.

The Commission Report states: "It was clearly shown before us that native public opinion generally condemns the habit as disreputable, mainly, perhaps, from its associations; and this opinion is shared by the great majority of European witnesses, official and private, including the medical practitioners."[1] Sir William Roberts says, "The practice of opium smoking is generally looked down upon in India as a low and vicious habit."[2]

"Whilst we are not prepared to recommend measures of restrictive legislation, we are in favour of making it difficult for the smokers of chandu and madak to indulge in the habit. We recommend that the Government should abandon in all provinces the licensing of shops for the manufacture and sale of these preparations, showing thereby that they are in sympathy with public opinion.[3] In the Panjab, Bombay, North-Western Provinces, and Oudh, this has already been done, and in those provinces individuals, though they may manufacture the preparations for their own use, are not permitted to possess a larger amount than 180 grains weight. We recommend that these provisions be extended to the other provinces of British India. . . . The general adoption of this system, which is undoubtedly repressive, so far as it can be enforced, will tend to prevent the spread of the habit, and lead, it may be hoped, to its ultimate extinction."

The Royal Commission therefore pronounced in favour of the ultimate extinction of opium smoking in India. The two Indian commissioners and Mr. H. J. Wilson went much further than this.

Mr. Haridas Veharidas, in his memorandum, says: "Under the present state of law, the opium smokers

[1] *R. C. Report*, vi. 23. [2] *Ibid.*, vi. 118. [3] *Ibid.*, vii. 72.

can indulge in their vicious practice with impunity." [1] "A strict law should be made, prohibiting opium smoking in any form, and under any circumstances. Knowing as I do, as a native of India, the feelings of the natives in general regarding the habit of opium smoking and its effects, I do not feel myself justified in entertaining any fears like those expressed in sect. vi." ("The authoritative imposition of prohibition by the British Government would be keenly resented by the races among whom the use of opium is customary; . . . and would be followed by widespread discontent.")

The Maharajah Bahadur of Darbhanga states that he is in agreement with Mr. Haridas Veharidas on the subject.[2]

Mr. H. J. Wilson, in his Minority Report, which is a model of compression, fairness, and clearness, says: "It is almost universally admitted to be injurious and demoralising, is practised by the vicious and degraded, and is generally reprobated. I consider that nothing short of absolute prohibition will satisfy the requirements of the case." [3]

The condemnation of opium smoking in India is at once forcible and complete. The burden of proof weighs heavily upon those who, whilst joining in this condemnation, make light of the same practice in China.

[1] *R. C. Report*, vi. 134. [2] *Supplement to R. C. Report.*
[3] *R. C. Report*, vi. 137–161.

CHAPTER III

BURMA

BURMA occupies a distinct position in regard to the opium habit. Its people are said to be peculiarly susceptible to the drug. They are certainly very averse to its spread amongst them. Here the Chinese first appear as colonists. The British officials in Burma have sought to restrict the use of opium as much as they possibly could. The Indian Government has thrown its influence heavily into the opposite scale. The position in Burma is best explained by the memorandum (1881) of Sir C. U. Aitchison, published by order of the House of Commons. It states: "When reviewing the report on the Administration of Criminal Justice for the year 1877, my attention was drawn to the change which was alleged to be gradually coming over the Burmese national character under British rule. One of the principal causes assigned was the growing habit of opium smoking. . . . Shortly afterwards, when on a visit to Akyab, I was waited on by a large deputation of the most influential natives of the town, who presented a petition describing, in very forcible language, the misery entailed on the population by opium, and praying that the traffic might be altogether abolished in Arakan. . . . The papers now submitted for consideration present a painful picture of the demoralisation, misery, and ruin produced amongst the Burmese by opium smoking. Responsible officers in all divisions and districts of the province, and natives everywhere, bear testimony to it. . . . These show that among the Burmans the habitual use of the drug saps the physical and mental energies, destroys the nerves, emaciates the body, predisposes to disease, induces indolent and filthy habits of life, destroys self-respect, is one of the most fertile sources of misery, destitution, and crime, fills the jail with men of relaxed frame, predisposed to dysentery and cholera, prevents the due extension of cultivation, and the development of the land revenue, checks the natural growth of the population, and enfeebles the constitution of succeeding generations. That opium smoking is spreading at an alarming rate under our rule, does not admit of doubt. . . . Native opinion is unanimous in favour of stopping the supply altogether, and no measure we could adopt would be so popular with all the respectable and law-abiding classes of the population." For many years the Government of India did not yield to these representations. When they did yield, it was done grudgingly.

Sir A. Mackenzie had again to urge, fifteen years later: "With all deference to the view taken by the Government of India, I am content to rest the case against opium in Burma on the consensus of voices condemning it, extending as this does through a long series of years, and emanating as we know from authorities of every shade of opinion, official and non-official, European and native. . . . The statistics afford, however, I think, strong confirmation of the accepted and authoritative opinion to which I refer.[1] The papers bring out, moreover, very

[1] *R. C. Report*, ii. 537.

clearly the fact that the evil is a rapidly growing one in many parts of the lower province. . . . I agree with the Financial Commissioner (Mr. Smeaton), that the best policy is 'thorough.' . . . I would close every opium shop both in Upper and Lower Burma. . . . We are not bound to ruin the indigenous race because a handful of foreigners finds our excise system disagreeable." When the draft rules were sent for the approval of the Indian Government, the latter decided "that the extent of the evil has been exaggerated," and refused to sanction a rule requiring the registration of non-Burmans.[1] The Burma officials said of the alteration: "That it will render the enforcement of restrictions on Burmans much more difficult and far less certain, goes without saying. Some of the worst smugglers have been found to be natives of India." But the Calcutta Government was not to be moved. At last, on the 1st January 1894, new rules became law. Burmans may not now purchase or possess opium for other than medical purposes, except those in Lower Burma who have been officially registered as consumers. Non-Burmans may purchase and possess opium for private consumption. The total number of legal consumers in Lower Burma was estimated at 17,000. For these the Government allows the very liberal maximum allowance of 45 grains per head per day. Thirty-six shops were still put up to auction, and in four additional places in Lower Burma opium was sold retail by Government officers.

It is startling to find that the controversy between the Indian and Burmese Governments was reopened and vigorously carried on by the section of the

[1] *R. C. Report*, ii. 489.

Royal Commission which visited Burma through its Chairman, Sir J. Lyall. Addressing Mr. Smeaton, he said, "I wish to *cross*-examine you upon your printed note of 27th April 1892, because it is an exceedingly strongly-worded document, and one which when it comes into the possession of a certain part of the English public, will be much used and much relied upon.[1] I must say that, after carefully reading it, it seems to me, particularly for an official paper, to be exaggerated and sensational in tone. I therefore think that it is right to cross-examine you to a certain extent upon it." The Chairman then asked, "Do you not think that the heading 'Physically or morally wrecked' is sensational?" and Mr. Smeaton's answer is, "It is the heading prescribed by the Chief Commissioner."[2] English readers, whatever be their opinions as to the effects of opium, will be surprised to learn that the Chairman of the Royal Commission for the time being publicly announced that he should *cross*-examine a witness who came to give information in the course of his official duty; that he charged the witness with being guilty of exaggeration and sensationalism before he had been heard in his defence; further, that the rock of offence was this, that a strongly-worded official document would be much used by a certain part of the British public; and lastly, that the Chairman asked an official to pronounce the heading of a column for inquiry, prepared by his superior officer, to be "sensational." The whole proceeding can only be described as a travesty of the ordinary course adopted in conducting public inquiries.

The spirit of the Chairman seems to have been shared by the officer deputed by the Government of

[1] *R. C. Report*, Q. 8080. [2] *Ibid.*, Q. 8081.

India to select the witnesses to appear before the Commission. The two witnesses selected to voice the sentiments of the Chinese against opium were both liquor sellers, and therefore open to the charge of trade jealousy. By way of protest at this misrepresentation, a memorial was drawn up and quickly signed by some 300 Chinese in Rangoon, and presented by a deputation of 60 persons, stating that amongst the Chinese opium is considered as poison of very subtle power, which plays sad havoc among its consumers.[1] "The ruination opium has brought upon all people is manifest enough," and concluding, "we shall be very thankful if opium is suppressed entirely." Another memorial was signed by 286 Chinese residents or business firms at Moulmein.[2] It concluded as follows:—"We resent the imputation of being unable to do without opium, and do not want the door to be left open, or even half-open, to this vice in Burma on our account. We will not be the pretext for the ruin of this country, but want opium altogether forbidden." At a meeting at Pegu, the leading members of the Chinese community agreed that opium should be absolutely prohibited after six months.[3]

It was generally allowed that prohibition had been successful in Burma so far as it had been tried. Sir C. Aitchison in 1880 said, "One fact is worth a bushel of argument. We succeeded in almost stamping out ganja, although the plant from which it is made grows wild in Burma."[4] Mr. Bayne, revenue secretary, was asked if the prohibitory legislation with regard to Upper Burma is satisfactory and effectual, and replied, "That is the general tenor of

[1] *R. C. Report*, ii. 526. [2] *Ibid.*, v. 346. [3] *Ibid.*, ii. 560.
[4] *Ibid.*, Q. 2468.

the reports."[1] Mr. Bridges, Commissioner of the Eastern Division, was of opinion that the prohibition in Upper Burma has been effectual, except in the larger towns, where there are a number of Chinese.[2] Mr. Smeaton thought the law had been successfully enforced, but that the loopholes left by it were open to great objection.

Those who make light of indulgence in opium will find matter for grave reflection in the Burmese evidence placed before the Commission; much of it relates to the jails. Of 937 persons in Bassein jail (3 only being women), 111 took opium. Of these, 48 were in bad or indifferent health when admitted.[3] But all were then well, except 4. Surgeon-Major Dalzell said this proportion was "much larger" than amongst the other prisoners. When persevered in "it seems to bring on an untractable form of diarrhœa, which is generally the ultimate cause of death." Surgeon-Captain Davis, of the Rangoon jail, said of the opium habitual, that "about a month or six weeks after his admission he appears to turn the corner. I do not say in every case, but in a great number of cases, and he begins to gain weight. I think it predisposes to disease."[4] Mr. Jennings, inspector of police, said of the men who acquire the habit, "They get fever and dysentery.[5] Many of them die if they do not get it." In the Arakan jails in 1891 more than one-half of the Burman inmates were opium consumers. The proportion of deaths amongst these in the Akyab jail during the then previous four years was "200 per cent. higher than that of abstainers."[6] In the Maubin and Myanaung jails the disease to which Burman con-

[1] *R. C. Report*, Q. 6568. [2] *Ibid.*, Q. 7585. [3] Q. 6704.
[4] Q. 7448. [5] Q. 7634. [6] *Ibid.*, ii. 542.

sumers are observed to be most liable is dysentery, and most of them suffer from extreme debility. The majority of the deaths in these jails are of Burman smokers and eaters of opium. Of the four jails of the Tenasserim division, 61 per cent. of the Burmese convicts suffered injury from the effects of the drug, against 48 per cent. of non-Burmans. From the Kyaukpyu district it was reported that nearly 69 per cent. of the prisoners "are addicted to this pernicious habit, and with very few exceptions almost all came in in an indifferent or bad state of health."[1] Deputy-Commissioner Houghton writes from Sandoway: "These figures fully support the common idea that an opium eater (or smoker) is a scoundrel and a thief, whilst there can be only one opinion as to the general effect physically and morally on persons of Burman race."[2] Deputy-Commissioner Wilson and Deputy-Commissioner Batten testify to the same opinion. With regard to the extent of the habit amongst the Chinese in Burma, Mr. Irwin represents the general impression given in the remark, "I think most of the Chinese consume opium." Surgeon Dalzell puts it at 75 per cent. Mr. Weidemann said from a third to over a half. "I find that even the Chinese connected with the opium farm are not smokers. The headmen do not smoke themselves. I think the best men avoid it."[3]

From the evidence of nine Chinese witnesses, apparently the proportion is much nearer one-third than one-half of the adult males, and this third includes the idle, the broken-down, and the criminals of the Chinese settlement. The pro-opium testimony of six Chinese consumers was a little mixed. Mr. Takkyu had smoked for twenty-six years. "Those

[1] *R. C. Report*, ii. 551. [2] *Ibid.*, ii. 553. [3] *Ibid.*, Q. 6731.

Chinese who do not take opium (he said) are physically stronger than those who take opium. Mentally, I consider opium smokers are improved by taking opium."[1] The Chairman improved upon this by saying, "You say you think that opium smoking makes men weaker in body, but it makes them *quicker* in mind; how does the quickness in mind show itself?" Answer: "It makes them good-tempered—they are even-tempered." Then this Balaam was asked, "Do you think a man who does not take opium can do his business as well as a man who does?" and the reply was, "A man who does not take opium is much better than the opium smoker." Others observed: "Those who are poor people, and have no money to smoke, will borrow of their friends, or turn thieves." "It does harm to poor people." Mr. Sit Kaung said opium smokers "can meditate better." He spent four hours a day over smoking, adding somewhat needlessly, "My work is not very hard."[2] A Chinese merchant who followed, said, "The Chinese suffer as much as the Burmans . . . and it will be a kindness to the Chinese to prevent them from procuring the drug. The respectable merchants are all against the habit."[3] A consumer who finished by saying, "I would not like it if my son smoked," represented apparently the opinions of almost every person addicted to the habit who came before the Commission, whether in Burma, India, or from China. Dr. Cushing said in all cases under his ten years of observation in the Shan States, opium coolies "went on from bad to worse. There is universal condemnation of the habit among the Shans."[4] The Sawbwa (Chief) of Thebaw was in favour of "total prohibition of

[1] *R. C. Report*, Q. 7108. [2] *Ibid.*, Q. 7140. [3] Q. 7401. [4] Q. 6947.

opium" in his State. He said, "They have very short lives if they smoke opium. No old people eat it."[1] The ex-Sawbwa of Nyaungywe said people "lose their strength by using opium. . . . Their mind becomes slow and indolent. Their lives are shortened." A captain of cavalry from the Shan States said, "The opium consumers are lazy men, and are no good." The Burmese witnesses may be briefly represented by a sentence from one of their merchants: "I would say in Burma that total abolition would be the best thing to be done, as they have done in the case of ganja. It is desirable to prohibit the sale of opium. People of Burma would hail such a measure with delight."[2]

The Royal Commission sums up the matter by saying—

"*The Burmans are specially susceptible to injury from opium, and there is among them a popular sentiment against the habit. Special regulations have therefore been introduced, which, short of universal prohibition, seem to us as restrictive as it would be expedient for any Government to attempt to enforce.*"

In the report of the Excise Department, Burma, 1899–1900, it is stated: "The sale of opium from the Kyaukpzu and Sandoway treasuries was maintained. In Sandoway it was anticipated that the consumption was increasing, and to provide for the needs of legitimate consumers the annual allowance was raised from 240 to 320 seers, but the quantity sold, which receded from 260 to 252 seers, does not justify the increase. The official vendor endeavoured to prevent non-Burman consumers from buying more than their actual requirements, in order that the chances of selling the surplus to non-registered

[1] *R. C. Report*, Q. 6961. [2] *Ibid.*, Q. 7232.

Burmans may be reduced to a minimum. The Financial Commissioner has informed the vendor that this interference is unwarranted, and that any registered Burman or non-Burman is at liberty to buy the maximum quantity which the law permits him to possess."

The action of the Financial Commissioner has since been justified by the Secretary of State for India. New regulations have been made in Burma doing away with the farming of the drug, but increasing the number of shops to be held at a high licence, by traders selected by the district officers. Early closing is compulsory, and every evening the stock must be removed to the nearest police station. The prices of raw opium and cooked opium for smoking purposes are fixed by law.

The persistence of the Indian Government is the unpleasant feature in the history of the Imperial drug trade in Burma.

CHAPTER IV

STRAITS SETTLEMENT

IN dealing with the opium habit to the east of Burma, the Commission relied on the answers received to schedules of questions. There was, of course, no possibility of cross-examination. The Straits Settlement includes protected Native States, along with the British colony. Its population consists of Malays, Hindoos, Chinese, and a small ruling minority of British. The opium question touches the finance of the Settlement deeply, and the presence of the Chinese brings the inquiry into the scope of this work.

The estimated revenue of the colony for 1893 was 3,635,780 frs., whilst the sums annually paid by the opium and spirit farmers for the three years, 1892–94, were 1,820,400 frs.[1] According to one witness, two-thirds of the revenue came from the opium, spirits, and pawnbroking licences. This probably accounts for an added note of bitterness in the conflict of evidence. Mr. Wray, official Protector of the Chinese, seems to have been troubled with no difficulties on the subject himself, though grieved at the errors of others. The moderate use of opium, he says, "does not more than does the moderate use of food and drink, affect the moral and social condition of its consumers, and is beneficial physically."[2]

[1] *R. C. Report*, v. 152.

[2] *Ibid.*, v. 171.

"The drug appears to compensate for the poorness of the rice diet, with savouries." "The Chinese, whose anti-opium opinions are quoted by agitators, are mainly the converts of European missionaries, whose intolerant views they have adopted." An Assistant-Protector writes, it is "taken occasionally by way of being sociable, *e.g.* when visiting a brothel with friends."[1] The habitués do usually desire to get free from the habit "in a feeble kind of way, and they no doubt would be able to do so if they had sufficient strength of mind." Whilst an Acting Assistant-Protector thinks "an opium smoker under press of work will outlast another man who goes without the stimulant," and says, "The habit is easily learnt. . . . The gay young man about town will take it, believing in its aphrodisiac virtues."[2] The morals of their wards do not seem to give any uneasiness to their protectors. Other witnesses state that mortality and sickness amongst opium-smoking coolies on unhealthy work is much less than amongst non-smokers; that injury by taking too much opium is comparable to taking "too much butchers' meat," etc.

The Colonial Secretary of the Settlement sums up the case thus: "In moderation opium smoking is not injurious; it is, in fact, held by several witnesses to be beneficial, and one medical witness declares that it increases the capacity for muscular exertion."[3] Loss of flesh there may be, but leanness is not always a disadvantage. A Civil Service table, showing that twenty-five opium-smoking prisoners gained on an average 5½ lb. weight by short prison sojourns, he speaks of as "not very instructive, for the difference may in some cases be referable to

[1] *R. C. Report*, v. 156 [2] *Ibid.*, v. 180. [3] P. 148.

improved diet and a healthy life, rather than to the mere discontinuance of opium smoking." Neither are the moral effects believed to be injurious; "a healthy man who only spends on opium what he can afford, is not necessarily tempted to steal." As to social effects, "there is little evidence." Probably the utmost that can be said is, that "there is a prejudice against smokers." This it would seem to be the business of British rulers to endeavour to dissipate.

It will be noted that the foregoing conclusions assume the general prevalence of the habit amongst the labouring Chinese. If this foundation belief proves to be illusory, then the comparison to the alcoholic habits of Europe, to the ordinary use of food and drink, etc., is vitiated. It has been pointed out that in India the use of the drug is very exceptional indeed. The difficulty of testing the number of consumers in the Straits is greater, but stored away in another part of the volume are some valuable statistics. First, be it observed, that at least sixteen witnesses, including several officials, intimate that a majority of the outdoor Chinese coolies are opium smokers. One says, practically all; another, 85 per cent.[1] Special stress is laid on the prevalence of the habit amongst miners. By general agreement they head the list. The Colonial Secretary gives the reason. In the mining districts there is no monopoly of the sale or manufacture of the prepared drugs, so the consumption is much larger than anywhere else. An opium farmer further explains that mining labourers, from their vocation in damp surroundings, generally cannot work without it. To prove these propositions, statistics were

[1] *R. C. Report*, iv. 170.

ordered to be collected. The result showed that out of 15,000 miners, there were 2988 smokers. The collector says this "seems very low," but he cannot believe the average exceeds 25 per cent. At Kinta, out of 5262 coolies, the district magistrate was surprised to find that under 25 per cent. were smokers.[1] Turning to plantation coolies, Mr. Vermont, J.P., sugar planter, states that out of 400 Chinese coolies in his employ, only 15 were regular smokers.[2]

These figures, it must be noted, apply to the men and districts where the opium habit is supposed to be practically universal. They are not without their bearing on the figures supplied from one of the principal hospitals of these regions. During 1892, and up to October 1898, the number of fever cases admitted were—

Opium smokers	269
Non-smokers	270

Of 5147 general patients there were—

Opium smokers	2929
Non-smokers	2218

The mortality was—

Smokers	489
Non-smokers	218

Dr. Fox suggests that when they become ill, then they resort to opium.

Of beri-beri admissions he had—

Opium smokers	74
Non-smokers	137

According to the ratio given above, the comple-

[1] *R. C. Report*, v. 346–349.

[2] *Ibid.*, v. 178.

mentary number to the 74 smokers would be 296 non-smokers.

Mr. Swettenham, British Resident at Perak, forwarded the mining returns to the Commission after he had told them, "I can only make a rough guess; but my own view, and that of well-informed natives, is that 60 per cent. of the Chinese in this State are opium smokers."[1] In forwarding the returns, the Resident wrote: "It can be stated that 25 per cent. of our Chinese population are opium smokers."[2] The Resident might have acknowledged his previous error. In reducing his estimate by more than half, he falls into another mistake. He has previously admitted, as every witness does, that the habit is exceptional amongst Chinese women and Chinese merchants, and that fewer artisans than labourers are smokers. The 25 per cent. on which he now founds himself is not a percentage of the Chinese population; it is a percentage of a class of men only, put forward as of all classes the most given to opium smoking. But this is not all. Mr. Swettenham, in writing to the Commission, said: "The hospitals . . . are largely patronised by the Chinese labouring classes, the majority of whom are opium smokers. I recently called by telegram for a return of the Chinese patients in all the State hospitals at noon on that day, and the result was, that with about 1000 Chinese patients, just over 50 per cent. of them were opium smokers. The conclusion to be drawn is, that proportionately fewer opium smokers than non-smokers are obliged to seek the hospital." On finding that his major premise was wrong, and that instead of a majority, only a quarter of the

[1] *R. C. Report*, v. 160. [2] *Ibid.*, v. 346.

labourers can be said to be smokers, the Resident should have withdrawn this misleading sentence.

Mr. Anderson, Consul for Siam, an apologist for the habit, estimates the consumers amongst the Chinese clerks, storekeepers, etc., as not exceeding 7½ per cent.; the fairly well-to-do traders at between 15 to 20 per cent.[1] Respectable women and children are said not to use opium.

Coming to the Malays, even the strongest apologists for the drug condemn opium smoking.

Mr. Swettenham writes: "The effect on Malays is decidedly worse than on the Chinese, because the Malay is naturally indolent, and the smoking of opium makes him more lazy and indolent than he would otherwise be." Mr. Clifford says: "Their natural indolence is considerably increased; they appear to degenerate physically." Mr. O'Brien, Acting Auditor-General, says: "I look upon a Straits Malay who takes to opium in any form as a lost man."[2] The estimate of the number of Malays using it in different districts varies from ½ to 2 per cent. only. The consumption amongst Hindoos in the Straits is evidently very exceptional. It is quite clear that, so far as any general habit is concerned, so far from resembling the alcoholic habits of Europe, the facts are exactly reversed. But further, the admissions of the pro-opium witnesses already cited differentiate the habit widely from that of intoxicants at home. Mr. Skinner, Resident-Councillor, says: "The feeling against employing clerks and domestics who smoke is very strong, and, I think, is almost universal";[3] but the most apt proof of this feeling is mentioned by Mr. Shellabear, that "any employee of the opium farm in Singapore

[1] *R. C. Report*, v. 173. [2] *Ibid.*, v. 182. [3] P. 178.

who is known to smoke opium is at once dismissed."[1] The two apologetic "Chinese Protectors" speak of the disinclination of Chinese fathers to give their daughters in marriage to opium smokers. One further point only may be cited. It is an undoubted fact that, notwithstanding the comparatively very limited use of opium, there is a decided demand for a cure. A former opium farmer, now Municipal Commissioner, Koh Seang Tat, says: "The desire appears to be constant, but along with it there seems to be a conviction that they are powerless to free themselves." "Habitual consumers invariably desire to get free from the habit, at such times as they exercise the prerogative of looking before and after." Mr. Hare, the Assistant-Protector, excuses this weakness as follows:—"I have often heard of consumers trying to break off the habit, but on inquiry it turns out that they usually have some strong personal grounds for trying to do so!"[2]

One of the peculiarities of the Report is, that it seldom appears whether a witness is pecuniarily interested in the trade. In any case, there are a few independent Europeans who take a very different view of the habit and its consequences from those already cited. Mr. Haviland, formerly a medical officer, says: "When taken in moderation, not much effect. When taken in excess, very bad; the consumers then lose all self-respect, are much more given to deceiving and stealing . . . and become miserable objects." "The present method of letting opium farms gives a strong inducement to the farmer to push the sale of the drug."[3]

Mr. Riccard, superintendent of police, says:

[1] *R. C. Report*, v. 166. [2] *Ibid.*, v. 180. [3] P. 156.

"Opium consumers of the poor class soon become physically unfit for labour, owing to not having means to support themselves with proper food. The majority become slaves to the drug, but a considerable proportion of the consumers are moderate."[1]

Surgeon-Major O'Sullivan writes: "Generally speaking, opium smoking in those who persist in its use leads to moral, physical, and social deterioration."[2] The universal opinion in Penang is, that opium smoking is a great and degrading vice—75 per cent. of smokers acquire the habit in brothels. Every prostitute in every Chinese brothel in Penang is furnished with an opium pipe by the brothel keeper." "No smoker will get domestic service in a Chinese house." The Hon. C. W. S. Kynnersley: "Although opium smoking does not lead to crimes of violence, the craving for the drug is so strong among habitual smokers of the idle class that they are driven to steal in order to satisfy this feeling."

Two missionaries were allowed to have schedules. No answers bear the trace of closer knowledge of the people. Mr. Shellabear served in Singapore as lieutenant and local captain in the Royal Engineers.[3] On returning as a missionary, he made a personal study of the question, because of the violent attacks on missionaries in the local papers, on account of their opposition to the opium traffic. His conclusion is: "The Chinese are ashamed of the opium habit, and many try to conceal the fact. When going long ricksha rides, I am always careful to avoid smokers, because after the first mile or two they are very slow runners, and seem to have no strength. When opium is taken to excite the sexual passions, as it

[1] *R. C. Report*, v. 167. [2] *Ibid.*, v. 176. [3] P. 166.

most frequently is, the object is to produce a kind of intoxication, which, as I understand the word, is inconsistent with moderation. In the native mind, the use of opium appears always to be connected with debauchery. I have heard Malays complain more than once of the extension of the opium habit among their race, by the agency of the opium farm."

Mr. Lamont, Presbyterian, says: "The effects of opium are degrading in all three senses, morally, socially, and physically. The phrase "moderation" is most misleading. Opium is indulged in mainly for purposes of intoxication. The opium vice is less palpable, assuredly, yet it is more inexorable than drunkenness. There is no hope to be entertained for the present generation of opium consumers."

Munshi Ismail, formerly interpreter at the Supreme Court, spoke very bitterly of the way in which the farmer sent opium up the rivers, giving it away to the Malays, knowing that if they acquired the habit he would have a sale for his opium on a second occasion.

The British apology for the opium habit in the Straits rests wholly on the supposed needs of a section of the Chinese. One of their "Protectors" says nearly three-quarters "of the property trade and business is in Chinese hands." Their opinions, therefore, should be of importance. Only four were cited as witnesses; two of these are opium farmers, and one an ex-farmer.[1] The first two extol the use in moderation, believe the effects to be the same on consumers of every race, and say that excess produces various ill effects. Mr. Koh Seang Tai, ex-opium farmer, says his observation convinces him that "when used to any considerable extent, the

[1] *R. C. Report*, v. 155.

consumer becomes worthless, morally, physically, and socially."[1] Demoralisation is the first effect; beginners use it to increase the desire for sexual intercourse. There is "an ever-increasing desire and a proportionate increase in the consumption." "It is felt that the opium traffic is a stain on the fair fame of the British people, and that, owing to her power in the matter, it is England's duty to mankind to efface the stain, if it be within the limits of possibility to do so."

Mr. Seah Liang Seah, J.P., says: "Opium affects consumers morally and physically; they have lazy propensities always."[2] Only two other native witnesses appear. Shaik Eusoff says: "The smokers ruin their health. Almost all the races consider the habit of consuming opium to be condemned and injurious."[3] The Hon. Minister of the Sultan of Johor observed: "Opium consumers generally become weak and emaciated." "The opium and alcohol habits are looked upon by the Chinese, Malay, and other Asiatic races as equally degrading and injurious."[4]

When financial interests are eliminated, and the people concerned are heard for themselves, it is as clear as noonday that they are face to face with an insidious vice, carrying great evils in its train. After making all due allowance for the superiority and good intent of Western rulers, it is difficult to understand their persistent advocacy of an indulgence which they carefully avoid for themselves and their children. There is also an unfortunate contradiction between the apologies for the drug as beneficial to the least-favoured sections of toiling humanity, and the self-congratulations on the restrictive influences

[1] *R. C. Report*, v. 158. [2] *Ibid.*, v. 173. [3] P. 172. [4] P. 181.

of a highly profitable system of excise. The tenders received for opium and spirit farms in Singapore, Penang, and Malacca for three years from January 1901, showed an increase to Government revenue of 1,500,000 dollars per annum.

CHAPTER V

HONG KONG

THE Report of the Commission has been shown to be of value mainly in so far as it may send the reader to search the evidence behind it. The difficulties in the way of such search are great. There is no relationship between the number of answers sent in and any of the main facts regarding the people of China. Everything is haphazard, both as to the distribution of schedules and the results of such distribution, except that copious supplies either of missionary or of native opinion were apparently deprecated. It is impossible, generally speaking, to focus the information from any city or district, and so obtain a clear idea of the actual state of things there. The one place which invites any such attempt is Hong Kong. A Chinese population is there, living under British rule; and though the rulers are represented in greater proportion than the ruled, some of the latter are included; and some idea of the diversity of opinions and of standpoints is possible.

Hong Kong, then a barren rock, was ceded to Great Britain in 1842. Though a Crown colony, it remains a station, rather than a home for British subjects. The population of some 300,000 is largely an overflow from Canton, with 10,000 Europeans added. As a port, it has thriven greatly. It is generally supposed to have outlived its past reputation as a nest of smugglers, but Sir Robert Hart clearly speaks of the present in this sentence: "Hong Kong has long been the centre of opium smuggling, and trade in arms and contraband salt; and round this lawlessness flock all the adventurers of the south."[1] It now ranks amongst the busiest harbours of the British Empire. After British shipping, Chinese shipping is far ahead of the tonnage of any other country. Two Chinese are on the Legislative Council. Mr. Colquhoun writes of the colony: "The Chinese merchant, by reason of his shrewdness, perseverance, ability, and honesty, stands very high in the commercial world, and is the most formidable rival to the Anglo-Saxon race. The English are aware that while the Chinese could accomplish nothing without them, on the other hand they themselves would accomplish nothing without the Chinese; they are mutually necessary."[2] Hong Kong has been described as the headquarters of the Indo-China opium trade.

The retail sale of opium is let to an individual or firm described as the Hou Fook Company. These opium farmers grant licences at their own free will. The sum received from them amounts to between one-fifth and one-sixth of the colony's revenue.[3] The opium farmer estimated that 10 per cent. of adult Chinese men smoke. The Colonial Secretary gives an approximate estimate of three chests per day for the colony. At one mace per head, this would represent some 32,000 consumers.[4] The Puisne Judge, speaking from a case that had come

[1] *These from the land of Sinim*, p. 128.

[2] *China in Transformation.*

[3] *R. C. Report*. v. 188.

[4] *Ibid.*, v. 189.

before him, estimated only one and a half chests per day, as prepared and sold in the colony. It is open to the farmer to export any quantity of boiled opium he pleases without rendering any account, so accurate statistics are not available. The ex-Governor, Sir William Des Voeux, considered it probable that the population at Hong Kong smokes more opium than any other equal population in the world, and yet has a comparatively low death-rate. Some reports from districts in China indicate that the first part of his proposition is wide of the mark.

The Governor of Hong Kong was asked to obtain information from (*a*) the most intelligent and trustworthy gentlemen of Oriental races; and (*b*) officials, medical men, merchants, and others, conversant with Chinese and other Asiatic consumers of opium. The questions were sent to sixty-one persons, including one missionary. There are thirty-eight replies, from English, Indians, Persians, and Chinese. If the reader asks himself, Does this witness condemn the habit, or defend it? he would probably say, Twenty condemn, and eighteen defend. If he asked, Do these witnesses believe the habit to be good, or bad, or indifferent? he would table the replies as, Good, three; bad, twenty; indifferent, fifteen. Then comes the question, What is the personal knowledge of these different classes of witnesses? Do the apologists for the habit represent those who have most to do with the revenue or profits; or those who have the closest knowledge of the users of the drug?

The English officials are divided. On the whole, they lean to the pro-opium side. The ex-Governor concludes his letter thus: "Opium, no doubt, does harm in a few cases of inordinate excess, but to the great majority of consumers it is, to say the least, innocent." He explains at some length that it is "only natural" that missionaries "should incline to a view which so conveniently accounts for, or diverts attention from, the enormous disparity between the efforts and money spent upon missionary enterprise in China, and the results obtained."[1] "But for the anti-opium agitation, it can scarcely be doubted that funds for Chinese missions would cease to flow in equal profusion." If the ex-Governor had devoted himself to ascertained facts, he would have aided the inquiry better, and have done more justice to British officialism in the East. The Chief Justice answers few questions. He is favourably impressed with the marked absence of opium crime.[2] The Puisne Judge confirms this view, and thinks the great majority of smokers do not become slaves to the drug, or suffer harmful effects. The Colonial Treasurer says: "Drink maddens, opium soothes. The Government should be thankful that they have imbeciles rather than maniacs to deal with."[3] The Colonial Surgeon, Dr. Ayres, thinks it a ridiculously lazy habit, but defensible, as indulgences go.[4] He stands alone in his opinion: "With opium smokers there is no such thing as becoming a sot. No one dies of it. I cannot find it is so injurious as tobacco smoking in some cases." The swallowing of the drug he has elsewhere characterised as a "terrible vice."[5] A surgeon-colonel thinks the moderate use, both of alcohol and opium, beneficial.

A doctor in private practice says: "Moderate opium smoking has no evil effects, morally, physically, or socially"! The Superintendent of the Government Civil Hospital considers that the habit,

[1] *R. C. Report*, v. 144. [2] *Ibid.*, v. 189. [3] P. 190.
[4] P. 193. [5] Appendix I. note 9.

"in moderation, is certainly not injurious, and, in many cases, is decidedly beneficial." "They very rarely leave off."[1] "The general opinion amongst Chinese appears to be, that if they leave off the habit they will die. Even leaving it off for a day brings on severe diarrhœa, and I can easily understand this proving fatal if not properly treated, not to mention mental disquietude," etc. "The Chinese know of no substitute for opium; the craving seems to be so great, the habit having been once established, that they would do anything to obtain it in one form or other." The reader is left to harmonise these somewhat conflicting statements as he may. The Government Analyst says that, with the exception of poor coolies, an opium smoker appears to be as good a man, morally, physically, and socially, as a non-smoker; but that the baneful nature of the taking of opium internally, and the injecting of morphia, is not open to question. These leading official witnesses are supported by the opium traders, who do not add anything to the argument, unless it be that those who look thin and emaciated are not necessarily weak.[2]

Then there come upon the field other English witnesses, some of them official also, who are either more imaginative, or who probe further into the social conditions in Hong Kong, who see evils in the habit, grave and forbidding.

Mr. Wodehouse, police magistrate, writes: "With regard to Chinese, the effects of any kind, whether moral, physical, or social, from taking opium, are in the direction of deterioration proportionate to the extent to which it is taken. . . . In every instance the adoption of the habit is a wound to the moral

[1] *R. C. Report*, v. 205. [2] *Ibid.*, v. 209.

instincts of the individual, and lowers his self-esteem, to the general weakening of his character.[1] . . . The habit of opium smoking is condemned as both degrading and injurious by the great majority of Chinese." Referring to the possibility of making good the opium revenue, Mr. Wodehouse concludes: "If it could be done consistently with the large questions of policy and expediency involved in its adoption, it would be infinitely preferable to the present method of obtaining a revenue by means of an opium farm, which is attended with many hardships and irregularities falling entirely upon the Chinese population."

The Acting Registrar-General says: "The Chinese become weak and anæmic, lazy and shiftless . . . will steal in order to obtain opium, if not able to continue to buy it. The majority are inclined to be sots." "The opium-smoking divans are a disgrace to the colony."[2]

Dr. Eitel, the Inspector of Schools, says: "There cannot be, in my experience, frequent indulgence without a corresponding degree of physical, moral, and social injury."[3]

Mr. Lockhart, the Protector of the Chinese, said: "It is the desire of the Government to limit consumption, so far as it possibly can consistently with the raising of revenue"![4] "Chinese popular opinion in respect to the opium habit is decidedly against it. There is a common Cantonese saying: 'The Ten Cannots: He cannot (1) give up the habit, (2) enjoy sleep, (3) wait for his turn when sharing his pipe with his friends, (4) rise early, (5) be cured if sick, (6) help relations in need, (7) enjoy wealth, (8) plan anything, (9) get credit, even when an old customer,

[1] *R. C. Report*, v. 191. [2] *Ibid.*, v. 191. [3] P. 207. [4] *Ibid.*, i. 100.

(10) walk any long distance.' That, I think, sums up the popular view of the Chinese with regard to the opium habit." Mr. Lockhart is quoted in the Report as saying that, in his opinion, it would no more be possible to enforce the prohibition of opium in Hong Kong than that of drink in the United Kingdom.

Mr. Stanton, Police Inspector, says: "None of those who consume opium appear to be benefited by it, while the wives and children of poor opium smokers necessarily suffer deprivation . . . in conversation, the people complain that England derives a great deal of money from the Chinese for supplying what is baneful to them."[1] Dr. Chalmers is "amazed that any honest man can utter a word in its defence."

But the evidence entitled to most weight as to the effect of the habit on the Chinese, is that of the Chinese themselves.[2] The evidence of nine Chinese witnesses is given. One of these says: "Opium smoking does not affect the morality or sociality of the smokers, but it affects the constitutions. It is like gambling, same as drinking with Europeans, it is a national vice, and it can never be altogether done away with."[3]

Law Wai Chun says its effects are deadly. "In thus stopping the supply of opium, the whole of Asia will be benefited, and England will be carrying out the will of Heaven in protecting its children, and will receive in return infinite blessings." Chin-u-Tin knows of no case of consumers who have taken opium for years without doing any harm. "The Chinese are only too glad if the Government would adopt any method to exterminate this evil."[4]

[1] *R. C. Report*, v. 197. [2] *Ibid.*, v. 202. [3] P. 187. [4] P. 188.

Lum Sin Sang, the opium farmer, gives his evidence with much candour. He says (and he ought to know): "About 10 per cent. of the Chinese adult males are consumers, few women, and no children. As a rule, the Chinese consumers are inactive, and their bowels are costive. . . . The majority eventually become 'opium sots.' The habit is condemned as injurious by the Chinese." Leung Piu-Chi, bankers, say: "Great moral, physical, and mental deterioration take place in the case of consumers of opium. All Asiatics are anxious that the sale . . . should be altogether prohibited, and the evil effects arising from it removed."[1] Dr. Ho Kai, member of the Legislative Council, says: "Smokers may hide the degrading effects from casual observers, and often succeed in deceiving their European employers and friends, but in their homes . . . their degradation is only too painfully apparent . . . though certain, it is very gradual.[2] There is no comparison between the moderate use of alcohol and opium. The latter (is) baneful in all instances. The Chinese Government must co-operate, and that earnestly and faithfully, in stopping the habit. The Chinese admire and appreciate the equitable and just rule of England too well to be stirred up into hostility against her people concerning even a great wrong—the opium traffic." Tong Singe, Director of the Tung Wan Hospital, writes: "The wealth of England is so great that it ought not to wish to derive advantage from an article so injurious."[3] Chan-u-fai, a director of an influential Chinese society, denounces the drug as prejudicial in every respect. Pun Pong, a member of the District Watch Committee, says: "In the case of habitual consumers it

[1] *R. C. Report*, v. 189. [2] *Ibid.*, v. 199. [3] P. 203.

has undoubtedly a deteriorating effect on the constitution."[1] The general opinion of the Chinese is, that habitual smoking is injurious to all.

In May 1893, a new form of the opium habit was discovered in Hong Kong. Establishments had been opened for providing injections of morphia. The ostensible reason was to get rid of the craving for opium. The immediate result was that the craving was satisfied at one-sixth of the cost of Government opium. It was reported that "poverty on the one hand, and the exorbitant charge made by the opium farmer for the smoking extract on the other, are the chief causes of the introduction of this practice."

The first persons to call out against this innovation were, very naturally, the opium farmers. As the charge for each injection was very small (1 cent.), large numbers of persons went; and it was believed that a considerable diminution in the receipts of the farm was owing to this cause. They asked the Government to step in and stop the practice. The police, colonial surgeon, and Government analyst were then communicated with. It was at once agreed that "there can be no two opinions as to the baneful nature of this practice, and that no effort should be spared to stop it." The consumers were apparently driven back into orthodoxy, for the Royal Commission was informed, "There is every reason to suppose that the practice of morphine injecting has been practically stamped out in this colony, an ordinance having been introduced to effect that object."

The Anglican Bishop of Hong Kong is not in the list of names to whom questions were sent. The

[1] *R. C. Report*, v. 204.

reason is not given. In an appendix to the evidence from China, the Bishop, however, heads a noteworthy memorial to the commissioners from British missionaries in China of twenty-five or more years' standing.[1] The memorialists state their firm belief that the consumption of opium is exerting a distinctly deteriorating effect upon the Chinese people, physically, socially, and morally; that the conscience of the Chinese people, as a whole, is distinctly opposed to the habit, and that the trade is highly injurious to the fair name of Great Britain.

The incompleteness of this inquiry is evidenced by the proceedings of the Annual Meeting of the Hong Kong Chamber of Commerce, in April 1899. The published report of the Chamber contains the following sentence:—"The present system of licensing an opium farmer leaves much to be desired, and the Committee would suggest that the Government should give its consideration to the formulation of some other scheme which will not only provide an *effective check on the import* of the drug, but will trace it also to consumption or exportation.

The Hon. J. H. Whitehead, representing the Chamber of the Legislative Council, said: "In some respects the Government's opium farm has been, and is, a great curse to the colony . . . it is attended with grave abuses; it is the cause of much State-created crime, and it is most objectionable on political as well as commercial grounds; the system of farming out the opium tax is bad, and is directly opposed to the established laws of Great Britain."

Readers of Lord Charles Beresford's book on China may remember that he bluntly says: "The opium farmer is known to be the largest smuggler of

[1] *R. C. Report*, v. 353.

opium into the country. If he did not smuggle he could not afford to pay the large rent demanded by the British Government. Such a state of things is in direct opposition to the sentiments and traditions of the laws of the British Empire." Students of this drug trade can only wish that this was so.

Dr. Kate Bushnell and Mrs. Andrews, in returning from a visit to Hong Kong, speak strongly of the inseparable connection of opium and vice in that city. Mr. Arnold Foster has mentioned that in passing through Hong Kong in 1899, a competitive examination for a Government clerkship had just been held. One of the subjects given was an essay on opium smoking. The lucrative Government income notwithstanding, all the five young Chinese who competed denounced the opium vice as the ruin of China.

It seems clear, then,—That where opium is a principal source of revenue, the trend of those responsible for the finances of the place is apologetic as to its use; that the paper inquiry of the Commission was valueless as to local methods of dealing with the sale of the drug; that there are grave objections to the farming system in force at Hong Kong and the Straits Settlement (they seem to combine the worst features of municipalisation and of private trading in one); that the ill results of the vice are not obtrusive. It leads, not to violence in the open, but to decay in seclusion. It does not result in crime, though it does in petty thefts. In the mortality returns, again, it does not figure under the heading of deaths, but it lowers the vitality, the power of resistance to other diseases.

English witnesses too often take it for granted that a drug habit, or a drink habit, must prevail.

They prefer that Easterns should keep to the former, whilst they hold by the latter. Easterns, on the other hand, see no necessity for either alternative, and continually denounce both.

The European is not ashamed of his wine, and sees no reason why the Chinese should be of his pipe. Herein is a cleavage between the fundamental thought of the two continents. The Chinese almost without exception are uneasy at the opium habit. No one has yet produced a Chinese author who defends it.

The Chinese are not supposed to be sensitive to the conception of sin. All the more is it self-evident that the spread of an indulgence of which every individual is ashamed, is of necessity injurious to the bearing and moral character of their people.

The main question at issue was well put by a Governor of Hong Kong, Sir John Pope Henessy, many years ago. "The British officials and the opium merchants," he said, "are constantly asserting that the smoking of opium does not injure the health of the Chinese, . . . but the real objection of the governing classes of China to opium has hardly been noticed, namely, that it injures the intellect, and impairs the moral character."[1]

[1] Social Science Congress, 1882.

CHAPTER VI

CHINA

CHINA was not referred to in the instructions to the Commission. The commissioners, however, "thought it impossible to form a complete judgment on the moral objections raised against the Indian opium revenue system, without considering the effects of that trade abroad." [1] With regard to China, therefore, they requested Her Majesty's minister there "to obtain the evidence of competent witnesses, in the forms of answers to interrogatories." The Commission state that "the quantity of both Bengal and Malwa opium exported to China and the Far East is . . . far larger than that consumed in India, to which it bears the proportion of about 12 to 1." [2] The Report continues: "The moral and physical results of the use of opium in China must be gathered from the evidence of witnesses, and, with few exceptions, we had no opportunity of seeing these witnesses, and of cross-examining them upon their statements." The gist of the evidence so collected is summed up in the following extracts from the Report [3]:—

"By the majority of the missionaries of every Christian communion, the use of opium is strongly condemned." "In the British consular service, the prevailing opinion is that opium smoking in modera-

[1] *R. C. Report*, vi. 1. [2] *Ibid.*, vi. 48. [3] P. 50.

tion is not harmful, and that moderation is the rule. The evil effects of excess do not thrust themselves prominently on the notice. A minority of the consular service condemn the use of opium in any form as essentially bad." "The medical opinions were in general accord with those of the consular body." "We conclude that the habit is generally practised in moderation, and that when so practised the injurious effects are not apparent; but that, when the habit is carried to excess, disastrous consequences, both moral and physical, inevitably follow. We may fairly compare the effects of opium smoking among the Chinese population to those of alcoholic liquors in the United Kingdom."

It will be noted that the Commission set out with the good intent of forming a complete judgment on the moral objections to the opium trade. As twelve-thirteenths of it directly affected China and the Far East, it would seem that these could hardly be equitably ascertained and examined, unless some twelve-thirteenths of the time and thought of the Commission was bestowed upon the peoples who consume this overwhelming proportion of the drug prepared for their use. Nothing of this kind took place. The Commission saw few Chinese witnesses personally. It added some written evidence collected in a very casual manner, and finally did not think it necessary to present a "detailed report"! The majority decided, however, that the evidence was "conflicting," and that the responsibility for anything which is not as it ought to be "mainly lies with the Chinese." For themselves, they would leave everything alone. From pressure of time, or other reasons, the moral objections to the trade abroad had to be largely jettisoned.

They are never even stated fully or clearly, and the reader has to infer their existence mainly from the counter-evidence put forward on behalf of the trade. Not a single quotation is given from any evidence whatsoever, except by way of defence, or in mitigation, of the opium habit. This remark applies also to the whole of the Report of the Royal Commission. Not one of the leading witnesses who appeared in person and gave evidence as regards the evil in China proper is cited in the Report. The one quotation set forth in it from the evidence received in London is from a letter sent by an ex-opium trader, who afterwards appears in another volume, giving his evidence twice over. In the written answers sent from the East, the reader is continually kept in darkness as to whether they are from persons pecuniarily interested in the trade.

Some apology is needful for the contentious character of this chapter. Wherever two sides of a case are pressed, it is well to let each plead for itself in its own terms, and leave the audience to judge. In this instance the evidence is offered in scraps and fragments from very varied districts. It hardly can be collated. It is a hopeless tangle, if treated separately. Little is attempted here beyond setting out the singularly unsatisfactory character of the inquiry, and of some of the conclusions alleged to be founded upon it.

The schedules of questions were sent from Calcutta to be answered by the consuls and any Chinese officials thought to be desirable, and "by medical men, merchants, and others . . . specially conversant with any part of China in which opium is grown and consumed." A few additions were suggested by the Government of India, and adopted by the Commission.[1] No equivalent opportunity of making suggestions was offered to any representative of anti-opium opinion. It will be seen that missionaries are not mentioned. Several of the consuls refer to the special knowledge of missionaries as the reason for seeking their aid. Consul Scott, after alluding to the long experience of two missionaries, writes: "It was my intention to have answered the questions myself, but, on consideration, I find that my information and opinions are for the most part second-hand. I have never turned my attention directly to the subject of the effects of opium on the Chinese."[2] Consul Bullock "can testify to the experience and competence of the writers. The papers are for the most part furnished by missionaries. But missionaries in China, speaking the language, constantly moving about, and always in close contact with the people, are able to give far more trustworthy opinions on such a subject than any other class of persons can, though many of them, of course, have strong prejudices concerning it.[3] The Report, in summing up the consuls' evidence, says: "The evil effects of excess do not thrust themselves prominently on the notice."[4] This ought to be borne in mind when comparisons with the alcohol habit are instituted. A striking proof may be found in Consul Allen's replies. Two sentences read as follows:—"As a private resident in China, my experiences have not the weight either of those of a medical man or those of a missionary. We consuls have little private intercourse with the natives outside our homes and offices."[5] "I held the post of mixed Court Assessor for two years, and

[1] *R. C. Report*, vi. 145. [2] *Ibid.*, vi. 213. [3] P. 266.
[4] P. 51. [5] P. 239.

certainly there were considerable numbers of opium sots brought before the Chinese magistrate and myself every week." Consul Fraser seems to have understood that the verdict of men in the trade was especially sought for. He writes: "Here is only one European merchant, a German, and even if he were present instead of absent, he has nothing to do with the opium trade, which is passing into the hands of the Chinese."[1] Answers were sent by officials, missionaries, medical men, merchants, and Chinese. If personal knowledge is the first qualification, the order of precedence would be—Chinese, missionaries, medical men, officials, and merchants.

According to the Report, the majority of missionaries of all Churches "strongly condemn" the habit. "Others take a less decided view. Of these, two may be quoted."[2] The majority who strongly condemn are 49 to 3. Fifty-one are distinctly adverse to the habit, as against one who is not. Why the Commissioners decide that they *may* quote two out of a minority of three, and none out of a majority of forty-nine, is not explained. Why, when they do quote two they do not quote them correctly, is not explained either. The Report runs: "The Rev. W. Ashmore states that some men will use opium for years, and not show marked results." What Mr. Ashmore does say is: "Some men of vigorous vitality will use opium for many years, and not show marked results." He goes on to write: "With great injury?" . . . "nearly all of those with whom the habit is fully formed, and whose regular recurrent daily craving has attained the mastery over the man. There is no such thing as an assured moderation."

[1] *R. C. Report*, vi. 288. [2] *Ibid.*, vi. 50.

The Report then quotes a long sentence as if it was complete in itself, from the Rev. A. Bone.[1] In the original, another long paragraph giving a darker side to the habit occurs within the sentence professedly quoted. In the omitted paragraph, Mr. Bone says: "Those who become in any sense 'victims' of the opium pipe have their moral sense greatly impaired."[2] Mr. Bone afterwards adds: "I never will allow an opium smoker among my crew if I can avoid it. I regard the smoking of opium, speaking in general terms, as baneful." Such methods of quotation can only be described as garbling. The Commissioners tell the public that "the prevailing consular opinion is that opium smoking in moderation is not harmful, and that moderation is the rule." This, no doubt, is the opinion that prevailed with the compilers of the Report, but it should not prevail with the public. The Indian Government has published a review of the Report.[3] It is not likely to err on the anti-opium side. It classifies the consular evidence thus:

1. Those who have expressed no opinion	3
2. Those who regard opium smoking as a serious evil	5
3. Generally condemnatory, but not strongly so	5
4. Consider that moderation is the rule, and that moderate opium smokers suffer no *apparent* injury . .	13

These figures need one correction: Of the twenty-eight schedules sent to consuls, five (not three only) sent no answers. Five, then, express no opinion;

[1] *R. C. Report*, vi. 51. [2] *Ibid.*, v. 218.
[3] *East India Opium*, 1896, p. 47.

ten condemn; thirteen say moderate smokers suffer no *apparent* injury. This is not saying that the habit "is not harmful." But when the answers under the fourth list are examined, it becomes clear that some of the thirteen answers cannot be fairly described as they are described in the Report. Mr. C. M. Ford of Amoy, for instance, is one who is cited as saying that "moderation is not harmful," and that "moderation is the rule."[1] His evidence is this: "Perhaps 30 per cent. use it without any injury, 40 per cent. with but slight injury, and 30 per cent. with great injury."[2] Consul Parker, instead of saying that a majority go unscathed, suggests that 50 per cent. do so.[2] Mr. Cockburn expressly limits his opinion as to a majority, to *apparent* injury, adding his belief that the number who smoke in excess is much larger in proportion than that of drinkers of alcohol at home.[3] Consul Mansfield, another of the thirteen, says: "It is to be deplored that the populations of the towns in this district are so much addicted to opium smoking.[4] The people are too poor to be able to afford the luxury, except at the expense of proper nourishment, and the effects on the race *generally* of under-feeding and diminished reproduction should be ultimately disastrous." The "prevailing" opinion of the Report dwindles into a minority opinion when examined.

The Report claims that "the medical opinions were in general accord with those of the consular body."[5] It proceeds, "we *may* quote, for instance," and then follow two quotations in mitigation of the vice. Again, it is to be asked, Why *may* the Royal

[1] *R. C. Report*, v. 310. [2] *Ibid.*, v. 316. [3] P. 232.
[4] P. 336. [5] *Ibid.*, vi. 51.

Commission never give a quotation, except in excuse of the drug?

The Indian Blue-Book classifies the doctors as—

Favourable to the habit	8
Unfavourable	9
Doubtful	5

This certainly does not entitle the Commission to claim a prevailing opinion in favour of the drug. Four of the "doubtful" give evidence as follows:—

Mr. Young, M.B.C.M: "*Moral*—I would trust an opium smoker less than a non-smoking Chinaman. *Physical deterioration*—without injury, 2 per cent.; with slight injury, 75; with serious, 15; sots, 8. I consider opium an unquestionable evil in China."[1]

Dr. Molyneux: "Probably two-thirds of those who smoke opium do so 'with slight injury'; . . . it is to the Chinese almost as demoralising a drug as morphia is to people of more enlightened countries."[2]

Dr. Underwood: "The Chinese in conversation condemn generally the habit of opium smoking, and they are always more or less ashamed to confess that they indulge in it."[3]

Dr. Cox: "About 20 per cent. smoke without injury, about 60 per cent. with slight, about 20 per cent. with great. It is universally condemned."[4] These opinions are classed among the "doubtfuls."

But the Report founds itself on "the medical opinions" as a whole. The Indian summary, for the extraordinary reason apparently that they are connected with missionary societies, has omitted—as the Rev. Arnold Foster in his very able analysis points out—to refer to the evidence of eighteen medical practitioners, all engaged in Chinese

[1] *R. C. Report*, v. 232. [2] *Ibid.*, v. 305. [3] P. 315. [4] P. 332.

practice, and many of them in charge of hospitals in different parts of the country.[1] Classifying all the medical witnesses together, and accepting even the Indian returns referred to above, so far as they go, the result is, that of forty medical witnesses, five are doubtful, nine are favourable, and twenty-six are decidedly unfavourable, to the use of opium. Mr. Foster, summing up the evidence, rightly puts the number in favour of the moderation theory as eleven, and against it, twenty-nine. Thus the Report is in direct and absolute contradiction to the evidence on which it is assumed to be founded.[2]

Coming to merchants, twenty-two are classified by the Indian authorities as follows:—

Favourable to the use of opium	16
Doubtful	2
Unfavourable	4

When a witness is pecuniarily interested in the trade, as many of these are, the fact should be stated. In most cases it cannot even be guessed. Mr. M'Kie, assistant to Messrs. Jardine & Co., opium merchants, is announced by the Commission to have had "unusual opportunities of seeing the better class of Chinese merchants." His own more modest statement is, "I do not possess sufficient knowledge to make my opinion on these questions of any reliable importance."[3] Messrs. D. Sassoon, Sons, & Co., the oldest-established house in the opium trade, say: "The social contact between foreigners and Chinese is so slight, that it becomes rather difficult to answer such a question" (as to moral effect).[4] In their opinion, 75 per cent. smoke

[1] *An Examination and an Appeal*, p. 27.

[2] *Contemp. Review*, July 1898. [3] *R. C. Report*, vi. 252. [4] *Ibid.*, vi. 255.

without injury, 23 per cent. with slight injury, and 2 per cent. with great injury. They think that the slight injury "does not in any way imply injury to health, but certain physical inconveniences." Mr. Duff says: "Being in demand, and so largely required, it must have some beneficial effect."[1] "Opium to them (the Chinese) has no deleterious effects, quite the contrary, for it is a positive need, and they could not do without it." How the nation managed to exist before the habit became frequent, is not explained. "Fully fed and stimulated faddists" can, he thinks, do without opium; missionaries, he suggests, "are not sincere," etc.[2] This is the witness previously referred to as honoured by special mention, and appearing on two occasions.[3] Many of the answers from the merchant class do not contain replies to all the questions, or indicate any general personal acquaintance with the subject. The class whose evidence must carry the most weight is the Chinese. The Commission specially asked for replies from desirable Chinese. Having obtained them, the Report makes no allusion to them whatever. Eleven Chinese replies are given. Two are forwarded through Europeans, and both are favourable to the habit. Another is non-committal. Eight are distinctly hostile. All the quotations from Chinese books, which are anywhere cited in the evidence, are without exception condemnatory of the habit.

One other statement in the Report must be noticed. The fifteenth of the Commissioners' questions runs as follows:—"Is there among the Chinese, in the part of China with which you are acquainted, any wish that England should not allow opium to

[1] *R. C. Report*, v. 259. [2] *Ibid.*, i. 112. [3] *Ibid.*, vi. 49.

be exported from India?" The Commissioners are made to say, "There is *no* evidence from China of any popular desire that the import of Indian opium should be stopped."[1] This clear and definite assertion is inexplicable to any one who studies the evidence, as the following quotations may serve to show:—

Hu Li Yuan replies to this question: "Yes, among the literary class."[2] Sub-prefect Sheng Fa Hai: "Some wish, but not all."[3] Dr. Edkins: "My Shanghai informant says, that hereabouts the feeling is general, that the stoppage of opium import from India would be an immense benefit . . . all feel it, in his opinion."[4] A Chinese General says: "For some inscrutable reason Heaven has sent down this curse; in the interest of the race I earnestly pray that the plans of Heaven may be changed."[5] Yu Keng Pak: "I hope you will forward it (his answer) to the Government of your country, and to all true gentlemen,—that they may take the opportunity of joining heart and soul in the suppression of the cultivation and sale of opium . . . let them make haste to help China, and do away with this huge evil."[6] Lu Pao Yu, official writer at H.B.M. Consulate, Chefoo: "The inhabitants of Shantung naturally do not like England to import Indian opium. Every chest of opium imported is so much injury to the people, and the flood of poison is never-ending."[7] Consul Hurst: "The Chinese dealers would regret the stoppage of the importation from India, the non-smoking population would approve the step."[8]

Consul Fraser: "I have on a few rare occasions become aware of such a wish being expressed by a

[1] *R. C. Report*, vi. 61. [2] *Ibid.*, vi. 314. [3] P. 300. [4] P. 249.
[5] P. 223. [6] P. 227. [7] P. 281. [8] P. 323.

few persons among the Chinese on moral grounds. It is often expressed in the native press of Shanghai. On grounds of political economy the wish is, I believe, generally—in fact, perhaps, I may say universally—entertained among the so-called educated classes."[1] The Rev. J. Macgowan furnishes a very representative extract, viz.: "In travelling in the interior and preaching to heathen audiences, the missionary is continually being twitted with the charge that his practice is not consistent with his teaching.[2] They say that his countrymen having brought opium to destroy the Chinese, he is so far involved in their wrong. The masses know nothing about India, or the exportation of opium from that country to China. They believe it comes from England, and that Englishmen bring it from there to sell for gain, without any regard to the morality of the question at all." It will be found that some thirty-five replies testify to such a wish, and yet more to a wish to get rid of the opium, from whatever source it may come. It is impossible to avoid the conclusion that the treatment of the evidence from China is discreditable to a Royal Commission. The transient desire to form a complete judgment on the moral objections to the trade ended in complete failure. The substitute for a detailed report is hopelessly misleading.

It seems impossible to obtain any accurate data as to the consumption of native opium. China is in the main an empire of villages, divided into eighteen provinces (now nineteen?), with separate governments, and possessing no trustworthy statistics in common. In 1881 the Inspector-General assumed that the native supply did not exceed the foreign,

[1] *R. C. Report*, vi. 280. [2] *Ibid.*, vi. 313.

and from this estimated the number of opium smokers at 2,000,000, or less than 1 per cent. There is evidence of a very great increase of the native growth of the poppy during the last twenty years. Consul-General Hosie, in reporting last year (1904) on the province of Ssŭch'uan, writes: "It (the province) was at one time a great wheat producer and exporter, but since the rapid extension of poppy cultivation that export has ceased, and has been replaced by opium."[1] He thinks it is well within the mark to say that in the cities 50 per cent. of the men and 20 per cent. of the women smoke, and in the country not less than 15 and 7 respectively. At 10 oz. (Chinese) to every fifty smokers, and allowing for a large export trade, he estimates that the province alone produces more than double the quantity of Indian opium brought into China. These are the most startling semi-official figures yet given to the public, and more than justify the laments over this "opium-cursed" province, to be found in a succeeding chapter.

[1] "China," No. 5, 1904.

PART III: PRESENT POSITION

CHAPTER I

INDIA

IN sketching the present position of the Indo-Chinese drug trade, it will be well first to attempt to realise the industry in India, before passing on to the recent evidence as to the effects of the trade in China.

The revenue in question is derived from a monopoly of the growth of opium in Bengal, and its sale both for export and for home consumption; and in part by the levy of a heavy pass duty on all opium entering British territory from the Native States. No Native State has access to the coast, except through British territory. This duty once stood at Rs.700 per chest, but in consequence of the decline in the cultivation has been lowered to Rs.500. Though the poppy can be grown in most parts of India, its cultivation in British territory is everywhere prohibited, except in parts of Bengal and of the North-West Provinces and of Oudh. The produce from these districts is known as Bengal opium. The opium grown in the Native States (*i.e.* of Rajputana and Central India) is known as Malwa opium. The vast majority of Native States, either by express or tacit agreement with the

Government of India, do not allow the poppy to be grown on their territory.[1]

The administrative head of the Bengal opium monopoly is the Board of Revenue at Calcutta. The poppy is grown and the opium manufactured under the control of the Government of the Bengal Presidency. The crops are sown chiefly in garden plots close to the villages over a large irregular territory, mainly in the valley of the Ganges. There are two separate opium agencies, termed Bihar and Benares respectively, with separate factories at Patna and Ghazipur. Each agency has its independent staff of European officers supervising large native establishments of sub-officials of various grades.

The evidence collected by the Commission as to the profit or loss of the cultivators was conflicting. The zemindars, with little exception, spoke in favour of the poppy crop. The personal knowledge of the large landowners was evidently not extensive. Other witnesses gave more detailed information. Patel Sheobaksh, a cultivator from the Bundi State, and a man of comparative means, warmly defended the crop as a very profitable one.[2] In addition to opium, he said they cooked the young leaves as vegetables, the poppy heads were fried and eaten, the seeds were used for making pottage, and a useful oil was obtained from them; the oil cakes left were the best food for cows and buffaloes, and the shells, when rubbed in water, made a kind of drink. It appeared that he grew ten times as much as the average British ryot, and employed paid labour. Another cultivator from Merwara testified that the prohibition of the cultivation would create great dissatisfaction in that district. A petition from

[1] *R. C. Report*, i. Q. 100.

[2] *Ibid.*, iv. Q. 20,951.

twelve residents in the Umballa district set forth that "the income from other produce is very limited, whereas opium yields us a handsome income, so that no other produce comes up to it. The large yield of opium was taken into consideration when the revenue of our villages was fixed at the recent settlement. If the cultivation be stopped we shall be ruined, and the Government will be obliged to revise the assessment of revenue."[1]

Other villages petitioned in a like sense. The ryot, generically a somewhat inarticulate person, amongst other things, said that wheat, potatoes, and sugar-cane are more profitable—there is not so much labour and cost required as in growing poppy—but they grew some "because we are poor people, and it is the order of the Government that we should cultivate poppy."[2] They had seen crops uprooted because poppy was not grown. They wished "that the opium should be stopped by the Government." A petition by cultivators confirmatory of this evidence was presented, to the following effect:—"To Lord Brassey, President, etc.—Cherisher of the poor, our salutations. We have heard that your honours have come to India to ask us whether we like to cultivate opium or not. . . . Sugar-cane and potato cultivation we find much more profitable. We cultivate the poppy under pressure from Government, otherwise we would not do it, and our prayer is that we be released from this trouble." This was signed by 89 in one village, 171 in another village, and 55 in a third village. Petitions from fifty villages were presented, asking that the poppy cultivation be altogether abandoned, or that the rate paid by Government be raised from Rs.5 to Rs.15.

[1] *R. C. Report*, iii. 260. [2] *Ibid.*, Q. 11,353.

As stated, the rate was raised shortly afterwards to Rs.6, and some of the villagers are said to have petitioned to grow the poppy again. It is freely admitted that the spread of railways and other causes have seriously trenched on the popularity of the poppy. Mr. Christian, a department officer, wrote: "The crops that are competing with poppy, in fact I ought to say, that have swamped and overcome it, are tobacco, potato, haldi, chillies, and other garden produce."

Unhappily there is no dispute over the fact that "the vast majority" of the ryots "live and die in debt," and that consequently "the advances of Government cash, free of interest at the time of sowing, are of the greatest importance."[1] The Report of the Bengal Department for 1896–97 states that "the increased area obtained was doubtless largely attributable to the necessitous condition of the cultivators, . . . on the verge of famine." Indian officials have worked in a manner beyond praise for their famine-stricken people in times of need, and these, unfortunately, have been frequent of late years. It is rather ghastly to find that throughout these years the permanent policy of the Government has been to make money advances, free of interest, on the sowing of the poppy, and for wells for poppy cultivation only. In ancient times Government advances known as takàvi, are said to have been made to food cultivators at seed-time, and recovered at the harvest.

It was at first denied before the Commission that any compulsion was ever used to induce the ryots to cultivate the poppy. The fact was speedily proved by eye-witnesses. It was afterwards ex-

[1] *R. C. Report*, iii. Q. 12,172.

plained thus: "Market-garden produce has admittedly of late years begun to compete successfully with opium. Cases of this kind must therefore be expected to occur."[1]

The manufacture of the drug for China, described long ago by Mr. Julius Jeffrey, still holds good.[2] He wrote as follows:—

"In passing by water the chief opium magazine of the East India Company at Patna, I paid a visit to a friend who had charge of the scientific department of it. After he had led me through storey after storey and gallery after gallery of the factory, with opium balls right and left, tiered in shelves to the ceiling; upon my expressing amazement at an exhibition of opium enough to supply the medical wants of the world for years, he replied nearly in these words: 'I see you are very innocent; these stores of opium have no such beneficent destination. It is all going to debauch the Chinese, and my duty is to maintain its smack as attractive to them as possible. Come to my laboratory.' There I saw broken balls of opium, procured, I understood, from China by the Bengal Government, as approved musters for imitation by the cultivators."

This "provision" opium is finally offered for sale by auction at Calcutta.

The fact that the growth of the poppy and manufacture of opium in British India (the supply of Malwa opium is becoming relatively less important) is a strict monopoly wholly in the hands of the Indian Government, has often been animadverted upon and strongly condemned. The great name of Lord Lawrence can be cited amongst those who wished to dissociate the drug trade from the

[1] *R. C. Report*, v. 355. [2] *British Army in India.*

Government.[1] The prime mover in the matter was Sir William Muir, a member of the Supreme Council, who in 1858–60, in 1864, and in 1868–69, advocated this change on account of the moral objections to the present system.[2] Sir Charles Trevelyan favoured the abolition of the monopoly on economic grounds. It is said that with one exception all the advocates of change have recognised that cultivation in British territory must be limited and licensed. The authorities, we are told, had little difficulty in proving that the change of system would be financially disastrous. Sir H. Maine, in opposing Sir William Muir's suggestion, wrote: "The British Government is sufficiently despotic to effect this (prohibition), and for moral purposes there is no distinction between what a despotic government does itself, and what it permits its subjects to do."[3]

The necessity for imposing restrictions on the free growth of the poppy, and the free manufacture and sale of opium, is in truth the justification for the monopoly of the Indian Government. If the present monopoly was abolished, stringent conditions on individual traders or trading companies would become necessary, and would in truth form a monopoly under Government auspices.

Where a government becomes the manufacturer or trader in an article liable to great abuse, its responsibility to use such privilege for the public well-being only, is very great. The temptation to push sales in either drink or drugs for profit, is one of the standing difficulties of all communities alike. The empire is justly proud, as a whole, of the character and purity of its administrators in India. But few

[1] Turner, p. 197. [2] *R. C. Report*, iv. 372. [3] *Ibid.*, iv. 376.

will claim that the Government has proved itself exempt from this particular form of temptation. Mr. H. J. Wilson, in his Minority Report, calls attention to the change which has come over official statements in reference to opium within the last few years.[1] Formerly there was perfect freedom of expression, and the general tone was distinctly condemnatory of the use of the drug. Now, it appears to be expected that the Civil Service shall, with one accord, uphold the Government monopoly. Other observers have insisted that our rule has become more commercial during the last thirty years; and that our commercial policies have an unfortunate tendency to neglect the necessaries of life, and "to stimulate the stimulants."[2] It would be easy to give many illustrations of this from the steady and formidable growth of the excise system in India. *Abkari*, the organ of the temperance movement, which owes so much to the generous efforts of the late Mr. W. S. Caine, is continually notifying cases of the planting of licences, to the dislike of the native thought of a district; and the stand the Hon. J. Ferguson has made against the serious growth of opium sales amongst the Singhalese, where the drug was formerly almost unknown, bear witness to the danger.

"In India, drink is mostly used by way of imitation," was one of the messages sent to the Royal Commission.[3] It adds to the regret that must be felt in many quarters at the aggressively pro-intoxicant character of the Report.

It has been said that "the hand of the ruler is

[1] *R. C. Report*, vi. 137.

[2] Carpenter, *From Adam's Peak*, p. 273.

[3] *R. C. Report*, iv. 510.

chiefly felt in the way of repression and restriction."[1] The Excise Reports, and the anxiety displayed to provide for a sufficient sale of opium in Burma, Ceylon, and elsewhere, in the face of strong opposition, do not bear this out as might be desired. Yet this is the *raison d'être* of the Government monopoly. How inconsistent, moreover, is a rule of repression and restriction at home, and the pushing of a wholesale export trade in the same drug for the sake of profit at the expense of a neighbouring people!

Any one who examines the statistics will see that the opium trade has been managed with as little regard either for the good of the ryots in India, or for the people of China, as could be shown by the most indifferent of syndicates or trusts. The number of chests produced was increased from 7565 in 1829–30 to 53,321 in 1853–54.[2] Then the Government altered its policy, and sought for higher prices on reduced sales by restricting the cultivation to less than half. In 1859–60 the production was brought down to 21,357 chests, at the enormous price of Rs.2000 per chest. But fear seized the administration that they were going too far, and the production was pushed up to 64,000 chests in 1863–64; and finally a third decision was come to, which has been fairly maintained, to try and steady the market by keeping reserve stocks in hand, and so endeavouring to avoid great variations; the main motive again being purely financial.

It is not the monopoly, but the use of it for the greed of gain which is objected to.

The suggestion of one of the representatives of India on the late Commission, that it might be

[1] *R. C. Report*, vi. 94.

[2] Fry, *England, China, and Opium*, pp. 31–33.

permissible for the British Government to give a direct assurance to China that she was now free to deal with the opium difficulty as she judged best, vanished under the spell of the authorities at Calcutta; and no British statesman has yet ventured on this initial instalment of elementary justice.[1] The Indian Treasury still rules the trade and Great Britain. The growth, culmination, and decline of the trade are set forth in Appendix II.

The position between Great Britain and China is now this. China can terminate the Chefoo agreement by giving a year's notice so to do. In that case the arrangement with regard to opium under the Treaty of Tientsin revives. Article XXVII. of that Treaty provides that either of the high contracting parties may demand a further revision of tariff at the end of ten years; but that if no such demand be made within six months after the end of the first ten years, then the tariff shall remain in force for ten years more, "and so it shall be at the end of each successive ten years."

[1] *R. C. Report*, vii. 28.

CHAPTER II

MEDICAL AND MILITARY EVIDENCE

THE physical effects of opium have been known and studied for generations, and Englishmen are generally under the impression that science has unhesitatingly condemned any resort to it as a dietetic. The late Sir Benjamin Brodie, and many of the leading London physicians with him, went so far as to declare that they could not "but regard those who promote the use of opium as an article of luxury, as inflicting a most serious injury on the human race";[1] and 5000 members of the medical profession declared in 1892, that "the habit of opium smoking or of opium eating is morally and physically debasing." It does not appear that any further discoveries have vitiated these pronouncements. But when the inquiring layman turns to the evidence collected by the Royal Commission, he finds that, so far as it is semi-official, it inclines to range itself, though with many important qualifications, on the side of the drug, and, moreover, that it can be just as obscure and non-luminous as the most unskilled humanitarian testimony.

The members of the medical profession combine personal knowledge, of a different kind to the missionary, with a training which should confer upon them scientific precision of statement. The

[1] Broomhall, *The Truth about Opium Smoking*, p. 73.

ability with which this precision has been successfully concealed by some of them in speaking of the opium habit, cannot be too frankly acknowledged. No better illustration can be given than Sir Wm. Moore's reply to the question: "Sir William, if I understand rightly, you think on the whole it (opium) is a good thing?"[1] The answer runs: "I will not go so far as to say it is a good thing, because I think we should be better all of us without any liquor or opium, or anything of the kind; but I mean to say this, that the use of opium does more good than it does harm." Yet Sir William would not advise the acquiring of the opium habit.

Somewhat similarly Surgeon-Captain Walsh endorsed the view that sufficient stress had not been laid on the use of small moderate doses of opium as a dietetic amongst the poor. But later on he said, "One must admit that it would be far better if they (the poor) would buy more food and no opium.[2]

It happens also that medical apologists for opium smoking strongly condemn the eating habit; whilst apologists for eating, where it is prevalent, as strongly condemn the smoking of the drug. All medical witnesses agree, however, in reprobating the introduction of preparations of opium by injection. When there is no disturbing environment of any kind, and science is not polarised by the exigencies of governments, its evidence can be both clear and strong.

In 1898, upwards of one hundred medical opinions on the use of opium in China were collected by a committee of medical missionaries, and edited by Dr. Park, surgeon in charge of the Soochow Hospital,

[1] *R. C. Report*, ii. Q. 1067. [2] *Ibid.*, Q. [illegible]59.

and surgeon to the Imperial Maritime Customs.[1] Questions based on those of the Royal Commission were sent to every known physician in China.[2] Answers were received and tabulated from members of the medical professions of various nationalities, chiefly British and American, but also including some German, French, Swedish, and Chinese. Of these, ninety speak of ill effects—moral, physical, and social—on the regular consumers of the drug. Of the four or five answers more or less apologetic, the most definite is that of Dr. M'Phun as regards: "Moral effect—If smoker is well off no particular change, except, as the natives say, they are not so ready to get angry as formerly.[3] Physical—If well off, not much change, unless taken to excess." A thoughtful and detailed opinion by Dr. Lyall says: "Cases of idiosyncrasy, both with regard to toleration of the drug and the opposite, are not infrequent." "Opium smoking, like any other vice, weakens the will power, paralyses the self-control, blunts the moral sense, and surely, if slowly, demoralises the whole character of the man. . . . Apart from the moral degeneration of the opium smoker . . . the evil effects are those of poverty. Families are impoverished, and homes are broken up, leading directly and indirectly to a vast amount of misery and semi-starvation. . . . The digestion becomes weakened, the appetite fails, the liver inactive, and the bowels constipated. From the inability to get, or take, or digest sufficient food, emaciation results. The skin becomes dry and shrivelled, and the eyes ıll. The bronchial tubes become irritated, causing ?h and often an asthmatic condition."[4] The

[1] ?endix I. note 10.
[2] *Opinions of over One Hundred Physicians.*
[3] . p. 6.
[4] *Ibid.*, p. 5.

almost unanimous opinions of this body of evidence are represented by the following:—

Dr. Kinnear: "Unquestionably detrimental in every way, though effects are not marked the first few years, especially in well-fed subjects."[1] Dr. Squibbs: "Effects, moral—depravity; physical—debility; social—poverty, etc. Have observed no good effects."[2] Dr. Stuart: "Degrading, is the one word for all."[3]

In some sixty-six replies as to the proportion of those who smoke "without injury," "with slight injury," "with great injury," twenty-six say "none smoke without injury"; others, "1 per cent., or one-tenth, without injury." One answer runs: "Without apparent injury," a few; "without real injury," none.[4] No reply puts the proportion of smokers without injury at more than 20 per cent. The general drift is, that injury is "only a matter of time." To the question, "Is there a tendency to increase amount smoked?" ninety-five reply in the affirmative, none in the negative. When asked, "Is the opium habit condemned as degrading or injurious by the Chinese in general?" eighty-five give affirmative answers; four, a qualified affirmative; two, a negative; and four, a qualified negative. Seventy consider opium worse than alcohol. Three consider alcohol the worst. Eighty of the medical witnesses speak to the commonness of suicide through opium. The conclusion that this little volume points to is, that the opium habit is a grave curse to China.

Any one wishing to study the effects of the opium habit on troops will do well to turn to the military evidence given to the Royal Commission in India.

[1] *Opinions of over One Hundred Physicians*, p. 4.

[2] *Ibid.*, p. 7. [3] P. 7. [4] P. 10.

Sir John Strachey told the Commissioners in London: "The Sikhs in particular, who form so immensely important a part of our army, are almost invariably habitual consumers." He had often thought "the best practical answer to those who inveigh against the use of opium would be . . . to bring one of our crack opium-drinking regiments to London, and exhibit them in Hyde Park."[1] In the evidence in India no trace of any opium-drinking regiment is anywhere to be found. Sir Lepel Griffin said of the Sikhs, "our regiments are full of opium eaters."[2]

The evidence does not bear out these statements. It is one of the grave omissions of the inquiry, that although it is shown that the Indian Government, in preparing for the Royal Commission, sent out a circular letter to officers commanding regiments and batteries of the native army, inquiring as to the extent to which opium was used,[3] the returns as a whole were never forthcoming or accounted for. Such details as were given showed that the use is exceptional, not general, in the Sikh regiments; and that the habit has a prejudicial effect, in cases of pneumonia more especially. Colonel Biscoe stated, "It is fallacious to take a percentage of Sikhs, because it is very rare for a young Sikh to take opium at all."[4] The habit is chiefly amongst middle-aged and old men. The general evidence from the Sikh States shows that taking opium before forty is considered objectionable, and "a species of licentiousness." The Report of the Commission states: "The true number of habitual consumers in the native army is probably not considerable."[5] It was further

[1] *R. C. Report*, i. Q. 872. [2] *Ibid.*, Q. 1559. [3] *Ibid.*, v. 366.
[4] *Ibid.*, Q. 17,571. [5] *Ibid.*, v. 123.

given in evidence, that all opium shops are closed by the authorities, when troops are on the march.[1]

To the Chinese, peace-loving though they be, the humiliations of their army must be hard to bear. The more so when they associate them with the spread of the "foreign drug." As long ago as 1836, Choo Tsun, Member of the Council, prayed the Emperor to stop the import of opium; because, if the camp be once "contaminated by it, the baneful influence will work its way, and the habit will be contracted beyond the power of reform. When the periodical times of desire for it come round, how can the victims—their legs tottering, their hands trembling, their eyes flowing with childlike tears—be able in any way to attend to their proper exercises? Or how can such men form strong and powerful legions? Under these circumstances, the military will become alike unfit to advance to the fight, or in a retreat to defend their posts. Of this there is clear proof in the instance of the campaign against the Yaou rebels, in the twelfth year of our sovereign's reign (1832). In the army sent to Leënchow, on that occasion, great numbers of the soldiers were opium smokers, so that, though their numerical force was large, there was hardly any strength to be found among them." Ever since there have been continual attempts to purify the army from this debilitating drug.

The fears and predictions of the native statesmen are restated by British consuls and others in the evidence collected in 1894, without a dissentient note as regards the military; and the Japanese war fulfilled them to the letter. Seeing the importance attached to military prowess, it is well to cite some of the

[1] *R. C. Report*, v. 17.

superabundant evidence regarding it. Writing to the Royal Commission, Consul Bullock says: "Chinese, so far as I know, are unanimous in agreeing that there is some loss of physical power occasioned by opium smoking." Ask a Chinese, which would win in a fight, a regiment of men allowed to smoke, or one of similar men who were prevented from doing so, and he will laugh at the simplicity of the question."[1] Consul Allen says: "The Brigadier-General in charge of the troops told me that he dismissed at once any soldier caught smoking opium. For all that I believe the accusation brought against the soldiers and underlings is not undeserved."[2] Mr. Archibald writes the mischief is not so apparent in sedentary life, "but in cases where men are called on to put forth effort at a moment's notice, to be in the hands of opium smokers is to ensure disaster."[3] Mr. James Jackson says: "If the habit continues to spread, I regard the Chinese race as doomed to decrepitude."[4] Consul Hurst adds: "As long as China remains a nation of opium smokers, there is not the least reason to fear that she will become a military power of any importance, as the habit saps the energies and vitality of the nation."[5]

The following evidence bears also upon the causes of China's humiliation before the Japanese:—Mr. J. Graham Brown: "At the time of anti-Russian excitement—on the march of fifty-four days to the capital of Chinese Turkestan—they raised three regiments in Lan-Chan of 1200 soldiers each. Out of these 1200 soldiers the natives expected that about 300 would arrive at Urumtzi; the others would die or desert on the road. The Hunan Regiments

[1] *R. C. Report*, v. 266. [2] *Ibid.*, v. 278. [3] P. 293.
[4] P. 302. [5] P. 321.

nominally do not smoke opium, and their officers threw this question in our teeth most bitterly." Yu-Keng-Pak writes: "How can China help being weak? Those who discuss the opium trade say that it does incalculable harm to China; it is from it that China is reduced to poverty and weakness. Surely England must shrink from the judgment that is passed on her behind her back.[1] Dr. Dudgeon writes: "There does not seem much hope for the rejuvenescence of China so long as this terrible evil remains in their midst."[2] Mr. Starkey, merchant (twenty-nine years in China), writes: "The opium habit is undermining society in this province, and the people are surely deteriorating. The Chinese soldiery and the Tartars are all opium smokers if not checked. The officers in every camp indulge in the pipe. As long as the smoking of opium in China is tolerated, the people will remain inert, and will thus never be a danger to other nations in Asia."[3] A native author writes: "The Supreme Ruler must have a meaning in causing opium smoking. He must intend to destroy the nation. There is no other way of accounting for the love of the Chinese for opium."[4]

General Mesny of the Chinese army, who writes apologetically of the "king of drugs," says: "Smokers as a rule cannot hold out as long as non-smokers without rest." "It is also an undoubted fact that opium smokers do not relish the frugal fare that suited them very well before they indulged in opium," and concludes: "It is no doubt a great pity that the Chinese should be so addicted to opium."[5] And another Chinese General, whom Consul Brenan says

[1] *R. C. Report*, v. 227. [2] *Ibid.*, v. 231. [3] P. 261.
[4] P. 265. [5] P. 246.

"has seen much service and is thoroughly qualified to give an opinion on the opium habit," writes: "The pseudo pleasure is obtained at the expense of natural contentment. As years go on the craving increases."[1]

As bearing immediately upon the defeat of the Chinese, Prince Galitzin, who for months together was with the Chinese armies, said at Edinburgh in December 1894: "It is true that the Japanese armies were well armed, and well led, but it is also true that the Chinese armies were so demoralised by the use of opium as to be incapable of offering an effectual resistance to any army whatever."

Dr. Fryer, scientific adviser to the Kung-nan arsenal at Shanghai, in a letter to Dr. Maxwell (24th January 1895), wrote: "Japan, with her total exemption from the use of the drug, is proving more than a match for China, now almost overpowered by it. Hitherto the advances of Japan have been almost like a parade, and her measures have been slowly but effectually carried out, in spite of all China can do, with her opium-ruined and enervated army and navy." Superintendent Jürgens wrote from the South Yangtse Forts: "If there are useless men upon this earth, I would without hesitation say that the opium smokers are. . . . A soldier that smokes opium is frightfully lazy, the biggest liar and the greatest coward in the ranks. If such a fellow stands before me in the early morning, he looks a being that has lost all his wits in the sea."[2] C. C. Hwang, a surgeon of the New Chinese Army Corps, writes: "The rule is, that if any soldier is found smoking opium, he is at once dismissed from the service.[3] It is well known

[1] *R. C. Report*, v. 222.

[2] *Opinions of over One Hundred Physicians*, p. 78. [3] *Ibid.*, p. 79.

to the Chinese military authorities that a soldier who smokes opium is quite useless as such. The Japanese apparently know it also very well, and besides know the advance this vice had made amongst officers and men of the old Chinese army."

K. L. Kwan, Chief Surgeon, Yangtse Forts, writes: "Opium smoking also affects the nerves of their eyes, causing them to aim the gun untrue; moreover, it makes them feel lazy, and general weakness prevails, so they cannot stand up long enough to finish their gymnastic exercises. They also find it painful to throw out their chests, and have a shortness of breathing as well. This pernicious drug is a curse to the people of China."[1] Mrs. Bishop mentions that "Chinese several times said to me, that the reason the Japanese beat them was, that they were more vigorous men, owing to the rigid exclusion of opium from Japan."[2] And so the proofs might be multiplied.[3]

[1] *Opinions of over One Hundred Physicians*, p. 80.

[2] *The Yangtse Valley and Beyond.*

[3] Appendix I. note 11.

CHAPTER III

UNBIASSED WITNESSES

ON the general question of the effects of the drug on the people of the country concerned, it is possible to collect a great variety of opinions; but it is very rare to find authorities who speak with personal knowledge of the social life of the Chinese, who do not admit the gravity of the habit and the evils attending it.

An importer of the drug may say, "it must have some beneficial effect," and paragraphs may go the round of the press, comparing it to the smoking of tobacco, or the drinking of tea; but these cannot satisfy any serious inquiry. The evidence even of the casually selected witnesses of the Royal Commission is decisive as to great injury resulting from the vice, but it is well to go beyond this to authorities wholly independent of any such collecting and collating agency. The conclusions of present and recent residents and observers with unusual facilities for forming their opinions, given in this chapter, form a body of evidence which cannot, it is submitted, be shaken.

Mr. Archibald Colquhoun has been quoted as a vigorous defender of the Opium War. His personal testimony as to the habit is shown in the following passages, viz. :—

"I am not among those who can defend the

practice, for I have witnessed under exceptional circumstances—on the march with soldiers and muleteers, or living with peasant and trader, entertained in the official yamen, or lodging in the common hostelry—its evil effects on the people of China. On the more southern people of Tong-king, Hunan, etc., the result is more rapid, and the effect more fatal. . . . I am convinced that the habit is pernicious, capable of great abuse, and saps away the energies of body and mind." [1]

Mrs. Archibald Little's works on China are those of a British authoress with a great knowledge of the country on which she writes. Her descriptions of the people are evidently as impartial as they are full and accurate.[2] Mrs. Little speaks of travelling for five days through a perfect flower-show of poppies, and in pointing out the consequences, cites a friend who wrote ten years ago to the effect that rice was 7 cash per basin. Now the poppy takes its place, and the rice costs 20 cash, whilst the people are wretchedly poor and ill-fed. "As a rule," Mrs. Little says, "in the country each family tills its own bit of ground, and where opium has not spread its poisonous influence, has held the same for centuries." On entering a large provincial town, the writer continues:[3] "Inside the city it is still all dark and dank, and all is pervaded by a sickly sweet odour, the emanation from the opium pipe; while the lean ribs and yellow faces of opium smokers controvert, without the need of words, all the scientific assertions about non-volatilisation of opium poison. With opium dens all over the place, with exquisite opium pipes, and all the coquetries of the opium trade and other accessories in the houses of the rich, how is it

[1] Colquhoun, p. 74. [2] *Intimate China.* [3] *Ibid.*, p. 66.

that we all give warning to a servant when we hear that he has taken to opium? How is it that treasure on a journey is never confided to a coolie who smokes? How is it that every man shrinks with horror from the idea of an opium-smoking wife; and this in a land in which all important business dealings are concluded over the opium couch,—where, indeed, alone is privacy to be obtained; and in which all important military posts are confided to opium smokers, not to speak of most of the important civil offices. . . . There is, it is true, an immense difference between the man who smokes and him who has the *yin* (craving), that must at all costs be satisfied; just as there is at home between the moderate drinker and the dipsomaniac. But in China people refuse to employ a moderate smoker to sweep out their rooms."

Dr. Arthur H. Smith, from his American standpoint, holds apparently that the past wars had to be. His books embody very valuable studies into the sociology of the Far East. He speaks of "the disintegrating forces which operate in the Chinese family" as "more efficient in the homes of the poor than of the rich"; and adds, "but there are two of these agencies which imply a certain degree of prosperity ere they can be fully developed—the gambling and the opium habit, twin vices of the Chinese race. Each leads by swift and relentless steps to destruction, and in each case there comes at last what is virtually a paralysis of the will, making amendment impossible."[1]

The author carries this condemnation of the vice yet further, in another volume on the subject of "Physical Vitality," viz.: "The only permanent and

[1] *Village Life in China*, p. 321.

effective check upon the rapid increase of the Chinese population appears to be the confirmed use of opium, a foe to the Chinese race as deadly as war, famine, or pestilence.[1]

Consul E. H. Parker was classed by the Commission as an apologist for the drug. In any case, his works on China are valuable as those of a frank, fair-minded, and kindly observer. Writing of Ssuch'uan, Mr. Parker says: "Where opium was so cheap and easily obtainable, less harm seemed to be done than where the expensive Indian drug is imported."[2] One of the somewhat illusory excuses for native-grown opium has been that it was less deleterious than the Indian. Mr. Parker records "that both in Cheh-kiang and Fuh-kien, the evidences of misery caused by indulgence in expensive Indian opium seemed to me much plainer than elsewhere. My bearers were always half-starved, ragged ruffians, but almost always smokers. Often I reached a village where no fowls, eggs, or sugar were to be got, where not even rice was procurable; yet I invariably saw the inevitable garish lamp sign, with the equivalent for 'Indian opium' upon it."

Referring to districts in North Ssuch'uan, the author alludes more than once to the signs of great poverty.[3] "What struck me most . . . is the shabby and abject look of the people, compared with the richness of the land. Who enjoys all these rich crops?"

Perhaps no other writer refers more frequently, it may be said, curiously, to the sensitiveness of the Chinese regarding the habit. As an outsider, disposed to make the best of things, this fact

[1] *Chinese Characteristics*, p. 145. [2] *China, Past and Present.*

evidently puzzled him. "All opium smokers seemed to be rather ashamed of the habit. I never heard any one of either sex go so far as to praise or recommend it. . . . Certainly the feeling of shame, weak and unsteady though it may be, is much greater in the moderate opium smoker than in the excessive English drinker."[1] And again, "How is it all Chinese are ashamed of it, or, if not, why do all try to conceal and apologise for it?"[2] On this head—and the fact, if fairly considered, means much—no testimony could be more fair and conclusive.

In his many references to the vice, Mr. Parker continually insists on the joint responsibility of China along with England in the matter. "It is unquestionable that the smoking of opium does a great deal of physical harm, and causes a vast waste of money and energy; but even the Chinese admit that the initial responsibility for its use by smokers was as much theirs as ours. They have deliberately extended the evil by allowing the undisguised cultivation of the poppy on a wholesale scale. Indian opium does not represent one-fourth of the total consumption."[3]

When the evidence occurs in natural course from travellers, without any thought of results to the Indian revenue before their eyes, it is continually strong and sweeping in its condemnation of the opium habit. An interesting book, published recently, by Captain Welby, gives an account of an adventurous journey by himself and Lieutenant Malcolm.[4] On reaching Northern China, one page bears the heading, "*Opium, the Curse of China.*"

[1] *China, Past and Present*, p. 177.
[2] *Ibid.*, p. 190.
[3] *China, her History, etc.*, p. 92.
[4] *Through Unknown Thibet.*

Captain Welby says their Hindoo servant summed up the Chinese in the words: "All the women are lame, and the men rotten with opium." "As was shown before the Opium Commission in 1894, the good effects of the drug more than counterbalance the evil effects (in India), but there can be no mistake as to its being an unmitigated curse in China, where many of its slaves would gladly give it up if they could; but the craving it induces is too strong to be combated by nature alone."

The late Mrs. Bishop, a world-wide and clear-sighted traveller, bears witness. "There are no apologists for the use of opium, except among foreigners. The smokers themselves are ashamed of their slavery. All alike condemn it, and regard opium as a curse as well as a vice, and from all which came under my observation in fifteen months, I fully agree with them."[1] And again: "It is admitted by the natives of Ssuch'uan, that one great reason of the deficient food supply which led to the famine and distress in the eastern part of the province in 1897, was the giving up so much ground to the poppy, that there was no longer a margin left on which to feed the population in years of a poor harvest." Mrs. Bishop only repeats the desolate picture of another famine-stricken district, very vividly presented by James Gilmour of Mongolia. The explorations in China, in 1900, of Colonel Manifold, Indian Medical Service, described in a paper read before the British Association, confirm the previous writers quoted. The province of Yun-nan, according to Colonel Manifold "is very rich in minerals, which have as yet been worked by inadequate and primitive means. The

[1] *Yangtse Valley and Beyond.*

present population will never do much, as their energy is sapped by the abuse of opium." "A long acquaintance with the uses to which the people of India put the drug had led me to believe it did little harm, and to be sceptical of the stories I heard of it in China. . . . In Yunnan I saw practically the whole of the population given up to its abuse. The ravages it is making in men, women, and children are deplorable, and though entirely out of sympathy with violent views of faddists, and the extreme measures they would resort to in India, . . . in Yunnan I felt that any measures would be justified that would save an intelligent and civilised population from being wholly demoralised in physique and energy, and from being ultimately extirpated by the fatal abuse of a valuable drug. The soil and climate of Yunnan are suited to the cultivation of a good quality of opium, and little of the Indian product is imported into the province."

The great Asiatic explorer, Sven Hedin, when he reached the confines of China, wrote: "More than once, whilst resting in the mission stations, I have been awakened in the middle of the night by a loud knocking at the gate. In such and such a house a man lay dying. He had just taken a dose of opium. Off went the missionary in hot haste with the stomach-pump, and so saved the man's life. . . . The habit of opium smoking is fearfully common, and quite as much practised by women as by men. The number of children who have died from having crept up on their parents' opium sofa and sucked at their pipes, is little short of appalling."[1]

With this may be joined Mr. Parker's striking

[1] *Through Asia*, p. 1246.

statement respecting suicides. "When I was at Chung-king, the C.I. missionaries used to 'save' opium suicides at the rate of two or three a week; this number being a mere fraction of the 'short-sighted ones,' as the Chinese call them, in one ward of the city."[1]

It will have been noticed how frequently in all classes of evidence comparisons are made between the opium habit in China and drinking stimulants in Europe. Space will not allow of the repetition involved in bringing these together, but two or three further testimonies on this special head ought not to be omitted here.

Archdeacon Moule, speaking at Lambeth Palace in 1902, after more than twenty-five years' experience in China, said: "It has been said, 'You have your own curse of drink in England, you must let the opium trade alone until you have got rid of the curse of drink.' A strange piece of moral reasoning! But there is no comparison whatsoever between the two questions. . . . There is no use and abuse of opium; it is all abuse. In the eyes of the Chinese the use of opium as a luxury and stimulant, as distinguished from its use as a medicinal drug, is a vice from first to last. Alcohol and opium do not stand on the same platform at all."

Mr. Montagu Beauchamp, after fourteen years spent amongst the inland Chinese, in contrasting the hold of drink and of opium on their victims, said: "People are expecting to find the same troubles as come from drink—wife-beating, brawling, and fighting. I would say again and again, that the evils of opium are far worse than the

[1] *John Chinaman*, p. 20.

evils of drink. . . . The Chinese themselves not only regard opium as an unmixed evil, but incipient smokers are always ashamed of the indulgence."

Archdeacon Wolfe has described the degradation of an opium-smoking town as "of that peculiar and intensely low and hardened type, so that, humanly speaking, it seems almost impossible to make any impression of a moral or spiritual nature upon the inhabitants of a place given up to the vice of opium smoking."

Dr. A. G. Reid, of the Chinese Imperial Customs Service, Hankow, said: "Opium differs from alcoholic indulgence by the absolute necessity of having a daily quantity. A drunkard may abstain until means accumulate to enable him to purchase liquids, and may do his work efficiently in the intervals, but the opium smoker must have his daily stimulant, or he breaks down. To obtain it there is no sacrifice he will not stoop to; even his wife is readily lent out for prostitution, to provide means to buy the drug."

It would be tedious to the reader to present anew the evidence to be gathered wholesale as to the deteriorating effects of the drug on outdoor labour, and the wage-earning classes generally. One of the most telling and impartial of recent reports on the subject has been given by Mr. Ross Skinner to the mine-owners of the Rand, on his investigations in the East in search of labour for the gold mines of South Africa.[1] In concluding his remarks on the Chinese, the question is put, "Is opium necessary to the coolies?" The reply is as follows:—"According to the opinion offered

[1] *Affairs of the Transvaal, etc.*, 1904.

by many experienced Europeans, and nearly all the Chinese interviewed, it is not necessary. By its introduction, if it is permitted, the employer would only be lowering the standard of labour. All coolies showing signs of opium smoking should be rejected on the China side. Instead of opium, plenty of Chinese tobacco, for pipes and cigarettes, should be placed within their reach. This tobacco is very cheap."

So British capitalists in South Africa reject men in China as inefficient, by reason of a habit promoted by British opium, in the interests of the Indian revenue. Wherever the drug lowers the standard of labour, it is certain that it lowers much besides. If this Report had dealt with English navvies, it would not have advised the mine-owners to engage no labourers who were not teetotalers.

CHAPTER IV

SIR ROBERT HART AND HON. CHESTER HOLCOMBE

THE status and exceptional knowledge of two officials entitle their opinions to thoughtful consideration. No recent writer of other nationality than our own has given the conclusions of a long and responsible service in China with more freshness and force than Mr. Chester Holcombe, late Secretary of the Chinese Legation and Acting Minister of the United States. A new edition of his book, entitled *China's Past and Future*, has been made easily accessible by Mr. Broomhall, whose additions also add much to its value.

"No true picture of modern China, in its attitude toward progress, in the opinions and feelings which dominate the lives and control the conduct of the people, from the palace to the mud hut, toward all men and all things that are foreign, can be correctly painted unless opium is mixed with the colours."[1]

"It is quite unnecessary to vilify the missionary body, in order to discover the cause of this bitter anti-foreign feeling so universal in China." "While other causes have co-operated to generate and sustain it, the largest single cause, the most important factor, is the source, history, and results of opium. And that man must be blind indeed to the ordinary operations of human nature who could expect any other result. Let any intelligent, fair-minded reader put himself into the place of the Chinese, run over in his mind the history of the use of this narcotic poison in that great Oriental empire, and then decide what the resultant and inevitable feeling must be toward the authors of such a scourge."[1]

"The writer listened for some time one afternoon to a missionary, addressing a large gathering of natives upon the street of an interior city of China. Near by and upon the outskirts of the crowd stood a middle-aged Chinese, evidently of the literary class, and having a countenance of much intelligence. Physically he was a mere walking skeleton. The tiny opium jar in his hand, the expression of his eyes, and the brown stain upon one of his fingers, all marked him as a slave to the narcotic poison. After listening a few minutes to the preacher, he turned away with an indescribable scowl of hatred upon his face, and snarled out as he left: 'You foreigners exhort us to virtue! First, take away your opium, and then talk to us about your Ya Su' (Jesus)."[2]

"The modern great Chinese wall is mainly constructed of chests of opium."

As to possible remedies, Mr. Holcombe suggests: "The last and yet most important, as well as difficult of these preliminary measures of reform . . . consists in weeding out and removing from the official service of China every person who is a victim of the opium habit. . . . It means the retirement to private life of a startling percentage of the entire official staff of the empire. It is imperative, because honesty and efficiency of service and opium smoking

[1] *The Real Chinese Question*, p. 286. [2] *Ibid.*, p. 287.

are incompatible and contradictory terms. The two simply cannot exist in the same person. . . . No man of affairs in China or elsewhere trusts an employee who is an opium smoker, and never employs such a person if any other is obtainable."[1]

"An official warning, extending over some two or three years, to the effect that persons still using the drug after the expiration of the limit would be excluded from public service, would probably be necessary."[2]

"It is humiliating to any one who has English blood in his veins to recall the facts, and to discover that the British Government is loudest and most imperative in the demand for reforms, while that Government is, in the main, alone responsible for fastening a vice upon China which renders any reform difficult to the verge of impossibility."[3]

Finally, Mr. Holcombe urges: "There can be but one wise or politic rule by which to shape our conduct towards the Chinese: *To treat them as we expect other men to treat us.*"[4]

By universal consent, there is no person living, of Western birth and training, who can vie with Sir Robert Hart in his intimate knowledge and mastery of the civic side of Chinese life and character. On the opium question he long maintained an attitude of official reserve. The threatened disintegration of China has impelled him to express freely the convictions he has formed during upwards of forty years of official life in China, and his book is undoubtedly the work which should weigh above all others with Englishmen who desire wise guidance as to the relations between the two countries.[5] With regard to

[1] *The Real Chinese Question*, p. 382. [2] *Ibid.*, p. 385. [3] P. 385.
[4] P. 29. [5] *These from the Land of Sinim.*

the opium vice itself, it may be observed that Sir Robert Hart's views are in truth those of Lord Elgin and of Captain Elliot, before him. As we have seen, Lord Elgin when he reached China, referred to opium as "a thing deplorable from what he saw in the streets; from the emaciation and wretchedness of the opium smokers he came across." Sir Thomas Wade, though engaged, as he put it, on the British side, said: "No man who has lived the time that I have in China, and who has been in contact with Chinese of all kinds, can deny that the excessive use of opium in that country is an exceeding misfortune to that country." Sir Robert Hart's utterances are charged with a knowledge of the best native thought, endorsed by his own experience and conclusions.

In order that the reader may see the relative position which Sir Robert Hart assigns to the opium question, and give full weight to his opinions respecting the future relations of Europe and China, some lengthy quotations are unavoidable. The Chinese, Sir Robert Hart describes as an "intelligent, cultivated race, sober, industrious, and on its own lines civilised, homogeneous in language, thought, and feeling, which numbers some 400,000,000 lives in its own ring-fence, and covers a country made up of fertile land and teeming waters . . . this race . . . is looking forward to the day when it in turn will be strong enough to revert to its old life again, and do away with foreign intercourse, interference, and intrusion. . . . Every member is tingling with Chinese feeling—'China for the Chinese, and out with the foreigners.'"[1]

"In fifty years' time there will be millions of Boxers in serried ranks and war's panoply, at the

[1] *These from the Land of Sinim*, p. 51.

call of the Chinese Government: there is not the slightest doubt of that!"[1]

"At first, the foreign merchant was in China on sufferance, and had to abide by local practice, and accept local rule. Then came the opium and *Arrow* wars, and the reigns of the Emperors Tao-Kwang and Heen-fang saw, added to the original laws and tariffs of the empire, the tariffs and regulations of foreign trade, and the stipulations of treaties. . . . The most striking among the treaty clauses are those which, under the heading 'Extra-territoriality,' withdraw foreigners from Chinese control, and place them under their own national officials in China. . . . It has always been felt to be offensive and humiliating, and has ever a disintegrating effect, leading the people, on one hand, to despise their own Government and officials, and, on the other, to envy and dislike the foreigner withdrawn from native control."[2]

"The position the Chinese take up may be said to be this: 'We did not invite you foreigners here; you crossed the seas of your own accord and more or less forced yourselves on us.

"'To the trade we sanctioned you added opium smuggling, and when we tried to stop it you made war on us. We do not deny that Chinese consumers kept alive a demand for the drug, but both consumption and importation were illegal and prohibited; when we found it was ruining our people and depleting our treasury, we vainly attempted to induce you to abandon the trade, and we then had to take action against it ourselves. War ensued; we were no warriors, and you won, and then dictated treaties, which gave you Hong Kong, and opened several

[1] *These from the Land of Sinim*, p. 55.

[2] *Ibid.*, p. 65.

ports, while opium still remained contraband. Several years of peaceful intercourse followed, and then Hong Kong began to trouble us; it was originally ceded to be a careening place for ships simply, but . . . it became a smuggling centre; in your treaties you had undertaken a certain control of any junk traffic that should spring up, but when that traffic became considerable you dropped the promised control, and our revenue suffered.

"'Originally uninhabited, Hong Kong now became the home of numerous Chinese settlers, many of them outlaws who dare not live on the mainland; these became British subjects, and you gave the British flag to their junks, which were one day British and another Chinese, just as it suited their purpose, and out of this came the *Arrow* war, followed by new treaties, additional ports, legalised opium, and fresh stipulations, in their turn the causes of fresh troubles. Whether it was that we granted you privileges or that you exacted concessions, you have treated the slightest mistakes as violations of treaty rights; and, instead of showing yourselves friendly and considerate, you insult us by charges of bad faith and demand reparation and indemnities.

"'Your legalised opium has been a curse in every province it penetrated, and your refusal to limit or decrease the import has forced us to attempt a dangerous remedy: we have legalised native opium,—not because we approve of it, but—to compete with and drive out the foreign drug; and it *is* expelling it, and when we have only the native production to deal with, and thus have the business in our own hands, we hope to stop the habit in our own way.'"[1]

[1] *These from the Land of Sinim*, p. 119.

"Sixty years of treaty relations have culminated in this Boxer movement: how account for such a finale?"

Sir Robert Hart's warnings may close for us with the following:—"Russia may yet be the first to restore to China her sovereign rights, and so cement for ever her neighbourly friendship."

If, after all these wrong-doings and misunderstandings, it is asked, where is the possible remedy? this experienced Minister of East and West alike, replies: "The only satisfactory answer that much thought suggests, is, that the Golden Rule might be worth a trial; do away with the existing anomaly, and let 'Do unto others as you would have others do to you' be given an international application!"[1] The crucial point is the principle of extra-territoriality, and Sir Robert Hart advises non-China to meet China frankly in this matter. "Respect, and not contempt; conciliation, and not dictation; appreciation, and not differential treatment,—try this prescription, and you will have a healthy body politic. And until this is done, it will be the reverse."

[1] *These from the Land of Sinim*, p. 141.

CHAPTER V

THE VOICE OF CHINA

THE two countries have mismanaged many things because they have not understood one another. It is a question now whether the diplomatists of China have not a subtler insight into Western thought and conduct than is shown by our public men, with very few exceptions, into the minds of the Celestials. Until Great Britain respects Chinese opinion, the history of our relationship must ever be one of blunders and regrets. In matters of health, of excise, of custom, of morals, each people must be its own judge; it is a transgression of all right relationship between nations for one government to force its standards in any of these matters upon another. The old Confucian saying still applies: "A gentleman regards what is right, a vulgar person what will pay."

Sir Ernest Satow is reported to have said recently at Tientsin: "The Chinese intellect is in every way on a level with that of the West . . . whatever else might be responsible for keeping them apart, intellectual incapacity is not to blame."

All leading authorities, who speak from long personal knowledge of the people, give impressions of their capacity, industry, and self-governing qualities far beyond those ordinarily entertained by Englishmen. At present the West is filled with wonder at the startling progress of Japan. Employers of labour and commercial men, at home and in the Colonies, who have had dealings with both races usually give a decided preference to the Chinese, for endurance in sustained labour, and more especially for fidelity in fulfilling engagements.

The case for the opium habit in China must stand or fall by the verdict of the conscience of the Chinese people.

It is on record that the first Chinese ambassador to this country asked Professor Legge of Oxford, as an accomplished Chinese scholar, whether he thought China or England the better country from the moral standpoint. Professor Legge said "England," and, in describing the incident, adds: "I never saw a man more surprised. He pushed his chair back, got upon his feet, walked across the room once or twice, and said, 'Looking at them from the moral standpoint England is the better country of the two! How then does England insist upon our taking her opium?'"[1]

The greatest political figure of recent times in China, Li Hung Chang, was mistrusted by his own countrymen, because of his alleged friendliness to foreigners. According to the Empress, "he blazed his name at the Court, uplifted his country, and put down the Great Rebellion."[2] According to outsiders, he was a great opportunist, wishing well to his land, but willing to accomplish his aims by doubtful means. There is no reason to question the sincerity of his reply to a memorial of the Anti-Opium Society in 1881.[3] He spoke of the moral objections to the trade, while showing between the

[1] *R. C. Report*, i. Q. 181.

[2] Mrs. Little, *Li Hung Chang*, p. 328.

[3] *Ibid.*, p. 125.

lines that the financial aspects loomed largely with him:

"Opium is a subject in the discussion of which England and China can never meet on common ground. China views the whole question from a moral standpoint, England from a fiscal. England would sustain a source of revenue in India, while China contends for the lives and prosperity of her people. The ruling motive with China is to repress opium by heavy taxation everywhere, whereas with England the manifest object is to make opium cheaper, and thus increase the demand in China. . . . In discussing opium taxation, a strange concern has been shown in behalf of China, lest she should sacrifice her revenue; and yet objection and protest are made against rates which could be fixed for collection at the ports and in the interior. The Indian Government is in the background at every official discussion of the opium traffic, and every proposed arrangement must be forced into a shape acceptable to that Government and harmless to its revenues. This is not as it should be." . . .

That China is not free to deal with opium as she thinks fit, is the point to which Li Hung Chang returns in his negotiations with the Marquis Ito at the close of the China-Japanese war. The following conversation is taken from the official Report of the fourth interview at Shimonoseki (10th April 1895):—

H. E. Ito: "'Our naval and land forces can bear any hardship. It was cold last year in the north, and everybody thought Japanese soldiers could not stand it. But the whole winter through they suffered no disadvantage, and were successful everywhere.'

H. E. Li: "'Formosa is very malarious. You lost

many lives there before. Most Formosans smoke opium in order to counteract the effects of malaria.'

H. E. Ito: "'When we take Formosa we shall forbid opium smoking.'

H. E. Li: "'It is an old habit with the Formosans.'

H. E. Ito: "'Yet Formosa was populated before opium was produced. We have kept opium out of Japanese ports by the most stringent prohibitions, and have consequently no opium smokers.'

H. E. Li: "'I admire that. . . . Great Britain insists on bringing opium into our ports. We have increased the duties, but what more can we do?'

H. E. Ito: "'The duty is much too low. Treble the amount would be none too much.'

H. E. Li: "'We have spoken of it frequently, but Great Britain will not consent.'

H. E. Ito: "'Opium smokers are all indolent; you cannot make good soldiers of them.'

H. E. Li: "'Great Britain has forced opium on us and we cannot stop it.'"

Chang Chih-Tung, now declared to be China's greatest Viceroy, has probably ruled more subjects than any European monarch save those of Great Britain and Russia. Mrs. Little testifies that wherever he has held great place he has left a school of ardent reformers behind him. Intensely patriotic, and a devoted adherent of the Confucian wisdom, he fearlessly protected the lives of the Christians in the last Boxer outbreak. Like Sir Robert Hart, he came to the rescue of China with a book in the hour of her need.[1] This appeal, addressed to his own countrymen, contains passages which almost re-echo the warnings of the prophet Amos to his people.

In dealing with opium there is no uncertainty of utterance, no balancing of pros and cons. "Cast out the poison! The foreign drug (opium) is debasing the homes and sweeping away the lives of our people. Cut it off, root and branch. . . . Know the shame of not being like Japan."[1]

"It is not foreign intercourse that is ruining China, but this dreadful poison. Oh, the grief and desolation it has wrought to our people! Opium has spread with frightful rapidity and heart-rending results through the provinces. Millions upon millions have been struck down by the plague. In its swift, deadly course it is spreading devastation everywhere, wrecking the minds and eating away the strength and wealth of its victims. The ruin of the mind is the most woeful of its many deleterious effects. The poison enfeebles the will, saps the strength of the body, renders the consumer incapable of performing his regular duties, and unfit for travel from one place to another. It consumes his substance and reduces the miserable wretch to poverty, barrenness, and senility."[2] . . . "Many thoughtful Chinese are apprehensive that opium will finally extirpate the race, and efforts are being made to mitigate the curse."[3]

"All the countries of the world recoil with disgust at the idea of smoking this vile, ill-smelling, poisonous stuff. Mencius says, 'If one has not the sense of shame, in what can he be equal to other men? If a man will not understand in what misfortune consists, disgrace is sure to follow; but if he will only face the difficulty, happiness will ensue.'"[4]

Chang Chih-Tung faces the opium difficulty, and would master it through anti-opium societies, in which

[1] *China's only Hope*, p. 23.
[2] *Ibid.*, p. 72–3.
[3] P. 75.
[4] P. 77.

members pledge themselves against the habit, "masters prohibit their servants, teachers their scholars, generals their troops, landlords their tenants, merchants their assistants, and foremen their journeymen." He would also bring learning to bear on the opium evil for men of discernment and the younger generation. In ten years' time, when the young and wealthy have grown up and become established in life, they will be qualified to control the customs of their subordinates. In twenty years more opium will be eradicated. "In the deadly drug we are self-steeped, seeking poverty, imbecility, death, destruction. From these we might be delivered if Confucius and Mencius could live again to teach the Chinese a proper sense of shame, and inaugurate a better condition of things for our country now under the power of this awful curse."[1] An able and patriotic statesman would not write burning words like these, unless he felt the need of his country to be urgent.

With all his zeal the Viceroy shows marked fairness towards the foreigner. Indeed it is a question whether the Chinese are not much fairer to Western opinion than we are to the wisdom of the East. Take, for instance, the following passage written by the general manager of the Soochow Salt Gabelle:[2]—

"Yet again, there are those who say, 'Suppose . . . opium cultivation be prohibited in India; already throughout China its production has been established, and thus to prohibit in India and permit in China only cuts off a source of income, and the trouble is still not remedied.' This may be true, and yet the whole matter really depends upon the British and American Governments. If there is a desire to

[1] *China's Only Hope*, *p.* 77.

[2] *Opinions of over One Hundred Physicians*, Introduction.

prohibit opium they should communicate with the *Tsung-li Yamen*, and in concert come to an agreement concerning a restriction of poppy cultivation. The woe that comes to China is not only recognised by the Government, but every one that uses it is aware of its hurtfulness; thus when both rulers and people are of one mind it could most easily be accomplished."

"Now, in China there are very many among the upper classes who seem to be in ignorance concerning the true state of affairs, and are not willing to blame the Chinese for their fault in using opium, but ascribe the real cause of the whole trouble to the avariciousness of foreigners, and thus look upon them with hatred. Also, the ignorant masses, having even intenser antipathy toward them, we continually see anti-missionary outbreaks and riots, by which are caused much trouble and perplexity."

The way in which the food question keeps recurring in lamentations over the opium habit, is well illustrated by the Censor Yew-Peh-Ch'wan in a memorial written so far back as 1870:—

"The people are the foundation of the State, and food the heaven of the people, and no greater obstacle to the production of food exists than the cultivation of the poppy. Having spread into other provinces from Kan-suh, the original seat of its growth, the plant is now found occupying land to the extent of upwards of 10,000 mow in each district. According to the calculation that has been made, 3 mow (½ acre) of rich land will produce sufficient grain for one man's support; applying this calculation to a single province, where more than 1,000,000 mow of land are thus withdrawn from productive cultivation, hundreds of thousands of persons are found to be deprived in this way of the means of subsistence. . . . The very children have a rhyming proverb on this subject:—

> "'Everywhere the flower blows,
> Sleep, or waking, still it grows;
> Reap the profit while 'tis there—
> For the future who shall care?'

"In their greed of gain the inferior classes lose all sight of injurious consequences; but unless radical measures be instituted to cut off the evil at its source, and pluck it up by the roots, the people's food and livelihood cannot be duly fostered." . . .

"The Censor reiterates the statement that the poppy is usurping lands imperatively required for the production of food, to such an extent that people have actually committed suicide under pressure of starvation, with money in their hands ready to buy food where none was to be had; . . . the evil caused by opium smoking is worse than the destruction caused by floods, or the ravages of wild beasts. On these grounds the Censor beseeches the Empress Regent and the Emperor to proclaim stringent prohibition of the growth of the poppy."[1]

In gauging public opinion on topics of the day, the foreigner is handicapped by the absence of popular light literature. The newpaper press is still in its infancy, and literature the prerogative of university men. But every Chinese understands a picture; a poster on a wall has more than once been responsible for a rebellion. Prints on sale at every village bookstall furnish the most accurate outline of opium smoking in Chinese perspective. The popular biographer has illustrated scene by scene the

[1] Turner, p. 295.

stereotyped stages in the smoker's career, from luxury and independence to public disgrace, domestic squalor, and final destitution and death. Several sets are known of these Chinese versions of Hogarth's *Rake's Progress*. The baldness of execution only emphasises the moral of the tragedy. Missionaries have sometimes tried to discover the other side to this picture. The Rev. Arnold Foster tells how he picked up at random from a street bookstall, three tracts on opium; all were non-Christian, one strongly anti-foreign in tone, and all alike took up their parable bitterly against smoking. The missionary then applied to one of the opium-smoking literati for the other side, and was greeted with the response: "There is no other side; I never met with any book that spoke favourably of opium, I do not think you will find such a book." This view is confirmed by the late Professor Legge's evidence: "I never, even among opiumists themselves, heard a man who had a word to say by way of apology or excuse for his habit."[1] Another missionary states that "in the popular moral literature of the Chinese, sold in the form of tracts in the streets of all large cities, opium smoking is commonly classified with licentiousness, gambling, and vice."

In the modern revolutionary movements, whether Taiping or Boxer, the opium habit has been one of the existent evils denounced. Mr. Grant Duff speaking of the great Taiping uprising, said, "We know that hostility to the poppy was one of the many strange characteristics of that terrible rebellion, misnamed 'The Great Peace,' which lately desolated so many cities in the Flowery Land." The celebrated Hunan Tracts, which prompted the anti-Christian

[1] *R. C. Report*, i. 14.

and anti-foreign outbreak of 1891, contain, behind many scurrilous and hopelessly untrue accusations, glimpses of genuine sorrow and anger at the British drug trade. Japan is praised for having "bravely forbidden opium and Christianity!" The following is one of the calls to amendment:—

"India raises 30 million taels of revenue from the opium which the Chinese use. If China did not import it, she would be richer by so many millions annually. With the exception of Hunan and Kiangsi, every province raises opium, and the more they raise the more the people smoke, till the Chinese all become opium smokers when living, and opium ghosts when dead. The remedy is to stop collecting any revenue, and strictly forbid the use of opium among the officials and people, then the people will be universally benefited; otherwise the mischief becomes worse every year."

It will be seen that the reluctance to derive a revenue from opium which has marked the Chinese Government throughout the course of her relations with Great Britain, is here reproduced from the standpoint of the people. In a Chinese brochure, compiled in answer to Protestant propaganda, the writer declared, it was absurd that persons so miserably deficient themselves should pretend to improve the inhabitants of the Celestial Empire. Of the great cardinal virtues the foreigner lacked benevolence, because for his own profit he introduced a poisonous drug; he also lacked righteousness, because he sent his fleet and armies to rob others of their possessions.[1]

There has recently been published, in two volumes,[2] the life of a Chinese scholar of Western Chang, a

[1] Brinkley, xi. 161.

[2] Mrs. H. Taylor, *One of China's Scholars, Pastor Hsi.*

village in Shan-si, "the entire province once wealthy, now cursed with the opium habit." Hsi, the scholar, by birth one of the literati, was a proud Confucian, the headman of his village, and an opium smoker. In the terrible famine which desolated the province in 1887–88, he won some prizes offered by a missionary for essays on Christian subjects, including the means of combating the opium habit. He became an earnest convert to Christianity, and after, a life and death struggle with the drug, he emerged a free man. Hsi took the usual remedies, but none alleviated his distress. He was prostrated by extreme depression, giddiness, shivering, aching pains, and burning thirst. For seven days and nights he scarcely tasted food, and was quite unable to sleep. The agony became almost unbearable, and all the while he knew that a few whiffs from the opium pipe would waft him forthwith into delicious dreams. In his most painful moments he would often groan aloud, "Though I die, I will never touch it again." He attributed his final deliverance to an exercise of divine power, and ever afterwards held that man's aid alone was insufficient for the purpose. Any one who wishes to realise the extent of the vice, and its hold over its victims, will do well to read these volumes. Though the opium question is only introduced incidentally, it confronts the reader everywhere. Pastor Hsi, as he became, worked out his own line of service to his fellows with extraordinary wisdom and intrepidity. He established no less than forty opium refuges in different districts for the cure of the habit, and left two hundred native Christian workers engaged in this ministry of healing and of mercy. The account of this gifted Chinese gentleman may inspire hope as to the possibility of China's redemption, and, at the same time, no stronger proof could be sought for of the extent of the calamity brought upon China by the rapid spread of opium smoking.

Mrs. Taylor describes a visit of one of the ladies of the C.I.M. in the great city of Shaohsing in 1886. In a large handsome house three women listened to her attentively for some time, until one of them, an old lady in her ninetieth year, caught the name of Jesus. She rose at once, and, coming to the missionary, cried, "Do not dare to mention that name again! . . . I will not hear another word. You foreigners come with opium in one hand, and Jesus in the other."[1]

The authoress also describes a riot in the province of Honan, which led to the closing of the first mission station. An infuriated mob, led by the scholars of the city, drove out the missionary, crying after him: "You burned our palace; you killed our Emperor; you poison our people; and now you come to teach us virtue."

A Cantonese, speaking of England's action towards his country, exclaimed, "If you wish to purify their crimes, all the fuel in the empire will not suffice, nor would the vast ocean be enough to wash out our resentment."

The bitterness of this invective may be largely due to ignorance, which, as every nation knows to its cost, is one of the most dangerous ingredients in international quarrels; but even the uneducated and misinformed know that they suffer from a great evil called "foreign smoke," and this knowledge is a very real source of provocation.

[1] *Pastor Hsi*, p. 112.

The gradual process of deterioration in the individual, through the habitual use of the drug, is set forth by Mr. King, a wealthy Chinese gentleman, in these words:—

"Opium lowers a man socially. The opium smoker is ill at ease in the presence of respectable men, but is happy in the company of other smokers. Thus he daily withdraws himself further from proper associations, and comes in contact with bad characters, until he ends in becoming a low-class man. This shows that opium leads to social disgrace. . . . If your honourable country can think of a plan to prevent opium from continuing to enter China, and remove the evil of one hundred years in one day, it will truly be to the happiness of 400 millions of people."[1]

The more hideous side of opium smoking, without which the intensity of feeling sometimes manifested cannot be understood, is brought out clearly in the evidence of two trained medical observers. By the side of facts like these, the impatient charges of exaggeration, advanced by persons who have little familiarity with the darker side of Chinese social life, become hollow and futile. Dr. Park writes:

"While I am penning these lines (10th December 1898), the crying of a wife who has been sold by an opium-smoking husband can be heard on the street in front of our house. He is one of our nearest neighbours, and I have known his wife ever since I came to China, when she was a pretty young girl. When he first began smoking, his mother, who was a widow, and had some property, and was also a teacher of embroidery in our mission, seeing no hope in life, took opium, and killed herself. He

[1] *Opinions of over One Hundred Physicians*, p. 31.

then sold off the houses one by one, then the furniture in the house, then his wife's clothes, then his grandmother's grave-clothes she had prepared against her burial, then his own clothes, and now he has sold his wife. The two children born to him have fortunately died, else he would sell them next. This is not an isolated case, but can be duplicated in every street in every city and town of this vast empire."[1]

Dr. Beebe gives a similar instance from his own experience. "My nearest neighbour for some time was an opium-smoking coolie. One by one he sold his three children to gratify his habit. At last he sold his wife, quitted his desolate house of reeds, and wandered a vagabond and thief to prey on the body politic."[2]

Dr. Park states that one charitable institution in Soochow treated 111 cases of opium suicides in six months; whilst in Voosih, a city of 20,000 inhabitants, 350 cases were treated in different institutions in one year.[3]

This chapter may fitly close with an appeal from some women to the men of Canton:

"Bowing down, we humbly beg that regulations may be established for the prohibition of opium in the villages. When in youth we went to the homes of our husbands, we did not suffer cold and hunger; but from the time that our husbands smoked opium, the children that were dressed—our sons in red, our daughters in green,—in the twinkling of an eye came to rags. Ornamental halls and grand houses vanished in smoke. Those who before protected their families are themselves reduced to the appearance of beggars.

[1] *Opinions of over One Hundred Physicians*, p. 87.

[2] *Ibid.*, p. 75.

[3] P. 43.

The beds have no coverlets, the dishes contain no food. Hungry, there is nothing to eat; cold, there is nothing to wear. The fault is surely with opium. In our distress it is difficult to give expression to the feelings that rend the breast. There is no tear we shed that is not red with blood.

"We have been long looking to you teachers (scribes) as the hope of the villages. Bowing down, we entreat you to take the matter in hand, so that men and women may be preserved alive. In this way, those who receive blessing from you will be more than a thousand families; the women and the children will rejoice, and the people of the villages be happy indeed."

CHAPTER VI

THE MISSIONARY FACTOR

PRINCE KUNG'S remarks to the British Minister, "Take away your opium and your missionaries, and you will be welcome," merits more consideration than it can receive here. The Chinese are born traders, and yet the main article of British trade has been the source of endless strife and poverty. They are naturally tolerant of religions, and yet the religion of love has roused their extremes of ferocity. The explanation is not far to seek in either case. If the drug had been as beneficial as it has been baneful, its history to patriotic Chinese would still be a history of overflowing humiliation. The linking of the religion of Jesus of Nazareth with the British opium trade is as bitter an irony as professing Christians have ever brought on themselves, which is saying much. To the Chinese, they came together, spread together, have been fought for together, and finally legalised together. Nor can the natives know that the humiliation of the combination is felt by many on Western shores as keenly as it is in their own land.

So far as Britain is concerned, the grim sequence described by Lord Salisbury, of "missionary, trader, consul, and gunboat," has not been literally fulfilled in China. The trader came on to the field first, and was very loth to give the missionary a foothold.

The Northumbrian, Robert Morrison, had to reach China in an American ship, and to live at first in an American factory. The East India Company only relented when it wanted a translator, and the office enabled him to give to the world his grammar and dictionary, two links for which East and West may alike be grateful. The course of events, as well as the Company, was opposed to mission work, and the number of Protestant converts at the close of the opium war might, it is said, have been counted on the fingers of one hand.[1]

Medical mission work, which "does not despise toilsome, disagreeable, and even loathsome tasks, if only good may result," came to the aid of other agencies, and out of this sprang the China Inland Mission, with widespreading rivulets of beneficence, and hundreds of lay-workers. The total number of Protestant missionaries and their wives in China in 1900 was estimated at 2785, and the converts at 112,000. There have been great accessions since.

It has been made already apparent that one of the greatest difficulties in the way of foreigners in China was the insistence on extra-territoriality by the Western powers. They refused to allow their subjects to be amenable to Chinese courts of justice. There is much to be said for this refusal. The courts were tainted with corruption, and their punishments were often barbarously cruel. It was against the grain for any ship's captain to hand a countryman over to the risk of torture, and possibly unmerited death. On the other hand, China had bitter cause for complaint. Her pride in her ancient civilisation was cut to the quick by the withdrawal of barbarians, who came uninvited to her shores, from her laws, and too

[1] *Rex Christus*, p. 149.

often from any laws whatsoever. When this had become a burning question, Vice-Consul Meadows writes from Ningpo of the outrages and offences of individual foreigners: "The unpunished existence of which would shake the best institutions of any State, provided such outrages and offences be strictly repressed," he thought "free ingress of foreigners into the country would not be by any means necessarily destructive of its peculiar system of government." An extraordinary reflection for a foreign official to have to make. Sir Robert Hart, commenting on Prince Kung's declaration anent opium and missionaries, cites the authority of "the still greater" Wen Hsiang, Grand Secretary, for the saying: "Do away with your extra-territoriality clause, and your missionaries and merchants may go where they please, and settle where they please; if your missionaries can make our people better, that will be our gain; if your merchants can make money, ours will share in the advantage."

Sir Robert, and there can be no more trustworthy authority, says of Prince Kung and Wen Hsiang: "What both objected to was neither Christianity nor commerce, but the *imperium in imperio*, which makes such difficulties for a State, and the class exemption which has in it so much that humiliates and disintegrates."[1] A people must be very long-suffering who can see foreigners insist that Chinese shall be punished with death where foreign life has been lost, whilst expecting China to be satisfied with a small fine, or short imprisonment, if it is Chinese life that has been ruthlessly taken. Chang Chih-Tung expresses it: "The murder of a foreigner by a Chinese is a very serious matter, but the killing of a Chinaman by a foreigner is a trivial thing."[2]

[1] Hart, p. 124.

[2] *China's Only Hope*, p. 143.

Missionaries scattered far and wide inland naturally brought this vexed question of extra-territoriality into special prominence; but further, the Chinese complained to the Powers in 1878 that "among the missionaries are some who . . . arrogate to themselves an official status, and interfere so far as to transact business that ought properly to be dealt with by the Chinese local authorities; while among their converts are some who look upon their being Christians as protecting them from the consequences of breaking the laws of their own country, and refuse to observe the rules which are binding on their neighbours."[1] It is easy to see the temptation for servants and converts of a foreigner to claim a like exemption with him from the operation of the Chinese law, but it is quite as easy to see that such claims would be altogether disintegrating to any well-ordered community. Some of the best of men find no difficulty in defending the wars of the past (even under such a title as "Rex Christus"), as necessary for reducing "the intolerable assumptions of the Chinese" to a more teachable spirit. To how many thoughtful Chinese must the assumptions of the foreigner have appeared equally intolerable.

The astute materialism common in China (and where is the Western people who can throw stones?), appraises all foreign influence at a commercial value. The knowledge that the barbarians have untold forces behind them, which have prevailed against China, and which may at any time be the undoing of any local magistrate, leads to devices which puzzle the most observing of the missionaries. It is said, for instance, that a litigant has been

[1] Hart, p. 179.

known to come successfully out of a law case simply by carrying a Bible in his hand, and putting it down on a table without saying a word. The mere association of the book with foreign power sufficed to turn the scale.

The difficulty, then, is the foreign influence attaching to the missionary, and not his theology, which in truth matters as little to Chinese generally as it did to Gallio.

But the Chinese case against Christendom is stronger than has yet been stated. It has been mentioned that the Pekin Convention of 1860 gave to France, as the protector of the Catholic faith, certain rights to lands formerly owned by Christians, as a set-off to the concession of additional land at Hong Kong to the British. The clauses actually agreed upon were further improved by the French interpreter, who adroitly secured for missionaries the privileges of leasing land, or buying or building houses in all the provinces. Sir Rutherford Alcock comments on the restitution provision of the treaty, as follows:—"We must suppose a French army entering London, and there dictating the conditions of peace, and among others, that all Church property confiscated by Henry VIII. should forthwith be restored to the Roman Catholic Church by the present holders, however acquired, and without compensation; and that the French Government should be appealed to, in order to enforce the vigorous execution of the stipulation." A land question in China has its dangers, as it has in Ireland.

A series of outrages on missionaries began in 1865, and incendiary placards charged the Christians with kidnapping and vile offences, but also with claiming exemption from the laws by which men ought to be governed. After the massacre at the cathedral and orphanage at Tientsin in 1870, the Chinese Government issued a circular to its foreign representatives, proposing as a remedy, that all foreigners visiting or residing within the country for purposes of propagandism, should divest themselves of extra-territorial privileges, and become subject to territorial jurisdiction. The circular closed by claiming that the Chinese Government treats all its subjects on a footing of perfect equality, "that is the evident proof that it is not opposed to the work of the missions." It is needless to add that none of the Powers assented.

Then came the murder of two German missionaries in 1897. By way of punishment, Germany insisted on a special tax, a war indemnity, the rebuilding of the chapel destroyed, the handing over of Kiachow as a naval base, a coal-mining monopoly in Shang-tung, certain railway concessions, and the cashiering of the Governor. The said Governor, it is understood, forthwith devoted himself to fostering the Boxer movement;—who can wonder? Other "Christian" nations were fired by the great gains to Germany accruing from the deaths of her two missionaries, and ere long, as Captain Brinkley puts it, "the total results of the murder of two missionaries were, that three of the great European Powers had seated themselves permanently at the entrance to the Gulf of Pechili, commanding the maritime approaches to the metropolis," that Russia had Manchuria, and "Germany regarded as a legitimate hinterland the province of Shan-tung," with "its profoundly sacred character as the birthplace of Confucius and Mencius."[1]

[1] Brinkley, xii. 193.

It is evident that these irreligious aggressions by Europe have had much to do with the popular outbreaks. On the 15th March 1899, an imperial decree was published, conceding, it is understood at the request of the French ambassador, legal status to foreign ecclesiastics. The decree states that "Bishops being in rank and dignity the equals of viceroys and governors, it is agreed to authorise them to demand to see viceroys and governors; vicars-general and archdeacons will be authorised to see provincial treasurers; and priests to see prefects, etc. Under the "most favoured nation" clause, Protestants were acquainted with their new privileges. The matter was felt to be grave and far-reaching, and after serious consideration all the Protestant missions happily refused to avail themselves of official status, and notified their refusal accordingly. There have been so many self-denying servants of the Cross of the Roman Catholic faith, that it is hard for it to be associated with the arbitrary materialism of its European protector. But through the zeal of the French Government to secure concessions as a set-off to those obtained by England, and through the willingness of the Latin Church to avail itself of secular rank and privileges, the popular objection to foreign mission work has been undoubtedly strengthened. The Rev. A. R. Saunders, for instance, in describing the flight of a party of fourteen persons during the Boxer riots, says: "The enmity of officials and people alike seemed to be chiefly directed against Roman Catholics and railroad and mining engineers, and we had all along the road to prove we were neither one nor the other."[1] The following passage

[1] *Martyred Missionaries*, p. 74.

from the famous, or infamous, Hunan Tracts confirms this view:—

"France alone is bent on missions; other nations are indifferent about them. But the Chinese people do not know the difference; therefore, whenever they hear the name of a foreigner, they hate it at once; whenever they see a foreigner coming to them, they avoid him."

It is to the credit of many of the missionary bodies that they are alive to the danger of claiming special privileges for themselves or their converts, and take decided steps to prevent it. Two volumes have lately been published, preserving records of some of the many missionaries who suffered death in the late Boxer outbreaks, and of the experiences of some who escaped. The accounts consist largely of letters, copies of journals, and recollections hastily put together, and therefore in some respects are the more genuine, informing, and valuable. It may safely be said that they represent many heroic lives freely spent for the people amongst whom they lived, and for the Master whom they served. Some of the memoranda, penned in the very depths of the valley of the shadow of Death, are worthy of the highest rank in the annals of Christian martyrs. Nor should the splendid fidelity of many of the native Christians, and the kindness of many Chinese manifested at great risk to themselves, be disregarded.

From some of these records it might seem as if one of the principal services of the devoted women amongst the slain, was to attend to opium refugees and opium patients in various inland districts. If the stain of the "foreign smoke" can be washed away, it is by such lives—lived and sacrificed, as they have been. The Chinese Inland missionaries alone are maintaining fifty-two opium refuges, or hospitals, for the special cure of the habit at the present time.

Anything in the way of blood-money has been refused by all the Protestant societies, and many of them will have nothing to do with compensation for destroyed property either. It is doubtless easy for writers at home to lay down lines of stringent self-denial, which in their judgment missionaries and their families ought to live up to under all circumstances. It is enough here to urge that the missionary should remember the injunction first given under a heathen emperor, to give to Cæsar the things that are Cæsar's, and to God the things that are God's. The more the spirit of the Founder of Christianity is evidenced to the Chinese in the lives and conduct of its professors, the more likely are they to be attracted to it. The more this is obscured and defaced by the intervention of gunboats and Gatlings, by methods of revenge and violence, the more certain are they to be repelled. Sir Robert Hart goes to the root of the matter in his sentence, "Christianise, but do not Westernise."

It is said that the Chinese resent the teaching of women. On the other hand, the neglect of woman has been one of the gravest defects of Confucius and his teaching. There are already indications that directly and indirectly Christianity may bring hope and well-ordered freedom to the one-fifth of the women of the world, who have long been sorely in need of it.

Since the Boxer outbreak, with its cruel slaughter both of missionaries and of native converts, it is said there has been increased willingness on the part of the Chinese in many districts to listen to the evangelists of the new faith, and the number of its native adherents has grown largely.

One fact of some moment may be stated here. It is the practice of all the Christian Churches in China to insist on exemption from opium smoking, the cultivation of the poppy, or the manufacture of the drug, on the part of their members. Considering the great diversity of missionary work by very different bodies carried on in China, this is as strong a proof as could be asked for of their estimation of the habit. There is no evidence that this is a yoke imposed by Europeans upon doubtful or unwilling natives. It is rather a rule of conduct imposed and maintained by the opinion of the Chinese themselves, as essential to the recognition of any worthy ideal of religious life. As it may well be imagined that the Protestant bodies would be the most strict in any approximation to Puritan habits, it may suffice to quote an authority as to a Church that might be judged to be less particular.

In a recent lecture to the Pharmaceutical Society, Dr. Augustus Henry said, "The Roman Catholic Church is loath to oppose native practices, unless they are really vicious. It has never interfered with foot-binding in China; yet all Roman Catholics in China are forbidden to engage in the cultivation, sale, or smoking of opium."

Any one who studies the work of Christian missions in China, can hardly fail to find much to admire and to give ground for hope in the future. Christianity saved Europe from the decadence of the Roman Empire; it is earnestly to be hoped that it may yet save China from the decrepitude which seems to have befallen its ruling class, and the demoralisation which threatens its people.

When Prince Kung's remark is searched into, it becomes apparent that the Chinese objections to opium and missionaries are on totally different planes. The drug is objectionable for its own sake; the missionaries have to bear the blame of authority exercised on their behalf, often for ends diametrically opposed to the true aims and methods of their calling. The British Government has clogged the progress of Christianity by associating it in the popular mind with the ruinous spread of the "foreign smoke." The Governments of France and Germany have made it repugnant, the one by insisting on unjust privileges, the other by territorial aggrandisement. It is to be wished that the missionaries may yet be able to atone largely to the Chinese for the sins of their respective countries.

CHAPTER VII

THE EXAMPLE OF JAPAN

SO long as the Indian Government is tied hand and foot to a gigantic trade in opium,—so long must it necessarily be difficult for this country to judge the issues arising out of it in the white light of absolute disinterestedness. Many countries have bound themselves by prohibition treaties of one kind or other, but the most important object-lesson for the world to profit by in the case of China is furnished by Japan. No careful observer can help noticing how close are the links between the great Middle Kingdom of the East and its famous island neighbour. The smaller nation owes its civilisation to the larger one. Its language, laws, religious learning are substantially the gift of China. The experiences of its intercourse with foreign nations have much in common with those of the Celestials. Like China, Japan suffered from the contemptuous treatment of foreign nations in the past; and the memory of the evil times, it is said, still survives, though courteously screened off from observation. Christianity and foreign commerce presented themselves together. Both were welcomed, and throve apace. The latest historian of these countries suggests a reason for the sudden change to a hostile attitude. He says: "Had Christianity relied solely on legitimate weapons, the pulpit, education, and example, paying due respect to the laws of the land, and extending toleration to others, there is nothing to indicate that it might not have retained, strengthened, and extended the footing it had gained,—that the Japanese might not then have finally entered the arena of international intercourse, instead of isolating themselves for nearly three centuries."[1] So strongly marked was the repellent effect upon the islanders, that trade was interdicted with all Western people (save the Dutch), and the Japanese, who in 1541 were celebrated throughout the East as "Kings of the Sea," are said in 1641 to have built no ship larger than a coasting vessel. Eastern revenge too often has responded after its kind to the barbarities of Western aggression; but a despatch of the British representative in 1859 may be accepted as a fair statement of the obstacles to commerce between the two countries: "Looking at the indiscreet conduct, to use the mildest term, of many, if not all the foreign residents, the innumerable and almost daily recurring causes of dispute and irritation between the Japanese officials of all grades and the foreign traders, . . . the irregularities, the violence, and the disorders, with the continued scenes of drunkenness, incidental to seaports, where sailors from men-of-war and merchant ships are allowed to come on shore, . . . so far from sharing in any sweeping conclusions to the prejudice of the Japanese, I think the rarity of retaliative acts of violence on their part is a striking testimony in their favour."[2]

Any one wishing to understand what the humiliation of the Eastern countries has been under the superior forces of the West, and the intensity of their

[1] Brinkley, iii. 116.

[2] *Ibid.*, iii. 208.

desire to reassert themselves, and to claim at least the respect due as between equals, cannot do better than study the volume lately edited by Mr. Alfred Stead.[1] The Marquis Ito, for instance, writing on the growth of Japan, asks: "Is there any country in the Orient, except Japan, which preserves the full right of an independent State? A country cannot be said to have preserved the full right of independence unless it is able to exercise its own jurisdiction freely, and conduct its own administration without restriction in the interior."[2] Turning anxiously to their colossal neighbour, the Marquis adds: "It is very necessary for China to maintain her own independence, and to take steps to place her country on a firm foundation.[3] . . . Besides, we have a great interest in the changes of the political state of affairs in China, so that in some cases our country might stand in such a position as not to be able to look upon them with passive inactivity."[4]

The change over, when it came to Japan, was very sudden. The national impulse to reject foreign intercourse gave way in a few years to an absorbing purpose to assimilate Western civilisation. And yet the motive remained the same. Japan had only decided to exchange the protection of isolation for the "protection of mimicry." It is too soon yet to reach any final conclusions as to the results. It is greatly to the credit of Great Britain that it aided the change generously when it came. After devoting twelve years to the revising and modernising of her legislature, Japan resumed her request to the treaty nations for the abolition of consular jurisdiction,—a burning question with her then, as now in China,—

[1] *Japan by the Japanese.*
[2] *Ibid.*, p. 67.
[3] P. 70.
[4] P. 71.

and promised that this concession on the part of the Western Powers should be met by throwing open the country without restriction. Great Britain took the lead in freeing Japan from its old position of legalised inferiority, a fact the more grateful to the recipient, because, when the United States had previously moved in favour of Japanese complete sovereignty, Europe, headed by Great Britain, had resolutely opposed any substantial concessions, and refused, moreover, with an indifference to Eastern courtesies which added to the legacy of resentment. Some five years passed before the other European States came into line, and Japan began to feel that she was on the threshold of the comity of nations.

During all this period, whether looking to the East or to the West, Japan has never faltered on the opium question. English philanthropists have cried shame on the traffic, and English publicists have cried faddist and fanatic at the philanthropist in return; Japan cared for none of these things, but she cared very much for the health, for the character, and for the industry of her own people. Captain Brinkley, referring to the time of the opium war, writes: "In the midst of the discussion, China's neighbour, Japan, had to consider the opium question as applied to herself. She did not hesitate for an instant. Laws so stringent were enacted, and their observance was enforced with such stern efficiency, that the import and sale of opium for smoking purposes became an impossibility within her realm. No occidental nation would fail to take similar precautions in the face of a similar emergency. Academical discussions might be carried on with much show of earnestness, but when the practical test came to be applied, every civilised people would do as the Japanese did."[1]

In the light of the comprehensive evidence with regard to China, indicated in the previous chapters, Japan has been more than justified in the extreme position she has taken up. It is certain that if she had allowed her people and army to come under the influence of the drug as the Chinese have done, the whole course of modern history in the East would have been materially altered. Japan was severely tested again in this matter when it added Formosa to its dominions, at the end of the war with China. Formosa, as may be remembered, was the centre from which opium smoking spread into the mainland nearly two centuries ago. It has ever since been enslaved by the opium habit. The island is described by Dr. Maxwell as the most malarial district of South China. Japan found all the materials at hand for exacting a high licence revenue, and leaving the habit otherwise undisturbed. Instead of this, it has forbidden the sale of the drug, except to registered habitués. The experiment is an interesting one. Two British consuls speak very favourably of the persistence of the Japanese in their policy of repression, and of the success attending it. Consul Layard reported in 1902:—

"It is asserted by the authorities, and the figures would seem to bear out their assertion, that the consumption of this drug is decreasing in Formosa. They express their intention of gradually stamping out the practice of opium smoking, and the stringent regulations enforced for the licensing of smokers and for the prevention of smuggling, assisted by moral suasion, which at one moment took the form

[1] Brinkley, xi. 7.

of a regular crusade against the habit on the part of the Buddhist missionaries from Japan, all tend towards bringing about this consummation. It has indeed been brought to my notice that the general appearance of the Chinese in this district has improved, which, however, may also be due in some degree to a better regimen of food being obtainable, since the advent of the Japanese placed a higher style of living within their reach; or possibly to the fact that the more intemperate among the consumers of the drug may have left the island for other places, where they find more liberty to indulge; but it is certainly a fact, evident to any person's observation, that fewer faces than formerly are seen among them showing the unmistakable brand of the opium habit. In any case, everything points to the fact that at some date, sooner or later, the import of opium is destined to be reduced to the limits of the country's requirements of the drug as a medicinal preparation only."[1]

In his report for 1903, Consul Playfair wrote: "The authorities are doing their best to put down the opium habit, and appear to be meeting with a fair measure of success. . . . Only those proved to be addicted to opium are given permission to buy and smoke it. Exceptionally heavy penalties are inflicted on those detected in importing, selling, or smoking the drug without permission. . . . Agents and dealers in opium have to be non-smokers and persons of good character. They are licensed, as are the smokers, and the latter must always produce their licences when purchasing opium, of which, however, only a certain quantity can be bought. The price is fixed by Government,

[1] *Consular Report, Formosa*, 1902.

and the selling agent who supplies the retailer is only allowed a profit of 1½ per cent. . . . He . . . has to report monthly the quantity and value of the opium he has sold. The retailer . . . also has to keep a careful account of his transactions, and report to the police. The regulations control the agent, dealer, and smoker so completely, that, if well administered, evasion is almost impossible. Nevertheless, it is asserted that a large amount of smuggling is carried on. On the promulgation of the law it was translated and well circulated amongst the islanders. Officials acquainted with the vernacular went from village to village, gathered together the chief natives, and, pointing out to them the great injury done to mind and body by indulgence in the habit, at the same time expounded the law. Moreover, the native authorities generously assisted natives in the study of the Japanese language in order to qualify them as interpreters. Text-books on the subject were circulated for the benefit of children, and opium was made a special branch of study in schools. The attempt to control the opium habit caused at the outset many disturbances, which might easily have ripened into rebellion but for the policy of the administration. The authorities found great difficulty in ascertaining the number of smokers, as people refused to give information, and it was not until late in 1900 that it was believed that all the opium smokers in Formosa were registered. Since that date it is reckoned that the number of smokers has decreased by about 1000 a month."[1]

[1] *Consular Report, Formosa*, 1903.

OPIUM IMPORT IN FORMOSA.

Year.	Value.
1900	£360,464
1901	£240,669
1902	£153,822
1903	£116,819

LICENCES TO OPIUM SMOKERS.

Year.	Licences.
1900	169,046
1901	157,619
1902	143,492
1903	132,903

NOTE.—The latest returns give a total population of 2,925,072.

The *Times* made the following comments on Japan's policy in Formosa:—

"The method of dealing with opium smokers might possibly afford instruction to many of those amongst ourselves who are in difficulties with regard to the control of habitual drunkards. . . . The Japanese financial authorities are content to seek for compensation in directions not injurious to the people. It is, perhaps, to be feared that the tendency of some amongst ourselves to drink the country out of debt has not been similarly discouraged by the English Chancellor of the Exchequer."[1]

This uncompromising attitude of Japan has a double significance for us. It shows the determination of the strongest Power in the East, our own ally, to be in no way compromised with the opium habit. And it shows the nature of the influence Japan will exert upon China on this particular matter.[2]

"China," Captain Brinkley observes, "has taken Japan for model. That in itself is a striking proof of earnestness; for, as late as half a dozen years ago, she regarded her little neighbour with scornful dislike, counting her a renegade from the venerable teachings of the sages, and an upstart aping unlovely fashions. But now over six hundred Chinese students are acquiring Western knowledge in Japan; numerous translations of Occidental standard works, made by Japanese experts, are being put into a Chinese dress; many Japanese men of science are engaged as advisers in China; there has just been elaborated for the throne's approval an educational system closely following Japanese lines."[3]

This was written a couple of years ago. Events are moving rapidly in the East, and in September 1904 the well-informed correspondent of the *Manchester Guardian* learned that there were "over 1200 Chinese young men studying in Japan, exclusive of military students. A very considerable number of these—more than half, it is said—have no connection whatever with the Chinese authorities, although the Chinese minister in Tokio maintains a benevolent watch over them. These non-official

[1] Appendix I. note 12. [2] *Ibid.*, note 13.
[3] Brinkley, xii. 229.

students are, for the most part, studying languages, trade methods, engineering in its various branches, or medicine. The remainder are official students, despatched at the expense of the Chinese Government, the viceroys, or other officials, and are being trained for work of a public nature, and for public employment afterwards."

"A year ago the Viceroy Tuan Shi Kai adopted for his province a system of each district selecting and paying for the education in Japan of one student in some branch of Western knowledge. . . . These young men are selected from the principal school in each prefectured city, and the district magistrate is bound to provide the 400 dollars per annum which the maintenance and education of the youth are estimated to cost." (In some districts the local mandarins have secured funds for this purpose from the disendowment of Buddhist temples.)

"The Army Board in Pekin, which was formed recently to reorganise the whole Chinese army, has sent out orders to the viceroys and governors to select between ten and twenty promising young men each, and to send them to Japan to be thoroughly trained in modern military methods. If one may judge by such indications as these, there is a real movement in China, which cannot but be accelerated by the present political condition of the Far East."

This remarkable inversion of the old order, when Japan learned everything from China, is sure to be attended with important results. It is well known that intelligent Chinese attach much significance to the reform movement temporarily arrested by the Dowager Empress; and the infiltration of thousands of young students full of the progressive and patriotic fervour of Japan must have momentous developments. It will be noted that it fits in with Sir Robert Hart's serious warnings to the West, to be wise in time in their relationships with China. Mr. Henry Norman accentuates the position in his latest book,[1] by concluding some remarks on the close affinity between Japan and China with the words: "I am able to say, from positive knowledge, that the Government of Japan has conceived a parallel to the Munroe doctrine for the Far East, with herself at its centre." Mr. Norman's discovery may be only an anticipation, but in any case he and others are unquestionably right in pointing out the rise of a new Power in the East, likely to demand very different treatment to that which has too often been meted out by Europe in the past.

[1] *Peoples and Politics of the Far East.*

CHAPTER VIII

THE COMITY OF NATIONS

IT is not possible to reconcile the history of this great drug trade with the generally accepted usages of the comity of nations. Even in its present legalised form there is no other trade analogous to it. Yet it is carried on as an imperial trade in the name of the people of the British Isles, and can always summon to its aid able and powerful defenders, with the resources of the empire behind them.

The three strongest defences of the trade may be stated thus—

1. The profits are necessary for India.

2. If Great Britain sacrificed her drug trade, some other country would supply the deficiency.

3. Great Britain is not called upon to be a self-appointed custodian of Chinese morals. It is for China to raise the question of ethics.

1. With regard to India, it is admitted that the growing competition of foodstuffs and garden crops has seriously interfered with the popularity of the poppy. The Indian Government has to bestir itself vigorously, and to offer exceptional advantages to cultivators, to maintain its supplies. The people of India would in truth gain by the substitution of food supplies for opium.

If, however, the sale of the drug manufactured for the East were suppressed, there would be a present loss of from two to three and a quarter millions of revenue. This is the crux of the situation; except for the great profit, the traffic would have been ended long ago. Few observers doubt that this question must be faced ere long. Lord Curzon has said that "long before our domestic Puritans have purged the national conscience of what they style this great sin, the opium question will have settled itself by the rapid decline of the Indian import, and the acceptance by China herself of the undivided responsibility of her own moral welfare."[1] The poppy is an uncertain crop, and fluctuations in either country may delay or hasten the end. But the native drug is steadily increasing in quality, as well as quantity, and the end of a profitable import trade from over the sea cannot be long postponed. A business firm would be very short-sighted which left one of its main departments to die of a lingering decline. A great country might well seek to close with graciousness an account which should never have been opened.

It would be folly to dilate here on the best means of meeting the deficit. This must be left to those who are competent to advise on Indian finance. That some change in the recent policy of the great Dependency might be attended with advantages, economic and otherwise, must have forced itself on the minds of many onlookers of late; but this country must first make up its mind on the main issue, and then call in the best counsellors to advise as to the best means of giving effect to the same. At first it would be only equitable that Great Britain should bear the lion's share of the loss.

The probabilities are that British trade with

[1] *Problems of the Far East*, p. 283.

China would gain by the sacrifice. The statistics of commerce between the two countries have been very disappointing. Any opium traffic on a great scale must make the world the poorer.[1] Apart from the more friendly feeling to England, which might be counted on, the purchasing power of the Chinese would be augmented as the opium habit declined. On the other hand, a new policy of friendliness to the greatest race of the East would be likely to meet with no ungrudging response, and might do more to secure a pacific and economical frontier policy with the Buddhists of Thibet than any number of military expeditions.

A high Minister of State in China said recently to Gilbert Reid, "If we could only believe that foreigners were sincere in their friendship to us, we would in an instant open up the whole of our country, and let traders, as well as missionaries, go anywhere. It is not that we are unwilling to advance,—we are afraid."

By reversing its opium policy, Great Britain has an opportunity such as no other nation possesses, of proving its friendship to China in a manner which would appeal to her thoughtful and patriotic subjects all over her empire.

2. Turning to the second line of defence, namely, "that if India stopped her drug trade some other country would step in," it is at least doubtful if this proposition will bear the weight which has been so repeatedly laid upon it. It has not been true of Formosa, one of the most opium-ridden districts of China. The United States and Russia[2] are already bound by treaty not to import opium into China. All the great Powers of the world have bound themselves not to import the drug into Japan.

[1] Appendix I. note 14. [2] Appendix I. note 15.

New Zealand, the most enterprising island of the Southern Seas, has followed suit, and vigorously prohibits it also. All the treaty Powers of Europe, with the United States and Japan, have just bound themselves to prohibit the importation of morphia into China, except under close restrictions for medical use. By an international treaty of 1892, sixteen of the foremost nations of the world agreed to suppress any traffic in firearms and spirituous liquor over a large part of the Congo State in Africa. Prohibition laws against opium, intoxicants, and firearms, or some of them, are now in force over the Philippine Islands, Bechuanaland, British South Africa, and the Soudan; and, to come nearer home, Great Britain, Germany, Belgium, Denmark, France, and Holland, by concerted legislation, have put down cooperage, or grog selling, amongst the fishing fleets of the North Sea. These are only some of the proofs that could be furnished of the awakening of the nations to the injuries resulting from certain trades, and their willingness to combine against them. The old formula is now greatly discredited, and honest endeavours should be made to bring about concerted action with the Powers and with China herself before it is brought forward again.

The proposal to protect the Chinese against the invasion of a drug opposed to their best traditions and ancient standards of morality, would probably do more than anything else that could be devised to arouse China from her lethargy into determined efforts to conquer her besetting sin. Even if the attempt were to fail, England should not fail to set a worthy example to China before it is too late. A trader trading on the ruin of a customer, because if he desisted some one else would step in, is a person to be shunned, not imitated. A recent licensing law has intervened to prevent the serving of intoxicants to certain persons in this country. The principle rightly applies to nations, as well as to individuals.

3. The third defence throws the whole onus of resistance upon China. But how can the Powers take up this attitude after intervening in the internal affairs of China so often and so recently? They cannot disclaim all responsibility, as they might do in the case of a land with which they had never intermeddled. China is still in the meshes of the past; if she renounced the Chefoo Convention with Great Britain to-day, she would be worse off, because she would be thrown back upon the Treaty of Tientsin. The facts of history refuse to give Great Britain a clean sheet in this matter. It remains to create one anew with China herself.

But further, our treaty rights in China have been won by the power of the sword. If China has now ceased to struggle, and to resist a trade which she believed vitally affected the morale of her people, it would be mean to continue to take advantage of the quiescence we have done so much to create. Our policy has prevailed, and the result is painfully apparent. The drug, sold as a poison in England, specially prepared to minister to the weakness of the Chinese, has been poured into their country at the rate of a ton per hour for the twelve hours of every day for some sixty years; whilst, to add to the irony, the great Dependency which reaps the immediate revenue is united and emphatic in its condemnation of the particular vice from which it draws its profit.

What the inner mind of the Chinese Court may be on this matter, probably no European, unless it be Sir Robert Hart, really knows. It has been shown that various efforts have lately been made to raise the taxation on the drug for revenue purposes. There are those who think the existing dynasty absolutely hopeless. In any case it would not be wise to count on any moral uprising from it. But if the Imperial Government cannot, or will not, attempt to roll away this stone, this is no reason why Great Britain should persevere in adding to its weight, and sealing it more effectually upon the Chinese people.

Whether we will or no, the question of ethics faces Great Britain as well as the Chinese. Our influence goes along with every ton of opium bearing our brand, and is thrown against all that is best in the social, political, and religious life of the Far East. To ordinary observers the situation may well look forlorn; the enervating effect of the opium habit appears to be well-nigh complete. But to Sir Robert Hart, and other competent watchmen on the spot, a great change is already discernible, and new forces in the national life are being called into existence. Whenever any progressive wave of opinion has burst upon the usually silent sea of that great empire, the abolition of the opium habit has been in the forefront, and is likely to be so still.

Her greatest viceroy has pleaded for China's "only hope." An earnest provincial governor has just put forth a stirring proclamation enjoining reform from the opium habit, and against foot-binding. It is known that these appeals represent much of the truest patriotism of the land;[1]—why,

[1] Opium smoking is to be severely punished in the new model army. In the province of Hwpeh no smoker is to be allowed to qualify as a teacher (*China's Past and Future*, p. x.).

then, should the British Government persistently uphold a trade which helps to make the down grade for China so much easier, and the upward path so much more difficult for her people to tread? *Individually*, many Britons in the East have shown the finest characteristics. They have fostered self-respect and straightforwardness, refused to take advantage of the weakness of others, and recognised the principle of give and take in life.

The commanders of the smuggling clippers are said to have been very hospitable, of generous dispositions, of courage and boldness unsurpassed. Sir Harry Parkes, a typical representative of the proconsul period, was a most attractive personality, as any readers of his life may see. It is the mother-country, of whose fame her children are jealous, that comes out so badly in the retrospect. She, according to Sir Thomas Wade, has never had anything to offer China for all that we have taken from her. Time after time she has simply said, "This must be done because I choose"; and the choice has been dictated by monetary considerations only.[1]

Sir Robert Hart sums up the past in burning words, when he says: "Just as one can paralyse the body or corrupt the soul of a human being, so too it is possible to outrage the spirit and antagonise the nature of a people; and it is something like this which the West has done in the case of China, of course unintentionally, yet not the less effectually.[2]

Let Englishmen try for once to put themselves in the place of the Chinese. Suppose the French Government had had the absolute monopoly of the

[1] Appendix I. note 16. [2] Hart, p. 163.

manufacture and trade of brandy in France,—that it took some pains to restrict the sale amongst its own people, and even required it to be sold as poison, but poured twelve times as much as it used for home consumption across the channel into England; suppose that all that was best in England had strongly objected to the foreign dram, that for sixty years it had to be smuggled into our coasts against our laws by means of force, and by the corruption of our officials, and that it had only been legalised after disastrous wars in which England was hopelessly beaten; suppose it was manifest that through the spread of the habit the English army was enervated, our people impoverished, and our rulers discredited:[1] is it not certain that the curses of this nation would be many and deep against those who had so ill-used it for their own selfish ends?

The analogy may be brought home yet more closely. Two centuries ago, a series of statutes encouraged patriotic distillers, in order that "French and other foreign brandies" should be as far as possible excluded, and a "perfect pandemonium of drunkenness" ensued.[2] Happily we were never at the feet of France in the matter, and by slow and painful footsteps, with occasional falls, have been working towards better habits, though we are not yet entitled to preach temperance to the East. In making such a comparison, however, three facts should be borne in mind. It is admitted that before the spread of the opium habit China was a singularly temperate nation. The drug is more inexorable over its habitués than the drink. The

[1] Appendix I. note 17.

[2] Webb, *History of Liquor Licensing*, p. 22.

Chinese are everywhere ashamed of the opium habit.[1]

If these arguments are only partially true, persistence in the opium trade by Great Britain is, if nothing else, politically foolish. The one thing certain in the East is, that its future is not going to be as its past. The newspaper press is naïve in its admissions that the Eastern peoples must now be treated with respect. The days of consular intimidation are over. Japan arrests the attention of the world for the moment; but the forecast of a diplomatist, who knew both countries, was probably right when he said that China is the pivot of the Eastern question in the far future. The Chinese yamen told Sir Rutherford Alcock that "real friendship was impossible, while England continued responsible for the supply of the drug to the Chinese people." Chinese policy may have become more decadent since then, but there are signs that the statement is true still. Writers on the recent troubles of China are at one in lamenting the weak place Great Britain holds in her counsels. In the light of the past it could not well be otherwise.

It is not only in China and Japan that Great Britain would stand to gain by abolishing her opium trade. Wherever Buddhism and Mahomedanism have a firm hold, there would be the recognition of a generous advance towards what to them is a high ideal of statesmanship. Lord Curzon is no doubt right in urging that "moral failure alone can shatter the prospect that awaits this country in the impending task of regeneration in the East."[2] We forget continuously that "in countries abstemious by creed and by climate, it seems to the intelligent

[1] Appendix I. note 18.

[2] *Problems of the Far East*, p. 428.

native monstrous that the English Government should introduce a system for promoting the sale of intoxicating liquors and drugs.[1] Viceroys and Commanders-in-chief on occasion give admirable temperance addresses to our Indian army. The Oriental mind would be much more impressed by an imperial object-lesson in this direction made for the good of the peoples.

Such a policy, then, could not fail to strengthen Great Britain's position in the East. Her apologists have to describe her present opium policy as "ambiguous." Her rivals use much plainer terms. The best excuse for British statesmen is probably this, that the opium trade involved difficult questions amongst a race little understood and very far off, and that its discontinuance necessitated a great apparent pecuniary sacrifice much nearer home.

The East India Company, Lord Melbourne, Lord Macaulay, Lord Palmerston, Mr. Gladstone, Lord Salisbury have all expressed regrets or apologies for the trade; but the Indian Treasury remains unmoved, and can only repeat "the most solemn warning against any destruction of its revenue." The Duke of Devonshire, one of the most straightforward of English statesmen, wrote to India in 1882: "You should direct your attention to the practicability of any measure with the object of rendering the connection of your Government with the trade less direct"; as if any superficial change would essentially alter its realities. Even the last apologists for the business are made to say, "It is evident that the position of the Government of India . . . is to some extent invidious," and thoughtfully explain, that in the event of China again becoming

[1] *E. I. Finance Report*, 1871, p. 239.

restive, they will hold themselves "at liberty to reconsider" their conclusions.[1]

Queen Elizabeth hoped that by intercourse and traffic the princes and subjects of the two kingdoms might help and enrich one another in amity. For more than a century this great drug trade has poisoned the springs of their relationship.

This is no question, either of emotionalism on the one hand, or of opportunism on the other. Let the appeals of missionaries and the remonstrances of philanthropists be put altogether aside for the moment. Let the public be informed only from official despatches, the utterances of statesmen, and the journals of diplomatists, and yet the imperial drug trade stands hopelessly condemned.

It was illegitimate to begin with. It grew in dishonour. It lingers with discredit. It has enriched the one country, and impoverished the other. But poverty is the least of the ills it has helped to fasten upon China. It has enervated her people, corrupted her officials, undermined the authority of her Government, embittered the advent of the English, and of a nobler faith, and violated the moral sense of the Chinese.

When the last war broke out, Lord Salisbury, speaking as Prime Minister of Great Britain, said (June 1898): "If I am asked what our policy in China is, my answer is very simple—it is to maintain the Chinese Empire, to prevent it from falling into ruins, to invite it into paths of reform. . . . By so doing we shall be aiding its cause and our own." There is a saying by a greater parliamentarian even than the late Prime Minister: "He that taketh away weights, is the same as he that addeth wings."

[1] *R. C. Report*, vi. 60.

The drug we pour into China has admittedly a unique power of deadening the springs of life, of paralysing all reform. For a nation to invite another nation to reform, whilst continuously serving out to it an enervating and deleterious drug, is mockery.

On the other hand, to invite a people, patient, industrious, law-abiding, comprising one-fifth of mankind, and representing the most ancient extant civilisation of the world, into paths of reform by entering at the same time along with them, is an invitation worthy of the highest statesmanship of "a land of old and just renown," with, as its children hope, its best days still before it.

The words of Milton to Cromwell are not without a bearing here: "To guide mighty States by counsel, to conduct them from institutions of error to worthier discipline, to extend a provident care to furthest shores, to watch, to foresee, to shrink from no toil, to flee all the empty shows of opulence and power, these indeed are things so arduous, that, compared with them, war is but as the play of children." Arduous as the most weighty processes of peace may be, they are free from the cruel injustice that ever dogs the footsteps of war, and its victories are twice blessed.

It is true alike for the West and East that

> "by the soul
> Only, the nations shall be great and free."

APPENDIX I

NOTES

Note 1, p. 24.

Q. 455. *Inglis.* "I had frequently spoken to him (Elliot) about the dangers that were evidently about to arise out of the opium trade. I told him I was sure the thing could not go on."

Q. 458. *Chairman.* "What gave you that impression?"—"An immense quantity of opium being forced on the Chinese every year, and that in its turn forcing it up the coast in our vessels."

Q. 459. "When you use the words 'forcing it upon them,' do you mean that they were not voluntary purchasers?"—"No; but the East India Company were increasing the quantity almost every year, without reference to the demand in China; that is to say, there was always an immense supply of opium in China, and the Company still kept increasing the quantity at lower prices."

Q. 461. "I conceive that nothing but a monopoly could have forced the opium in the way in which it was done."—*Report of the Select Committee on China Trade*, 1840.

Note 2, p. 35.

The weakness of Elliot's position was of course understood and discounted by the smugglers. Captain Thacker, asked later by the Select Committee, 1840: "You hold the Chinese had a right to confiscate the opium if they could seize it, but you acknowledge that if they had attempted to do so, it would have been resisted by order of Captain Elliot?" replied, "No doubt Captain Elliot would have protected it."—*Report of Select Committee on China Trade*, 1840, p. 72.

NOTE 3, p. 47.

In his *Life of Gladstone*, Mr. John Morley gives a summary of the situation full and terse, in which he states that the orders not to protect the smugglers arrived too late. "The Chinese question was of the simplest. British subjects insisted on smuggling opium into China in the teeth of Chinese law. The British agent on the spot began war against China for protecting herself against these malpractices. There was no pretence that China was in the wrong, for, in fact, the British Government had sent out orders that the opium smugglers should not be shielded; but the orders arrived too late, and war having begun, Great Britain felt bound to see it through, with the result that China was compelled to open four ports, to cede Hong Kong, and to pay an indemnity of six hundred thousand pounds. So true is it that statesmen have no concern with paternosters, the Sermon on the Mount, or the *vade mecum* of the moralist."—*Life of Gladstone*, vol. i. p. 225.

NOTE 4, p. 55.

Mr. Innes went on smuggling at Macao, and Captain Elliot, moved by the Chinese, wrote to the Portuguese Governor at Macao (May 1839) to expel him.

"The undersigned cannot touch upon the shameless and unfeeling proceedings of some of his countrymen outside, at the actual crisis, without thanking Your Excellency for the great consideration extended towards them, a consideration, however, to which they are not entitled, and which he trusts will be effectually withdrawn from such persons."

The countryman, so referred to, retorted that his opium bore the mark of the East India Company; that it was specially prepared for the Chinese, and that he was therefore merely assisting the Government.—*Correspondence relating to China*, 1840.

NOTE 5, p. 64.

Mr. Inglis told the Select Committee, 1840, he believed the Chinese meant to give something for the surrendered opium. The despatches do not disclose any such suggestion.—*Report of Select Committee on China Trade*, 1840, p. 19.

NOTE 6, p. 67.

The narrative of the occurrences leading up to the war, attached to the Report of the Royal Commission (vii. 213), alleges that the remarkable growth of the opium trade, which forced the subject upon the notice of the Chinese Government, was not a matter for which the Government at home or in India was responsible. It is sufficient to give the opinions of two responsible officials, with personal knowledge of the circumstances.

Mr. St. George Tucker, Deputy Chairman of the East India Company, wrote in October 1839: "By promoting the growth of the poppy throughout Central India as we have done, paying high prices, and giving the native chiefs an interest in producing rather than restricting the cultivation, we became accessory to the probable extension of a pernicious habit among a race of men whose well-being ought never to be an object of indifference to us." Sir George Staunton said in the House of Commons (14th April 1843): "I never denied the fact that if there had been no opium smuggling there would have been no war. Even if the opium habit had been permitted to run its natural course, if it had not received an extraordinary impulse from the measures taken by the East India Company to promote its growth which almost quadrupled the supply, I believe it never would have created that extraordinary alarm in the Chinese authorities, which betrayed them into the adoption of a sort of *coup d'état* for its suppression."

NOTE 7, p. 122.

The fact that the Indian Government was one of the parties at issue before the Commission, was recognised by the Chairman early in the proceedings at Calcutta. Lord Brassey, addressing Mr. J. G. Alexander, the Secretary of the Society for the Suppression of the Opium Trade, at the conclusion of his evidence, said: "We all appreciate that in the encounter in which you are engaged with the Government of India upon its own ground, you are placed in circumstances of no ordinary difficulty."

NOTE 8, p. 131.

Chief Commissioner of Police, Calcutta: "Over 32 per cent. of the suicides . . . were from opium poisoning."—Vol. ii. p. 411.

Rev. W. B. Phillips: "In seventeen days there were 5 clear cases of suicide, and 3 of deaths from overdoses."—Q. 2605.

Surgeon Lieut.-Colonel M'Connell: "Last year in my own wards . . . we had 53 cases of opium poisoning."—Q. 3635.

Mr. K. K. Mistra: "In 1883, 25 per cent. of suicides were from opium; in 1892, 54 per cent."—Q. 8985.

Mr. G. D. M. Mchtaji: "About 80 per cent. of the suicides committed in Bombay and the Presidency are with the assistance of opium."—Q. 26,896.

Dr. Blaney, Coroner of Bombay: "There had been 463 inquests for suicide by opium in twenty-two years."—Q. 26,369.

Also Assistant-Surgeon T. M. Shah.—Q. 24,125.

NOTE 9, p. 168.

"Opium smoking bears no comparison with opium eating. The latter is a terrible vice most difficult to cure, and showing rapidly marked constitutional effects in the consumer." — Dr. Ayres, *Medical Testimonies as to the Effects of Opium Smoking.*

NOTE 10, p. 202.

The medical physicians report that over 750,000 visits are recorded to their hospitals every year.

NOTE 11, p. 209.

An English officer wrote of the native force under Gordon: "They drink very little, they are great hands at languages . . . their great bane is opium; and I do not think it is possible for any of them who have taken to it to give it up; consequently, by the time they are forty years of age, they are old men."—Brine's *Taiping Rebellion*, p. 152.

NOTE 12, p. 261.

Late reports from Formosa state that, owing to the financial pressure of the present war, the Government is granting licences for the sale of opium to the Chinese, whilst prohibiting any sale to Japanese on the island.

NOTE 13, p. 261.

In 1878 an Englishman named Hartley secretly imported opium in violation of the treaty, but Japan had no jurisdiction over foreigners, so the case was brought before the British consul, who acquitted the prisoner on some ground or other. This greatly enraged the Japanese public. The Minister for Foreign Affairs had to resign, and the negotiations for treaty revision, then on the way, fell through.

Note 14, p. 266.

"Intelligent Chinese ascribe the stagnation of foreign trade to the alarming progress which opium cultivation is making throughout the country. The easy production of the drug, and the remunerative returns it gives, they declare, tend to engross the attention of agriculturists, and to sap nearly every other industry. I look upon this suggestion as important, and I cannot but think that it indicates, at any rate, one source of the blight which seems to be affecting branches of the trade with China."—Medhurst, *Consular Reports*, Shanghai, 1873.

See also Tables of Statistics, Appendix II.

Note 15, p. 266.

Rev. T. Loegstrip, Secretary to the Danish Missionary Society, writes that in the district near Port Arthur, controlled by Russia, its authority is used to restrict the opium traffic to the utmost.—*Intoxicants and Opium in all Lands.*

Note 16, p. 270.

"What I do object to is, that being interested, as I have pointed out, in the sale of opium, the Government has worked both tax and monopoly alike for one purpose, and for one purpose only, viz. the requisition of the largest amount of gain, and that without regard to the moral results in China, and in defiance of the wishes of the Government and people of China." — Sir Edward Fry, *Contemporary Review*, February 1876.

Note 17, p. 271.

Mr. Gibb (opium merchant)—

Q. 723. "We have destroyed the power of the local governors (Canton) since the war."

Chairman. "The authority of the Government is exceedingly weakened by the result of their engagements with England?"—"No doubt."

Mr. Wilkinson, another witness, said—

Q. 14,013. "There has been a war since, and the officials have lost their power. . . . They have found that the fulminations of the Government are of no effect."—*Report of Select Committee on Commercial Relations with China*, 1847.

NOTE 18, p. 272.

"The evil of opium smoking in China I do not contest. I do not abate it by a parallel between it and the abuse of spirits even amongst hard-drinking nations. The smoker, to whom his pipe has become a periodical requirement, is more or less on a par with the dram-drinker; but the Chinese constitution, moral or physical, appears to me to be more insidiously invaded in the case of the first. The confirmed smoker is not, or is seldom, at all events, outwardly committed like the drunkard, to indecorum. The indulgence appears, at the same time, to present a special attraction to the Chinese as compared with other peoples. The use of it, in my experience, has become more general in the class above that in earlier times addicted to it."—Sir Thomas Wade, *China*, No. 5, 1882, p. 55.

APPENDIX II

STATISTICAL TABLES, SUPPLIED BY MAURICE GREGORY

STATEMENT SHOWING THE NUMBER OF CHESTS OF BENGAL OPIUM sold at the public sales at Calcutta of the East India Company, from 1787–88 to 1828–29, with the average price realised, and the gross price from the sales of each year. The first three columns are taken from pages 61 and 62 of the seventh volume of the Report of the Royal Commission on Opium.

Year.	Chests Sold.	Average Price of each Chest in Rupees.	Total Results of Sales each Year in Rupees.
1787–88 . . .	3693	470	17,35,710
1788–89 . . .	2330	569	13,25,770
1789–90 . . .	2467	588	14,50,596
1790–91 . . .	2839	553	15,69,967
1791–92 . . .	3220	525	16,90,500
1792–93 . . .	2982	632	18,84,624
1793–94 . . .	3860	569	21,96,340
1794–95 . . .	4650	559	25,99,350
1795–96 . . .	6026	245	14,76,370
1796–97 . . .	6564	264	17,32,896
1797–98 . . .	4172	426	17,77,272
1798–99 . . .	4054	750	30,40,500
1799–1800 . .	4570	718	32,81,260

Year.	Chests Sold.	Average Price of each Chest in Rupees.	Total Results of Sales each Year in Rupees.
1800–01 . . .	3947	831	32,79,957
1801–02 . . .	3292	1383	45,52,836
1802–03 . . .	2840	1378	39,13,520
1803–04 . . .	3159	1950	61,60,050
1804–05 . . .	3836	1608	61,68,288
1805–06 . . .	4126	1039	42,86,914
1806–07 . . .	4538	1583	71,83,654
1807–08 . . .	4208	1276	53,69,408
1808–09 . . .	4560	1460	66,57,600
1809–10 . . .	4968	1557	77,35,176
1810–11 . . .	4891	1549	75,76,159
1811–12 . . .	4966	1328	65,94,848
1812–13 . . .	4769	1955	93,23,395
1813–14 . . .	3672	2554	93,78,288
1814–15 . . .	4230	2257	95,47,110
1815–16 . . .	4318	2091	90,28,938
1816–17 . . .	3685	2289	84,34,965
1817–18 . . .	3552	1876	66,63,552
1818–19 . . .	3706	2221	82,31,026
1819–20 . . .	3999	2479	99,13,521
1820–21 . . .	3045	4283	1,30,41,735
1821–22 . . .	3900	3489	1,36,07,100
1822–23 . . .	3360	2062	69,28,320
1823–24 . . .	5390	1383	74,54,370
1824–25 . . .	3810	1990	75,81,900
1825–26 . . .	6570	1385	90,99,450
1826–27 . . .	6350	1846	1,17,22,100
1827–28 . . .	7461	1328	99,08,208
1828–29 . . .	8578	1357	1,16,50,346

STATEMENT OF EXPORTS OF OPIUM FROM INDIA IN CHESTS FROM 1829–30 TO 1901–02.[1]

Year.	Pp. 41, 42. Exports of Opium from India in Chests.	P. 40. Net Revenue therefrom to Indian Government in Rupees.
1829–30	9,678	...
1830–31	11,726	...
1831–32	18,186	...
1832–33	16,083	...
1833–34	22,785	...
1834–35	17,862	83,84,500
1835–36	14,807 [2]	1,49,20,070
1836–37	33,616½	1,53,49,680
1837–38	29,679½	1,58,64,450
1838–39	35,574	95,31,300
1839–40	18,510 [2]	33,77,770
1840–41	29,432½	87,42,770
1841–42	34,212	1,01,87,660
1842–43	35,887	1,57,65,810
1843–44	34,803	2,02,48,260
1844–45	36,942½	2,18,12,880
1845–46	20,553 [2]	2,80,33,500
1846–47	42,379¾	2,88,62,020
1847–48	23,877 [2]	1,66,33,848
1848–49	53,679¼	2,84,57,630
1849–50	51,606	3,53,02,810
1850–51	52,040	2,75,03,480
1851–52	60,474½	3,13,92,460
1852–53	61,157½	3,71,79,320
1853–54	66,908½	3,35,90,200
1854–55	77,379¼	3,33,36,020
1855–56	70,606	3,96,19,770
1856–57	72,385½	3,86,03,890
1857–58	74,966	5,91,83,750
1858–59	75,822½	5,34,63,910
1859–60	58,681½	5,16,97,780
1860–61	63,464	5,75,82,920
1861–62	62,362½	4,90,98,050
1862–63	82,217	6,19,91,980
1863–64	70,834	4,52,55,060

[1] *Financial and Commercial Statistics of British India.* Tenth issue. Office of Superintendent of Government Printing, Calcutta, 1903.

[2] The amount of opium sent to China from Bombay was not recorded in these years.

Year.	Pp. 41, 42. Exports of Opium from India in Chests.	P. 40. Net Revenue therefrom to Indian Government in Rupees.
1864–65	84,491	4,98,44,240
1865–66	88,439½	6,62,39,940
1866–67	74,855	5,72,50,170
1867–68	86,930½	7,04,80,650
1868–69	74,955½	6,73,13,300
1869–70	88,685	6,13,08,730
1870–71	89,074½	6,03,10,340
1871–72	88,797	7,65,72,130
1872–73	82,934	6,87,04,230
1873–74	88,724½	6,32,35,990
1874–75	94,745½	6,21,50,830
1875–76	88,354	6,25,28,600
1876–77	96,872½	6,28,08,130
1877–78	92,820	6,52,16,520
1878–79	91,200	7,70,06,790
1879–80	105,508	8,25,16,700
1880–81	92,192	8,45,12,940
1881–82	89,340	7,80,51,090
1882–83	91,800	7,21,67,780
1883–84	91,964	7,70,18,110
1884–85	86,579	5,85,06,320
1885–86	87,956	5,88,48,410
1886–87	95,839	6,21,39,130
1887–88	90,096	6,09,08,870
1888–89	87,789	5,96,44,140
1889–90	85,166	6,97,79,490
1890–91	85,753	5,69,83,850
1891–92	87,558	6,15,05,670
1892–93	75,384	6,39,06,840
1893–94	70,841	4,75,09,640
1894–95	68,838	5,70,76,520
1895–96	60,860	5,05,49,810
1896–97	62,258	3,92,25,460
1897–98	56,069	2,79,06,550
1898–99	67,128	3,35,20,400
1899–1900	67,350	4,01,22,417
1900–01	69,708½	4,97,45,509
1901–02	65,603	4,86,49,985

The highest revenue in £ sterling was £7,378,044 in 1871–72. The lowest in the last fifty years was £1,790,903 in 1897–98.

DECLARED VALUE OF BRITISH AND IRISH PRODUCE EXPORTED FROM THE UNITED KINGDOM TO CHINA AND JAPAN RESPECTIVELY.[1]

Year.	China (inclusive of) Hong Kong.	Japan.	Year.	China (inclusive of) Hong Kong.	Japan.
1859	£4,457,573	£2,917	1882	£7,645,337	£2,119,151
1860	5,318,036	...	1883	7,116,331	2,276,573
1861	4,848,657	43,100	1884	7,372,148	2,255,451
1862	3,137,342	21	1885	8,944,811	2,077,287
1863	3,889,927	108,897	1886	7,559,588	2,169,590
1864	3,711,478	627,383	1887	8,789,537	3,534,619
1865	5,152,293	1,576,794	1888	9,008,351	3,976,832
1866	7,477,091	1,444,539	1889	7,220,613	3,888,188
1867	7,468,278	1,545,386	1890	9,137,194	4,081,793
1868	8,498,147	1,112,804	1891	8,987,921	2,882,964
1869	8,973,677	1,442,104	1892	7,581,906	2,992,833
1870	9,547,563	1,609,367	1893	6,446,943	3,487,910
1871	9,415,950	1,584,517	1894	6,262,810	3,724,089
1872	9,497,184	1,961,327	1895	7,166,645	4,644,550
1873	8,294,669	1,680,017	1896	8,539,390	6,033,342
1874	8,402,066	1,282,899	1897	7,117,716	5,807,822
1875	8,528,311	2,460,227	1898	7,264,379	4,913,162
1876	7,691,556	2,032,685	1899	9,729,069	7,909,158
1877	7,912,663	2,203,153	1900	8,337,029	9,775,166
1878	6,608,921	2,615,616	1901	9,386,324	8,132,223
1879	7,597,962	2,638,002	1902	9,278,223	5,065,526
1880	8,842,509	3,290,906	1903	9,460,251	4,591,619
1881	9,579,387	2,824,620			

[1] Taken from *Statistical Abstract*, *United Kingdom*, vol. for 1870, pp. 62 and 63; vol. for 1877, pp. 52–54; vol. for 1890, pp. 84–87; vol. for 1904, pp. 120–123.

IMPORTS OF BRITISH PRODUCE INTO CHINA AND JAPAN.

The following are the figures worked out to show the imports into China and Japan of British produce per head of the population for the four decennial periods, 1870, 1880, 1890, 1900. The population of China is estimated at 350,000,000; of Japan, at 32,295,000 in 1870, and at 45,862,000 in 1900.

YEAR.	CHINA.	JAPAN.	
	d.	*s.*	*d.*
1870	6½	1	0
1880	6	1	9¾
1890	6¼	2	0¼
1900	5¾	4	3

APPENDIX III

AUTHORITIES QUOTED

ABEL, Dr. CLARKE. Narrative of a Journey in the Interior of China. 1816.

ALEXANDER, J. G. Substitutes for the Opium Revenue.

BARBOSA. The Coasts of East Africa, Malabar, etc. *Cir.* 1516.

BERESFORD, LORD CHARLES. The Break-up of China.

BISHOP, ISABELLA. The Yangtse Valley and Beyond.

BRINKLEY, Captain F. Japan and China. 12 vols. 1904.

BROOMHALL, B. The Truth about Opium Smoking. 1882.

" B. China's Past and Future. 1904.

" M. Martyred Missionaries of the C.I.M. 1901.

CARPENTER, E. From Adam's Peak to Elephanta.

CHANG CHIH-TUNG. China's Only Hope.

China, Friend of.

Chinese Repository. 1839, 1843.

COLQUHOUN, A. China in Transformation.

CRAFT, Dr. and Mrs. WILBUR. Intoxicants and Opium.

CURZON. Problems of the Far East.

DANE, R. M. Historical Appendices B and C. R. C. on Opium, vol. vii.

DEFOE. Robinson Crusoe. 1719.

Edinburgh Magazine. 1841.

EDKINS, Dr. Historical Note. R. C. on Opium, vol. i. App. II.

Encyclopædia Britannica. Tenth Edition.

FOSTER, ARNOLD. R. C. on Opium: An Examination and Appeal. 1899.

Fraser's Magazine.
FRY, Sir EDWARD. England, China, and Opium.
GORST, H. E. China. 1899.
HAMILTON, ALEX. A New Account of the East Indies 1727.
HANSARD. Parliamentary Debates.
HART, Sir R. These from the Land of Sinim. 1903.
HEDIN, SVEN. Through Asia.
HILL, J. S. The Indo-Chinese Opium Trade.
HODDER, E. Life of Lord Shaftesbury. 1892.
HOLCOMBE, CHESTER. The Real Chinese Question. 1901.
Hunan Tracts. 1876, 1892.
JEFFREYS, J. The British Army in India. 1858.
LANE-POOLE, S. Life of Sir Harry Parkes.
LITTLE, Mrs. A. Intimate China.
" " Li Hung Chang. 1903.
LOCH, Captain G. Closing Events of the Campaign in China. 1843.
LOVETT, R. James Gilmour of Mongolia.
M'LAREN, DAVID. An Inquiry into the Results of the Opium Trade.
Manchester Guardian.
MARTIN, R. M. China: Political, Commercial, and Social. 1847.
MARCO POLO. Voyages and Travels.
MEDHURST, W. H. China. 1838.
MORLEY, J. Life of Gladstone.
National Righteousness.
NORMAN, HENRY. The Far East.
PARK, W. H. Opinions of over One Hundred Physicians on the Use of Opium in China. 1889.
PARKER, E. H. Chinese Account of the Opium War. 1888.
" Up the Yangtse. 1891.
" John Chinaman and a Few Others. 1901.
" China: Her History, Diplomacy, and Commerce. 1901.
China, Past and Present. 1903.

PARLIAMENTARY PAPERS—

Report of Select Committee on Bengal, etc. 1783.

Papers on the Colonies. 1830–32.

Report of Committee on Affairs of E. I. Co. 1830–32.

" " " China Trade. 1840.

Hostilities between Chinese and British Subjects. 1840.

Correspondence relating to China. 1840.

Report of Committee on Commercial Relations with China. 1847.

Papers relating to the Opium Trade. 1857.

Correspondence concerning the Colonial Register, Hong Kong.

Correspondence relating to Elgin's Mission to China and Japan. 1857–59.

Correspondence respecting Revision of Treaty of Tientsin. 1868.

Report of Committee on East Indian Finance. 1871.

Correspondence respecting Agreement of Chefoo. 1882.

Correspondence respecting Duties on Opium. 1885.

Royal Commission on Opium, vols. i.–vii. and Supplements. 1894, 1895.

E. I. Opium. Correspondence regarding the Report. 1896.

Consular Reports on Trade in China. 1902–04. On North Formosa. 1903–04. On Ssuch'uan. (China, No. 5) 1904.

Royal Commission on Licensing Laws. Report.

Affairs of the Transvaal and Orange River Colony. 1904.

ROSS. Cornwallis Correspondence.

SMITH, ARTHUR H. Village Life in China.

" " Chinese Characteristics.

" " Rex Christus.

STANLEY, Dean. Life of Dr. Arnold.

STEAD. ALFRED. Japan by the Japanese. 1904.

TAYLOR, Mrs. H. One of China's Scholars. 1903.
" " Pastor Hsi. 1904.
The Times.
TINLING, J. F. B. The Poppy Plague. 1876.
TURNER, F. STORRS. British Opium Policy. 1876.
WALROND. Letters and Journals of Lord Elgin. 1872.
WEBB, S. & B. History of Liquor Licensing.
WELBY. Through Unknown Thibet. 1898.
WILLIAMS, S. WELLS. The Middle Kingdom. 1883.

INDEX